INFORMATION TECHNOLOGY
JOBS IN AMERICA

Corporate & Government Career Guide
Why You Want One, Where They Are, How to Get One
By The Editors of Info Tech Employment

An Info Tech Employment Publication
561 Hudson Street, Suite 23
New York, N.Y. 10014

Printed in the United States of America

ISBN 1-933639-74-1

ISBN 978-1-933639-74-1

Publisher: Louis R. VanArsdale

Cover Design: Cheryl Klinginsmith

Layout & Design: Pierre Studios

Table Of Contents

Chapter Three
Information Technology Jobs in Government

Paid Holidays
Sick Leave
Student Loan Repayment Program
Health & Benefits Package
Career Ladder
Union Representation
Union Benefits
Long Term Care Insurance & Flexible Savings Account
The Federal Flexible Spending Account Program
Federal Life Insurance Program
Survivor Benefits

Information Technology Jobs in U.S. State & Municipal Government

Information Technology Job Titles U.S. State & City Government – Salaries, 5-Year Salary
Projections & Estimated Pensions U.S. State & City Government
(Chart V - Sample U.S. States & Major Cities)
ARIZONA-PHOENIX
CALIFORNIA-LOS ANGELES
COLORADO
FLORIDA
ILLINOIS-CHICAGO
IOWA
IMARYLAND
NEVADA
NEW JERSEY
NEW YORK
NEW YORK CITY
TEXAS
Pay
Permanence
Annual Raises
Longevity Increases
Pension Plan
Vacation Days – Annual Leave
Paid Holidays
Sick Leave
Health & Benefits Package Health Care
Career Ladder
Union Representation
Union Benefits
Prescription Plan
Dental Care

The Civil Service Exam
Ranking by Score
Certified Civil Service Lists Created for the Job Titles
Job Hiring Pools
Types of Employment Status

Chapter Six

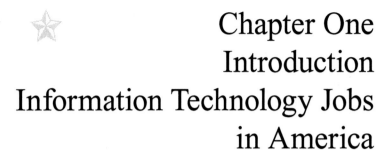

Chapter One
Introduction
Information Technology Jobs
in America

Introduction

Chapter One: Information Technology Jobs in America now exist in two main sectors 1) information technology jobs with the growing information technology professional services sector, and 2) information technology jobs with U.S. Federal, State and Municipal government. These sectors will continue to increase hiring. Prospective and seasoned employees will want to learn what drives IT hiring in these sectors, where the jobs are, and how to get the best career employment.

The IT professional services sector continues to hire and place for American companies and government agencies seeking expert staff.

A new government workforce has taken shape because of computers in Federal, State and Municipal government. The workforce is *leaner* and *greener*. It is characterized by a reduction of clerical level jobs, the creation of a new class of information technology employees with higher salaries, the creation of new Civil Service titles to cover computer and emerging technology jobs, and the incorporation of technology into all phases of government operations and business processes.

Hiring practices and opportunities in these two sectors open the field. The composition of the American workforce is changing; the nature of tech work is changing.

Companies Keep Hiring As Demand Grows. Career & Hiring Choices for Employer & Employee Expand. A New Workforce Model Presents Opportunities for Part-Time, Contracting, & High-Paid In-House Expertise. Tech Jobs with Government Are Lively Stable, Secure, and Well-Paid. Tech Jobs Emerge in All Sectors. Computer Jobs Are Changing in Nature- Less Programming – More Managing. Companies Hiring IT Staff from Third-Party Providers. Experience Is an Acceptable Substitute for Education. Core Skills Include Business-Process Understanding – Critical Thinking – Communication. Companies Are Attracting & Retaining Experienced IT Workers. The Climate is Favorable for Computer Professionals – Entry Level & Experienced. Tech Jobs are Lucrative. Technical & 'Non-Technical' Tech Jobs Are Available.

Good News. Companies keep hiring as demand grows. More Managing. Less Programming.

Chapter Two: IT Jobs in the Information Technology Professional Services Sector, explains the IT professional services sector. American companies and government

11

agencies seek to hire expert staff from the growing IT professional services sector or IT service providers. We recommend resources from Info Tech Employment, http://www. infotechemployment.com), an excellent source for identifying and contacting companies in this sector in your geographic region. Companies published in the resource have registered contracts with government agencies and American corporations to provide tech staff. Sample salaries are shown. We also recommend IT Staffing Firms (http://www. infotechemployment.com). The resource publishes contacts for over 2300 IT Staffing Firms in all 50 U.S. States and major U.S. cities. These resources also publish rates recently published under a real contract awarded to 23 companies (IT Service Providers) to supply tech staff. Job Classifications used by these employers to classify staff and determine pay are shown. The Job Classifications show how employers typically classify tech jobs to determine position and pay. We also recommend http://www.americasjobbank.com where employers post their job announcements.

"IT Job Titles – Tech Skill Sets", an excellent chart in Chapter Two, shows current information technology job titles, covering all aspects of technology within an organization. An array of Skill Sets for today's IT jobs accompanies the IT Job Titles. Employers increasingly want to see a bundle of Skill Sets. The Skills Set chart will help you think about your abilities and present your array on your Resume. How to prepare the E-Resume, a Scannable E-Resume, and contact companies in the IT professional services sector, helps you to complete the contact, application and hiring process.

Chapter Three: Information Technology Jobs in Government – U.S. Federal – State – City, provides an in-depth look at tech jobs in government, Federal, State and City. *Why You Want One - How to Get One,* indicates the reasons why a government job in technology is a sound career choice in today's global economy. With shifting markets, mergers and re-organizations, a government job is one of the best long term career choices. It is a sound career choice for economic reasons, as well as for reasons of career interest. To support this outlook, you will learn how the government workforce has taken a new shape in the U.S., becoming a *leaner & greener* workforce, with a new class of employees with higher salaries. Public Unions, Civil Service Commissions and Agency Personnel Departments have created new job titles to fill the need for a workforce in emerging technologies. A re-cap of major developments in the computer revolution and technology in government demonstrates the exciting developments surrounding today's IT jobs. Today's jobs in technology are certainly in one of the most interesting and exciting industries. Information Technology jobs in government brings the best of all worlds together – a public sector prosperous career in an exciting industry, with stability and new knowledge growth potential.

The New Face of Government describes *The New Civil Service & Public Unionism for Technology Jobs,* outlining the seminal role of the Civil Service in ensuring a qualified workforce. It explains how Civil Service Commissions, Personnel Departments and Public Unions have defined new job titles and work to fulfill staffing requirements for emerging technologies in government. This is a new class of employees with higher salaries. *Government Tech Jobs – Who is Qualified* demonstrates how, in today's market, there are opportunities in government for most people who wants a tech job. Experience is an acceptable substitute for education in almost all cases. Many tech jobs are managerial in nature, rather than programming in nature. There are technical and 'non-technical' tech jobs in government.

Technology in Government – The Computer Revolution describes the exciting backdrop to today's modern government. It outlines the major technological developments in the computer revolution that make possible the systems, methods, tools, and emergent technologies used in Federal-State and Local government today.   These developments include: the large integrated circuit computer, network computing & communications, the Internet, World Wide Web, email, Local Area Networks, Wide Area Networks, Relational Databases & Data Warehouse, Multi-platform Operating Systems and Component software, modern Telecommunications & Telephony, Speech Recognition, Computer Graphics and Geographic Information Systems, for e-business, e-commerce, and e-government.

Technology in Government – Computers in Federal, State and City Government takes you inside government. The shape and nature government have changed because of technology. Technology has made the "re-engineering of government" possible. It has modified the shape and nature of the workforce. It has modified business processes and government processes. This chapter describes these modified processes. It describes the function of technology in government. It describes some of the methods used to modify processes, and to create and maintain systems. Various major government systems are described.

Chapter Four: What Jobs Are Available – Federal-State-City, presents information on actual information technology jobs and job titles, in the U.S. Federal government, in U.S. State governments for all 50 U.S. States, and in Municipal government for the major U.S. cities.

"IT Job Title & Salary Charts" show Information Technology Job Titles and Salaries for U.S. Federal Government IT positions, for IT positions in U.S. State governments, and for IT positions in Municipal government in representative major U.S. cities. A Salary Profile and Salary Projection, for each job title, indicates current and estimated 5-Year salary projection for the job title. Projections are based on a survey of real raises over 5 years. Further, the Chart includes a 20-25-30 year Pension Projection based on the current salary, projected average raise, and the Federal Government's, U.S. State's or Municipality's' formula for determining pension.

The Job Package describes what benefits you can expect to receive with your Federal, State or City government job in technology.

Chapter Five: Completing the Application & Hiring Process-U.S. Federal-State-City, outlines the basic application and hiring process for U.S. Federal, State and City information tech jobs. It explains in detail: Learning about Actual Job Announcements, Completing the Application, Taking a Civil Service Exam (or writing an Experience and Education Exam Paper if it is required); and the Federal, State and City Hiring Process.

Chapter Six: Today's Tech Jobs, provides a career and job guide to specialties:
- C++ Computer Programmer Jobs
- Java and JavaScript Programmer Jobs,

- Visual Basic Programmer Jobs
- Sun Solaris, Unix, Linux, Operating System & Network Tech Jobs
- Oracle, SQL, FoxPro, Sybase, Database Management,
  Database Programmer Jobs
- Software Programmer Jobs; Software Engineer Jobs
- Network Programmer Jobs, Network Systems and Data
  Communications Analyst Jobs, Network Management
- Software Jobs, Network Engineer and Network
  Programming Consultants
- Telecommunications Jobs
- Web Developer Jobs
- Non-Technical Tech Jobs: IT Procurement Jobs, IT Training Jobs,
  Project Management Jobs, IT Security Jobs
- Computer Graphics Jobs, Computer Animation Jobs

Information Technology Jobs in America

Good News – Companies Keep Hiring As Demand Grows

There is good news for U.S. jobseekers. There will continue to be an abundance of tech jobs for U.S. jobseekers throughout the decade. There will be expanding U.S. computer job opportunities for those trained in fields such as software architecture, product design, project management, technical support and IT consulting. Tech jobs will continue to develop in all 50 U.S. States (BLS, 2007).

The fears of tech jobs migrating far outweigh the reality. According to a new study by the Association for Computing Machinery Computers released March 2006, the United States continues to increase the value of the work it is performing with its tech jobs in the national and global economy. The U.S. will be better off identifying the high-growth, high-value opportunities that lie ahead, rather than trying to hang on to work that's been commoditized by technology and the global dispersion of knowledge to low-cost countries. Therefore, U.S. tech jobs will continue to increase. The U.S. will see only 2 percent to 3 percent of its IT jobs shifted overseas annually over the next decade, according to the study (ACM, 2006). These jobs will be largely lower-end virtual 'rules-based' computer jobs (Levy and Murnane, 2004).

Tech jobs requiring teamwork, expert communication, and critical thinking—such as troubleshooting, making decisions, developing systems that are business-driven, and building and maintaining computer infrastructures will not be outsourced overseas. The study also finds that IT hiring is higher today than it was during the peak of the dotcom boom in the 1990's. U.S. IT employment was 17% higher two years ago than in the previous 6 years, according to the ACM study (http://www.acm.org/globalizationreport), and the U.S. Bureau of Labor Statistics data reveals that IT jobs are predicted to be among the fastest-growing occupations over the next decade (ACM, 2006).

Tech jobs with the growing information technology professional services sector continue to increase. The U.S. Bureau of Labor Statistics (BLS) predicts that approximately 1.4 million tech jobs will be created between now and 2015 in the U.S. (BLS, 2007).

Companies from a variety of sectors in the economy continue to discover greater efficiency and more competitive operations through investment in IT. Therefore, there will be continued growing demand for IT as underserved fields such as health care, retail trade, construction, and certain services make greater investment in technology. U.S. computer jobs will continue to increase.

IT Services Sector Grows Globally and in U.S.

IT employment in the U.S. is growing, even as more businesses outsource tech work overseas. Tech employment in the United States has been rising to a record 3.48 million people as of June 2006, as 185,000 jobs were added to the rolls over the past two years, according to *Information Week* (Chabrow, July 17, 2006; August 8, 2006.) The IT profession is growing faster than other occupations.

The IT gains don't surprise chief economists. Scott Brown, who tracks employment trends as chief economist for financial brokerage Raymond James & Associates indicates that U.S. employers with their eye on the bottom line are hiring more IT pros. "There's still a very strong emphasis on productivity growth, and that's how you get there--with technology," Brown says. The fastest growth in IT employment is among computer and IS managers, up nearly 15% the past 12 months. Other growing job categories include software engineers, up 3.6% to 853,000, and systems analysts, up 2.2% to 756,000" (InformationWeek, Chabrow, 2006.)

Why 'Outsourcing' May Lose Its Power as a Scare Word

IT employment in the U.S. is growing, even as more businesses outsource tech work overseas. Hudson, a professional staffing firm, reports in a July 2006 survey that hiring and pay in the tech sector is up, as is worker confidence. At the same time, India's revenues from outsourcing are climbing (McDougall, 2006).

How can these seemingly contradictory facts co-exist? If more tech work is going to India, shouldn't U.S. tech workers feel squeezed?

"Why Outsourcing May Lose Its Power as a Scare Word" reports the New York Times, is because "it's a win-win for both businesses and workers. Businesses cut costs by sending routine work offshore. Some of the money saved is then invested into more advanced projects that require higher skills, kicking off a new cycle of hiring. This may be what we're seeing now. The Hudson survey notes that the skills most in demand--Web services, .Net and Java programming--are those most applicable to the build out of cutting edge, service-oriented architectures. In English, Service Oriented Architectures allow computer applications to more easily amongst themselves" (McDougall, 2006.)

Shifting Occupations in the Industry

"Economists who focus on the big picture rather than on individual displacement say the labor market is working well," according to the *Chicago Tribune* (Rose, 2006.) Shifts in occupations reflect shifts in the industry. "Jobs in computer-related occupations [in the last five years] grew more than twice as fast as the average for all occupations, according to an analysis of U.S. government data by Robert Lerman, an economist at American

University and the Urban Institute, a think tank. The number of computer programmers fell by 22 percent, for instance [in the last 5 years], while software applications engineers grew by about 26 percent. Support specialists grew by a slim 1.3 percent, reflecting outsourcing. Overall, higher-skilled, higher-paid occupations grew faster than those requiring less skill. ``The data over the last four years have a broadly positive bent to them,'' Lerman said. ``We've created a whole new occupation in the last 30 years; people have gotten trained and found their way to achieve what's required. ``It fits very much with the economy's rising demand for skill, which in general is a good thing,'' he added. ``But it means that people who want to succeed have to learn something'' (Rose, 2006.)

More Managing – Less Programming
Computer Jobs Changing in Nature

Managers' ranks are swelling. People who once were programmers take on managing outsourcers or work in small teams that include IT and business-unit peers. As IT becomes ingrained in every aspect of an enterprise, more people are needed to manage the flow and integration of information, especially at companies that outsource. "As outsourcing relationships continue to evolve, the junior people or non-management people are gobbled up by sourcing relationships or farmed out to other parts of the organization…," says Scott Holland, a research director at the Hackett Group, an advisory firm. "You don't find too many computer operations jobs anymore. It's more about the folks who are business technologists, people who can obviously code but also have a stronger sense of the business" (Chabrow, 2006.)

More Americans were employed in computer jobs and information technology last quarter than at any other time in the nation's history. IT employment in computer jobs reached a record high of 4.347 million in the 12 months ending March 31, 2006, according to Information Weeks report from the Bureau of Labor Statistics (InformationWeek, 2006; BLS, 2006).

Computer jobs for IT managers grew by 91,000, or 31%, to 373,000 last quarter, according to Information Week. "IT management computer jobs appear to thrive in a global economy and appear to be increasing at a very healthy rate," says Roy Lawson, a software developer and board member of the Programmers Guild, an IT workers' advocacy group (Lawson, 2006).

With thousands of baby boomers retiring from the work force each day, the brain drain will prompt companies to hire for a new set of tech jobs. Hands-on mangers will handle projects that may be contracted out to third-party vendors or outsourced overseas.

The number of 'programming jobs' or 'software development jobs' may not keep pace with the development of other types of tech jobs. Often jobs will morph into a new type tech job, requiring IT computer jobs management ability, overall understanding of the Information Technology infrastructure or enterprise, technical support, or requiring you to be an overall IT player.

To plot a managerial career, hone application development skills, move into an information architecture area, possibly jockey for a senior operations position abroad and return to the States ready to grab your next job. Playing the field is another option. Become a free agent.

The successful management of new with older systems will require managers with experience in both. Fading fast is experience with older database systems, older middleware and development tools from companies such as IBM, and the former Digital Equipment Corp. and Data General Corp. IT staff with experience in many platforms will be able to move into management positions that call on expertise to integrate or migrate older applications to newer platforms, or maintain older systems along with new. Continued reliance on mainframes will buoy the careers of IT workers. For that reason, IT workers will be able to bargain for manager deals based on their experience with programming languages like Cobol and assembler. Expertise with IBM-specific operating systems such as DB2, z/OS and VSAM will also be in high demand. Integration of older systems with new or use of both is a live management issue.

IT Management jobs will be abundant especially with projects going to any outsourcers. In "Successful Program Management in a Complex Outsourcing Environment," Michael Latchford, Alexander Lowry and Ian Roberts, PA Consulting Group argue that "As outsourcing grows by leaps and bounds, its various forms call for a greater level of due diligence, strategy and management…. A complex outsourcing program consists of individual workstreams as well as a number of cross-program activities. Typical program management, communication, reporting and controls must be adapted to meet the requirements of this increasingly complex environment." Opportunities will exist for managers to meet the need to handle outsourced relationships (Latchford, Lowry, Roberts, 2006).

Career & Hiring Choices for Employer & Employee Expand

Companies and government agencies have a choice in who they will hire from and how they will hire to fill their computer jobs. They may hire from IT Service Providers, or Staffing Firms. They may hire to build In-house IT Staff or to have outside contractors develop and deploy their IT projects.

In 1999 when client-server technology first came in, hiring contractors or outsourcing seemed the solution for companies that had little trained staff. Today, IT environments have become more stable. The trust to develop IT departments and hire and maintain IT staff has become greater.

As the client hires IT experts from without, bringing new energy and knowledge into the organization, the client can also hire and maintain a core IT staff to be on payroll full-time permanent. Information technology hiring will place with an emphasis on core competencies in application development tools, database languages, operating systems and networking; operations; and user-support. These skill sets will permit the in-house IT staff to work with the IT service provider contractors and consultants, in a seamless way. Full-time company IT staff will implement custom-made applications. Often company IT management and planning staff will monitor work progress and contracts. In-house IT staff will take over and shepherd the application through to deployment.

Experts may be paid a lot to come in and jumpstart an organization, quickly put together infrastructure and a critical application. Entry-level information technology jobs are often filled by people hired in-house to supplement and expand the IT knowledge base, to bring skills from recent education, and ability to learn to grow with the organization in their skills, and learn from the experts who may stay or who may move on.

Where the cost of keeping IT staff on board full time is not deemed cost effective, or essential to the primary business of an organization, an IT Service Providers may be asked to develop and maintain a system or provide a service.

A case in point comes to mind with the development of website portals for several U.S. States. While digital government has increasingly come into play in government, IT is not the primary business of government. As States decided on the function and importance of their web portal in their relation to the public, they had to decide on how essential it was to develop the knowledge base within to develop and maintain their web portals. Kansas and Missouri went to outsourcers to develop and maintain their web portals. New York, California, Colorado and many other States kept the web developer jobs in the State IT departments (Franzel and Coursey, 1999).

Today companies and government agencies have a choice. Many of them will use a combination of IT personnel strategies. For projects where expertise does not exist in-house, companies will rely on IT service providers for staff and support. Often IT staff from IT service providers will develop and turn over a project to in-house staff, training them along the way. The IT service provider may carry an ongoing maintenance agreement that requires maintenance of a turnkey system, thus insuring the IT service provider of continued work. The client is relieved of keeping documentation and interacting with the intricacies of the application. The IT application developer job, database developer job, or web developer job may actually come in-house, with the client company hiring the team leader or project manager who worked on the project. The IT service provider continues to interface with the company. Thus there is a play of contract, contract-to-permanent, and permanent employment opportunities.

A New Workforce Model Presents Opportunities for Part-Time, Contracting and High-Paid In-House Expertise

As 77 million baby boomers retire over the next decade, the U.S. work force will not produce enough qualified workers to replace all of them. The boomer retirement trend will force businesses to rethink and adapt from their traditional work forces, which are likely comprised primarily of full-time employees from executive leadership all the way down to line-level workers.

American companies will need to restructure their staffing models. Because the generation of new employees place a high premium on the work-life balance, often more than did previous generations, they appreciate the flexibility offered by part-time, job sharing, outsourcing and contracting opportunities.

In order to operate and grow in tomorrow's economy, businesses will need to shift to a new work-force model that is comprised of a smaller group of full-time employees who perform core business functions.

Non-core competencies for many companies, such as information technology, accounting, human resources, call centers and marketing, will be contracted out to qualified third-party vendor partners or part-time contract workers. A generation of new employees will have a prime opportunity to fill these roles.

While contracting for niche talent is hardly a new concept, it will become the norm in the post-boomer workplace. As top talent becomes scarcer due to a shrinking national work force, it will also become more expensive.

Your expertise will be highly paid, whether working as an employee for a third-party IT vendor, or for core in-house and managerial tech jobs. With the law of supply and demand, American companies will be competing for a smaller supply of trained experts. This will be a prime opportunity for top talent to get top dollar and for new people to enter the IT field. These tech jobs will require an understanding of the industry, business processing knowledge, people and project management skills, technical know-how, and skill sets.

Experience Is an Acceptable Substitute for Education

Because demand exceeds supply, computer jobs, computer programming jobs and technical support jobs are available to people with experience, as an acceptable substitute for formal education, in almost all cases. The President of the Association for Computing Machinery reported recently that the number of American college students majoring in computer science is dwindling. David A. Patterson cited a survey from last year that found only 1 in 75 college students majored in computer science in 2005, compared to 1 in 30 in 2000 (ACM, 2006).

Government jobs in technology allow experience to substitute for formal college education in nearly all cases. Because of high demand, many jobseekers are moving into the industry by bringing experience, vendor-sponsored training or vendor product certifications. Because technology is changing so rapidly, it is difficult for college students to learn all products or new technologies. College students majoring in computer science and management information systems will bring principles of information technology and a mind-set capable of life-long learning to their tech jobs. Tech jobs will continue to go to people with a computer science or management information systems education. They will bring their educational success to their computer careers.

Now, a survey from the Society for Information Management (SIM) indicates that getting the best possible people on the payroll will become the challenge in coming years. In "The Information Technology Workforce: Trends and Implications 2005-2008," authors say that factors such as the shift from IT services to business-process services, imminent baby-boomer retirements and declining IT-focused enrollments in U.S. and European universities will change the IT employment landscape between now and 2008 (SIM, 2006).

Tech Jobs with Government Are Lively Stable, Secure, and Well-Paid

Public Unions, Civil Service Commissions and Agency Personnel Departments have created new job titles to fill the need for a workforce in emerging technologies. An explanation of major developments in the computer revolution and technology in government creating this need for technology staff is found in **Chapter III: Technology Jobs in Government**. Today's tech jobs in government are certainly in one of the most interesting and exciting industries.

The development of the large integrated circuit computer, data processing, office automation, network computing & communications, the Internet, World Wide Web, email, Local Area Networks, Wide Area Networks, Relational Databases & Data Warehouse, modern Telecommunications & Telephony, Speech Recognition, Computer Graphics and Geographic Information Systems, for e-business and e-government, create tech jobs in government

Information on actual technology jobs and job titles, defined by and for the Federal government, all 50 U.S. States, and major U.S. Cities shows what job titles exist to fill continued tech job placement. A Salary Profile and Salary Projection indicates current salary for the job title. Analysis includes a 5-year salary projection, based on 5-year average raise recorded. Analysis also includes a 20-25-30 year Pension Projection based on the current salary and that State or Municipality's' formula for determining pension.

A tech job career with Federal-State or City government is a sound career choice for economic reasons, as well as for reasons of career interest.

How Tech Jobs Emerge in All Sectors

Several types of business activities tend to create information systems employment for information systems staff and information technology consultants. Business expansions, technology rollouts, and IT project implementation produce information systems jobs. An expanding business may need additional information systems staff to fill new information systems jobs and handle increasing workload. Technology deployments are often complex and may require the expertise of information technology consultants to ensure they are carried out smoothly. Hiring information technology consultants can be productive for companies because learning curve and training are saved. Information technology consultants and contract staff can make quick deployments.

Tech Jobs emerge at each stage of the development life cycle. From Feasbility Study to Systems Analysis, Purchasing, Application Development, Business Process Engineering, Training, Infrastructure Implementation, Application Maintenance,

Infrastructure Maintenance, Network Maintenance, Help Centers, Ongoing Support – tech jobs are required.

In E-Commerce applications, Website Development and Maintenance, and ongoing data processing activities – tech jobs are required.

Companies Hiring IT Staff from Third-Party Providers
IT Staffing Industry Grows

Companies of all sizes expect to use more third-party providers. Business investment in new equipment and operations will probably play a large role in driving economic growth. Corporations in America have made huge profits. They will reinvest these profits in hiring and development.

Companies will be supplementing in-house tech staff with employees hired from IT Service Providers. Many of these employees will be hired to full-time tech jobs by the companies, to capitalize on the learning curve they have achieved in implementing a technology or application.

The Information Technology Services industry has demonstrated that technology, when used properly, is a key competitive advantage that can positively impact the long-term growth and success of organizations across our economy, from financial services and healthcare, to transportation, manufacturing, education, and scores of other industries. These companies provide a key link between a trained information technology workforce and the organizations that need the work.

In The World is Flat, Thomas Friedman, says: "In the flat world" "… a job and will go to the most talented and adaptive person." (Friedman, 2006). These specialized third-party IT service provider companies make it their business to get the most talented and adaptive people and to offer them and their expert services to clients.

The U.S. Bureau of Labor Statistics echoes the hiring news. Employers are hiring and using IT Staffing Companies to get the best talent. According to the U.S. Bureau of Labor Statistics (BLS), the staffing industry is expected to create more jobs than any other industry from 2007 to 2015. According to the BLS:

- more than 90 percent of U.S. businesses use staffing services;
- 71 percent of employers cite labor force flexibility as the number-one reason for using temps;
- 79 percent of temporary employees work full-time, virtually the same percentage as the rest of the workforce; and
- 72 percent of temporary employees obtain permanent jobs while working for a staffing company (BLS, 2007.)

Internships as Front Door to Hiring

Nothing can cement an IT career start quite like a good internship. Internships are a front door to hiring. Major companies, local businesses, and government agencies will take Interns with academic or computer-based training education. Typically, they will take on the Intern for 6 months to a year and assign them to an area and mentor employee. Internships can be key to getting the kind of business and industry understanding that business IT leaders say entry-level people often lack.

The Intern will be hired by the business or government agency. Some prospective IT professionals have an Internship every summer they are in school. This adds up to 3 or 4 Internships, paid or unpaid, with experience in 3-4 different companies. The IT staffer will have the Internship experience to put on a resume, and the references.

According to the Computing Technology Industry Association, Internships in IT are well up the food chain. Organizations are looking to fill entry-level jobs that require a broad base of skills. Internships that are available require candidates to have a mix of technology, business, and communication skills. This includes the ability to present well, write well, and speak well (CompTIA Online Survey Results, 2006, InformationWeek, 2006).

"Novell took on eight interns in one quarter, and is upping that to 12 because of the success they had, says Cheryl Williams, a Novell business analyst who's hired interns for Web services work. Projects include the development of an internal Web tool used companywide, which required interns to learn about the Sarbanes-Oxley regulations. Neumont students generally come better prepared than most others in their understanding of how a project fits into a business, says Williams, applying their technical experience with Web services, applications, and databases (InformationWeek, 2006)."

The Society for Information Management local chapters--whose members include IT leaders from local employers--have sponsored, along with Microsoft, events at U.S. colleges and universities, where college and high school students are invited to hear about IT careers and ask questions (SIM, 2006; InformationWeek, 2006) .

Companies are on the campus. Prospective IT professionals may contact companies while pursuing their education, seek Internships, and parlay that work into full time desirable employment.

Core Skills Include Business-Process Understanding – Critical Thinking – Communication

The core skills for U.S. jobseekers building a computer career are technical skills, as well as business skills. U.S. employers seek computer professionals who understand business processes. Computer professionals with business skills and excellent communication skills will be highly prized. The business and soft skills play key role in the tech job. The soft skills, such as oral and written communication, team working, critical/analytical thinking, problem solving, and adaptability, are cardinal. Business skills, such as project management, customer relations, needs analysis, and understanding of business-driven decisions and value cost-benefit analysis come into high play.

As Frank Levy and Richard Murnane indicate in The New Division of Labor: How Computers are Creating the Next Job Market (Levy and Murnane, 2006), while the lower-end rules-based virtual jobs may be outsourced overseas, jobs requiring critical thinking, pattern recognition, and symptom analysis, will not be outsourced overseas. Tech jobs requiring troubleshooting, making decisions, developing systems that are business-driven, and building and maintaining computer infrastructures require hands-on critical thinking and teamwork (Levy and Murnane, 2006). These tech jobs will never be outsourced overseas.

IT professionals need to acquire more knowledge of the business side of IT in order to advance their careers. Technical aptitude will always be a prerequisite for entry into the IT profession, but business skills account for five of the top 10 critical skills that organizations will require for their in-house staffs over the next three years.

The need to acquire business knowledge in addition to technical proficiency has been a recurring theme for IT solution providers during the past few years, and it's especially true for those who sell technology solutions.

"It's one thing to talk about the bells and whistles and what a technology can do, but you have to make a business case for it at the board level to get CEOs and CFOs to move forward," says Tony Vasco, vice president of the security division for Convergent, a systems integrator in Schaumburg, Ill, as reported in March 2006 *VARBusiness* (VARBusiness, 2006).

A successful tech career needs much more than studying computer courses and programming. The key values to build a successful tech career include working well individually and as a team member, embracing knowledge about computer skills, efficiency, demonstrating ability, troubleshooting efficiency, right attitude, hard work and coping with change and learning in the industry.

The professional education is the corner stone in building up a successful computer career. The technical postsecondary education is strongly recommended for starting up a tech career. A four-year degree in Computer Science, Computer Engineering, Information Technology, or Management Information Systems makes a professional eligible for the toughest of the tech jobs. These degrees offer enough advantage to a professional to edge out the rival job seeker from the competition. The postgraduate degree programs make the professionals eligible for higher-level tech jobs.

Vendor-related certification, such as the Sun Certified Java Programmer Certification or Microsoft's MCSE certification and the IT certificate programs offered by higher educational institutions are also highly recognized and give an employee an edge for the vendor-specific, product-specific tech jobs.

Companies Attracting & Retaining
Experienced IT Workers

By 2010, nearly one in three workers in the United States will be over the age of 50. As the relative proportion of younger workers declines, attracting and retaining experienced and reliable workers will become a core business strategy for all employers.

There will be new opportunities for experienced employees to get new tech jobs, to change companies, and to work as consultants for IT service provider clients.

Climate Favorable for Computer Professionals
Entry Level & Experienced

Tech job professionals in the U.S. are in high demand and will continue to be in high demand, with demand exceeding supply, for several reasons. An aging workforce is retiring, making it an optimum time for entry-level people to move into information technology. Entry level tech jobs are available, as well as advanced positions.

While the debate continues in the U.S. Congress about the number of H-1B visas, to allow foreign workers to work in the U.S., one thing is certain. Silicon Valley high-tech companies are strongly backing the proposed increase in H-1B visas, because the improving economy has made it difficult for them to find enough qualified Americans, they say, in fields such as math and engineering. Others argue that part of the reason high-tech employment has improved the past two years is because the annual allotment of H-1B visas has gone down.

This is certain - there exists a climate where demand exceeds supply for the tech professional. There are good opportunities for tech jobs for the U.S. jobseeker seeking to work in information technology.

Lucrative Jobs

Tech job careers are one of the most lucrative careers today. Tech job salaries will grow about 5% this year, according to InformationWeek (InformationWeek, 2006). While minimum wage in the U.S. is around $7.00, most tech jobs in median salary ranges pay an annual $15-$35. per hour, with an additional 33% vacation, and health care benefit package, making the job package equivalent to $45-75 per hour.

Information Technology jobs exist in all 50 U.S. States and most major U.S. Cities, in all government agencies and departments. A "Survey of IT Jobs in U.S. States & Major U.S. Cities 2006-2007" conducted by Info Tech Employment shows that most U.S. States and Major Cities offer between 10-35 Civil Service Information Technology Job Titles. The Salaries for IT Job Titles are higher than for many trade, labor and administrative titles. The Average Raise per Year for IT Job Titles, according to the Survey, is 2.25%, with a cumulative 5-Year Raise of 11.25%, and a Compounded Raise of 11.75%. In addition, many U.S. States and Major Cities have Service in Job and Service in Title Longevity

Increases, at 5 years, and at 10 years. These Longevity Increases, once earned, continue to be compounded as part of the Salary, and paid over the career of the employee. The Average Retirement Pension Percentage among the 50 U.S. States and Major U.S. Cities, found in the Survey, was found to be between 1.5%-2% (highest salary or average of 3-years highest salary times number of years worked times 1.50% to 2.0% (Info Tech Employment, 2007.)

Using the figures gathered in the Info Tech Employment Survey, a starting salary of $55,000 in an Information Technology job, and a 2.25% raise per year yields an 11.75% compounded raise over 5 years (or $61,475.). The 20-Year Retirement Pension for a career employee at a starting salary of $55,000 (without Longevity added in) is an estimated $27,369 per year. The 25-Year Retirement Pension for a career employee at $55,000 (without Longevity) is estimated at $45,876 per year. The 30-year Retirement Pension for a career employee at $55,000 (without Longevity added in) is estimated at $61,530 per year (Info Tech Employment, Survey, 2007; http://www.infotechemployment.com.). The Career Pension is in addition to Social Security Benefits. The Estimated Pension amount is in today's dollars.

Students have always poured into the most lucrative and promising careers. As IT salaries continue to be generously met by employers seeking to meet demand, college students will see the wisdom of that 4-year degree in IT. IT is a viable long-term career path. A four-year degree in programming or engineering will yield the graduate over 85% more in higher wages during his or her lifetime, than that earned by the high school graduate. Good jobs in the U.S. will not go offshore to foreign workers at very low wages. Whether someone qualifies for a tech job through a college degree or through on the job experience, the salaries are lucrative.

Types of Tech Jobs – Technical & Non-Technical

There are many types of tech jobs, covering many industries. Tech jobs can be classified as programming jobs, information technology jobs, IT jobs and internet jobs or technical support jobs. They can exist within the Management Information System department or within a Program Area department of Administrative department. The greatest benefits of tech jobs are that they offer excellent pay, exciting work challenges, opportunity for continued learning and plenty of opportunities for career advancement or movement. For a more complete look at Technical and 'Non-Technical' Tech Jobs – see Chapter Three.

The Top 8 Fastest Growing Jobs between now and 2015, according to the U.S. Bureau of Labor Statistics (BLS, 2007) are:

- **Computer software engineers, applications**

- **Computer support specialists**

- **Computer software engineers, systems software**

- **Network and computer systems administrators**

- **Network systems and data communications analysts**

- **Desktop publishers**

- **Database administrators**

- **Computer systems analysts**

One City's Example

The number of vacant information-technology jobs in the New York metropolitan area reached 11,000 in February 2006, up about 11% from last year, according to a study by two Manhattan research firms published in *Crain's Business* (Crain's Business, 2006).

"Because the economy improved, there is a need to invest in programmers and the IT area," said John Tepper Marlin, former chief economist for the city comptroller and founder of *CityEconomist* (CityEconomist, 2006). The study shows a shift in the type of computer programming jobs that are in high demand. Programmers skilled in Java, Unix, SQL and Html are in the greatest demand, with more than 24% openings for each than a year ago (Crain's Business, 2006).

REFERENCES:

Association for Computing Machinery (ACM), http://www.acm.org/globalizationreport.

Crain's Business New York, Number of Vacant Computer Jobs Rises: Survey, Amanda Fung, March 29, 2006.

Franzel, Joshua M. and Coursey, David H., Government Web Portals: Management Issues and the Approaches of Five States, in Digital Government, Principles and Best Practices, ed. Pavlichev, Alexei, and Garson, David, A., Idea Group Inc., 2004, 63-77.

Friedman, Thomas, The World Is Flat, Farrar, Strauss and Giroux, 2006.

Gross, Daniel, "Why 'Outsourcing' May Lost Its Power as a Scare Word," The New York Times..

Info Tech Employment, Editors, IT Jobs-IT Prospects- Companies-Contacts-Links: Get Hired by Companies Winning New Business and Requiring New Staff (2007), William Briggs Publishing, 2006, http://www.infotechemployment.com .

InformationWeek, More U.S. Workers Have IT Jobs Than Ever Before, Eric Chabrow, Apr 24, 2006, July 17, 2006; August 8, 2006.

Latchford, Michael, Lowry, Alexander, Roberts, Ian, PA Consulting Group, "Successful Program Management in a Complex Outsourcing Environment," quoted in CMP Global Services, July 24, 2006, http://www.globalservicesmedia.com/sections/sm/showArticle.jhtml?articleID=190500432

Lawson, Roy, InformationWeek, 2006, quoted in More U.S. Workers Have IT Jobs Than Ever Before, Eric Chabrow, InformationWeek, April 24, 2006.

Levy, Frank and Murnane, Richard, The New Division of Labor: How Computers are Creating the Next Job Market, Princeton University Press, 2004.

Marlin, John Tepper, City Economist, 2006, http://www.cityeconomist.com/pdf/CityEconomist06-04-01.pdf quoted in Crain's Business New York, February 2006, Number of Vacant Computer Jobs Rises: Survey, Amanda Fung, March 29, 2006.

McDougall, Paul, "U.S. Tech Workers In Hot Demand Despite More Outsourcing," InformationWeek, August 8, 2006.

National Research Council (NRC), Funding a Revolution: Government Support for Computing Research, National Academy Press, 1999.

Patterson, David A., Association for Computing Machinery, 2006, http://www.acm.org/globalizationreport; http://www.acm.org/pubs/cacm/

Rose, Barbara, Tech Workers Plugging Back in to a Changed Job Market, Chicago Tribune, July 2006

Society for Information Management, 2006, http://www.simnet.org/

U.S. Bureau of Labor Statistics, U.S. Government, 2006, 2007; http://www.bls.gov.

VARBusiness, March 2006.

Chapter Two
Tech Jobs in the Information Technology Professional Services Sector

Why You Want One – How to Get One

As outlined in Chapter One, you want a tech job because it is a sound and exciting career choice today.

To develop a sound strategy for finding the best employment, you need to consider the best, and best equipped employers for giving you career employment choices and a career. You have hiring options.

You can get "a" tech job. There are plenty. Or you can work with an IT Service Provider who gets continuous work, with major companies, and who you can develop a relationship with. IT Service Providers have contract-contract to permanent and permanent work. You can get an excellent tech job, as a sound career choice, also in Federal, State or Local government (Chapter III).

IT Service Providers for Information Technology Jobs

All over the U.S., Federal, State and City agencies and private corporations are hiring thousands of information technology specialists for various computer tech jobs. Be part of this and work for the leading organizations that are doing the information technology work for America.

The IT Service Provider business, a multi-billion dollar business and phenomenon, delivers the mother load of IT jobs and work in this country, for the nation's best employers. Government agencies and private corporations issue bids for IT services and staff and award contracts to IT Service Providers to create, deploy and maintain IT projects.

IT Service Providers are used to deliver expertise to the client, and Information Technology Jobs to the software programmer, database administrator, network engineer, or developer. You want to connect with these companies.

You Want to Reach the Client Companies

Companies have choices in how they will develop and deploy their IT projects, and in turn who they will hire from and how they will hire for their tech jobs. IT Companies with

The IT Service Provider business, a multi-billion dollar business delivers the mother load of IT jobs and work in this country.

29

Registered Contracts, IT Staffing Firms and IT Domestic Outsourcers are all providing IT services and staff to America's corporate and government sector.

Domestic hiring from third-party vendors will continue to affect the way some companies deploy their information technology jobs and handle their information systems work. Companies may not want to develop IT departments. If their essential service is banking, manufacturing, health or some other industry, companies may rely on IT outsourcing company experts to handle their IT services. Seeking an information technology job with an IT Company should be part of an effective IT job seeking strategy. IT Companies have divisions in IT consulting, IT management and planning, IT data center and operations, programming and network development, and tech support. IT Companies may specialize in a specialty of the IT industry such as data warehousing, help desk or call center technology. Getting placed with a U.S. based IT service provider provides an opportunity to work, whether at the client's workplace or at the domestic provider's workplace, to develop an industry specialty and work with a variety of clients.

IT Service Providers Have the Work

Businesses initiating new IT projects may find the task too complicated and important to be left in the hands of less experienced information systems staff. They enlist the aid of information technology consultants to plan, implement, and manage the IT project. They may hire from an IT service provider, domestic outsourcer, or staffing firm.

IT Service Providers appoint information systems technology jobs to contractual IT professionals, to work either on the client premises or at the vendor's premises. The client company pays the service provider, and the service provider pays the information technology staff person or information technology consultant. With IT staffing companies, the information technology consultant may be paid either by the staffing company or the client, depending on what arrangements are made. The in-house information systems staff can concentrate on core competencies, as new projects are brought on by new tech staff.

Clients find a cost-saving avenue in not setting up an IT department, or in jump starting a project with outside expertise. IT service providers have contracts to hire information technology staff and information technology consultants for the client's tech jobs. Clients realize the benefits of outside expertise and support. They avoid the learning curve it takes to train new employees. They may hire on a term basis and when the project is complete, they are not obligated to keep the information systems consultant on payroll.

When the expense of recruiting a fulltime, permanent employee with benefits outweighs the cost of hiring from an IT service provider, companies go with a service provider. Hiring information technology consultants for short-term information systems jobs makes good economic sense, especially when the IT project has a definite lifespan and limited resources. Another justification for hiring information systems consultants from an IT service provider is when a company would like to benefit from consultants' extensive experience of working on similar projects with clients of comparable resources. Information systems consultants can adjust tried-and-tested IT project management principles according to the current client's circumstances. They can bring their experience with similar applications to the current client. If the client company wants to bring the information consultant on payroll, they may make a job offer.

Seeking a tech job with an IT service provider should be part of any effective IT job seeking strategy. IT service providers have divisions in IT consulting, IT management and planning, IT data center and operations, programming and network development, and tech support. IT outsourcing companies may specialize in an area of the IT industry such as data warehousing, help desk or call center technology. Getting placed with an IT service provider or U.S. based IT outsourcing company provides an opportunity to develop an industry specialty and work with a variety of clients.

IT provider companies with contracts to supply information systems staff are authorized to hire information technology consultants on behalf of various clients.

Corporations and government agencies at Federal, State and Local levels are accelerating adoption of digital technology to transform their operations. The phenomenon of the digital government has created the need for thousands of computer jobs covering the whole spectrum of information technology to transform operations. Developers, programmers, computer security, network engineers, tech support, IT, and telecommunications engineers are required to get the job done.

To transform operations, Federal, State and City government agencies have gone out to bid and awarded contracts to IT service providers. These IT service providers are delivering services. They have won new business and are hiring contract, contract to permanent, and permanent personnel to work on new business with their government clients.

Corporate America alike has seen the advantage of hiring information technology consultants and information technology staff to reengineer its business processes and streamline operations. Cost-savings are achieved in downsizing, as business processes are automated and manual jobs eliminated. Investment is made in information technology staff who will create productivity gains for the entire company.

When new companies are formed or when IT companies win new business to supply computer-related products and services, these companies will go to an IT service provider or an information technology recruiter to manage the hiring process for information technology staff. IT service providers, IT staffing firms, and IT outsourcers represent a diverse array of clients. Professionals seeking technology jobs who contact a representative or information systems recruiter at an IT service provider, IT staffing company, or outsourcer, can gain access to many companies.

New Partnerships – New Players – Government Hires from Third-Party Vendors

Application of business principles to e-government has brought with it the cost-saving techniques of relying on expertise by hiring third-party vendors rather than retaining an in-house staff. Challenges involve 1) defining responsibilities that cannot go to third party vendors, 2) utilizing the available hiring strategies for building and retaining specialized staff; 3) assessing projects on the basis of development and maintenance needs and determining staffing requirements accordingly (Richardson, 2004, x; 200-217; Franzel and Coursey, 2004, 63-77).

Economical in Terms of Job Search Effort

If you have been like many in search of information technology employment, you probably have searched job boards and perhaps submitted your resume in the hopes of snagging one of the computer jobs these sites advertise. A national survey recently reported that only 3% of people who go to job boards actually find a job through one. The other majority find jobs by going directly to the company 1) through proactive contact with professional IT Service Providers and 2) through professional IT Staffing Firms.

You may still be waiting to hear from the job board ads you answered. Or, you only saw jobs that didn't relate to you or that were in some far off place. Or you answered less than 10 ads because that was what was available to you.

Tech jobs are available. However, they are not to be found on job boards. Most employers do not advertise on job boards, because it is expensive for them to do so. There is a known existing supply chain of jobs for the IT industry. It has been developed by the IT industry itself, as it has grown, and developed its own companies to provide specialists.

This supply chain represents the "hidden job market", hidden from job boards, yet in the mainstream of American business. Jobs are delivered by companies, IT Service Providers, with registered contracts to deliver services and staff to companies and government agencies. In addition, professional IT Staffing Companies provide IT staff.

Professional IT Staffing Companies

While IT service providers with contracts have a working relationship established with their clients to deliver services and staff, IT staffing companies receive orders on an ad hoc basis. Thousands of businesses require IT staff. They may or may not go through the bid process to try to lock in pricing for personnel for a fixed time period.

Searching tech jobs through IT staffing companies also puts you in touch with the "hidden" job market. IT staffing companies may or many not advertise. They often rely on networks of employees who know where to go to get IT work, and on networks of information technology staff telling other information technology staff about the IT staffing firm.

Going to an IT staffing firm also has several advantages over submitting resumes to Internet job sites.

First, their representative represents multiple technology companies. Through IT staffing companies, you save several weeks of researching company information on IT companies and interviewing for computer jobs.

Second, dealing with an information systems recruiter creates an opportunity for you to test your value in the IT market and use the information to raise your asking salary.

Third, an information technology recruiter can refer you to two or more companies that could be interested in hiring you. You can increase your salary when a "bidding war" develops between prospective IT companies needing information technology staff.

Fourth, dealing with an information technology recruiter can help you build your network of associates and contacts, thereby increasing your chances of finding the right computer jobs. And fifth, IT staffing companies have company information on companies that have immediate information technology recruitment needs. IT staffing firms are eager to contact the companies to make the right fit between you and the client they represent.

U.S. Federal Government
Information Technology Exchange Program (ITEP)

The ITEP is a new and exciting professional development opportunity. If you are already employed in IT in the private sector, or if you are currently employed in IT in a federal agency, you may be eligible to participate. This program allows exceptional performers from the Federal and private IT sectors to participate in temporary assignments of three (3) months to 1 year, in the other sector. ITEP promotes the interchange of IT workers to develop, supplement, and modernize IT skills to expand the long term competencies of the Federal IT workforce. While Federal agencies have a strong interest in the areas of Enterprise Architecture, Solutions Architecture, IT Project Management, and IT Security, ITEP exchange opportunities can exist in all IT disciplines. Please visit, http://www.opm.gov for more details about the program.

The following Federal agencies are participating in this program. To contact the ITEP representative for jobs for IT professionals from the Private Sector for this program with these listed Agencies, visit http://www.usajobs.opm.gov/itep.asp

- ☐ **DEPARTMENT OF COMMERCE**
- ☐ **DEPARTMENT OF DEFENSE**
- ☐ **DEPARTMENT OF HEALTH AND HUMAN SERVICES**
- ☐ **DEPARTMENT OF HOMELAND SECURITY (DHS)**
- ☐ **DEPARTMENT OF JUSTICE (DOJ)**
- ☐ **DEPARTMENT OF THE TREASURY**
- ☐ **ENVIRONMENTAL PROTECTION AGENCY**
- ☐ **FEDERAL BUREAU OF INVESTIGATION**
- ☐ **OFFICE OF PERSONNEL MANAGEMENT (OPM)**

To view ITEP opportunities in the private sector for existing Federal employees, visit http://www.actgov.org/ITEP.

How to Identify & Connect with Your Prospective Employers

You want to contact and network with the nation's best employers for IT jobs. This market sector has grown up to deal with the demand for computer tech staff. Companies seek to hire expert staff from the growing IT professional services sector or IT service providers.

We recommend resources downloadable at www.infotechemployment.com (http://www.infotechemployment.com) (Info Tech Employment, 2007), an excellent source for identifying and contacting companies in this sector in your region. Companies published have registered contracts with government agencies and American corporations to provide tech staff. You may boost your information technology employment prospects by building valuable relationships with IT service provider companies with contracts, and network with key information technology recruiters.

These companies are the real marketplace - the IT Service Providers, Computer Services Companies doing business for America. These Companies have known, existing high-profile government and private contracts to provide IT services and solutions, hiring and placing staff in their State and often in and outside their region, to get the job done for their clients. The company lists have been prepared by research using the latest information technology (Info Tech Employment, 2007).

Scouting single positions is often discouraging. These are companies, not single positions. Meeting with their representatives, representing multiple companies, multiple positions, saving you weeks of researching and interviewing.

This is an effective, proven, professional, method to target IT companies with computer jobs and tech jobs to get hired. You have a vast array of companies in your marketplace to work with. Books and other resources at http://www.infotechemployment.com will link you to companies serving clients in your State, and in and outside the region. Downloadable resources on *IT Staffing Firms* (http://www.infotechemployment.com) links you to staffing firm contacts for 2300 IT staffing firms. The lists do not duplicate each other. IT Outsourcing Companies (U.S.-based)) employ IT staff in the U.S. to work for U.S. companies, multinationals, companies developing IT for global economies, and government agencies. Links to over 1100 IT Outsourcing Companies are provided in IT Jobs & IT Prospects. The lists do not duplicate each other. Downloadable electronic editions will contain live hyperlinks.

We recommend that you use the source list for your U.S. State, and for your Regional hub as well. Since companies often hire and place regionally, we recommend you take a source list for your regional hub: New York for the NY, NJ, CT and New England area; Virginia for the Potomac Region, MD, DE, PA, OH; Texas for the Southeast; Arizona and Colorado for the Western States; California and Washington State for the Pacific Coast Region. Find Companies-Contacts-Links to get hired in all 50 U.S. States:

☐ **New England States**
☐ **Mid-Atlantic States**
☐ **Potomac Region**
☐ **Southeastern States**
☐ **Midwest**
☐ **Western States**
☐ **West Coast**
☐ **Pacific Northwest States**

IT service providers located in one State may place programmers and system engineers throughout their Region (the Tri-State Region for example, the Pacific Coast Region, the Mid-West Region). They may provide IT services and staff to government entities and companies both within and outside the State in which the IT Services Company itself is located.

It is to your advantage to contact IT service providers in your State, in your Region, and outside your Region, for the widest possible job choice and placement. The companies place programmers in long-term and short term assignments; they provide contract, contract-to-permanent, and permanent employment.

How to Contact Prospective Employers:

☐ Develop a "Prospect" selection of 10-12 company prospects from within your source lists. Choose your "Prospects" by clicking on the company URL link and learning more about them, if they seem like a good or the best "fit" for you and your skills, your interests, your region.

☐ Make a telephone call. Ask for the person in charge of hiring. Introduce yourself , giving them your skill set and number of years experience, and educational background. Ask about them - who they work for, what clients they have, what they are looking for now, and in the future. Take it from there.

☐ To use contact source list E-mail Links:
You may selectively send e-mails to companies you have made contact with, including your resume electronically. See material here on preparing the E-Resume. It is recommended you identify 10-12 "prospect companies" first, research who they are and what they are about from their website URL, make contact with a company representative, and ask if you may send your resume. Get the person's name and individual e-mail address. Send them your resume.Follow-up to see if they received it. Follow-up with a telephone call to talk more definitely about employment.

☐ If you want to do a mailing, and Mail your resume, you may obtain USPS Ready-to-Print Mailing Labels for the IT Service Providers in the Individual 50 U.S. States by purchasing individual U.S. State lists of companies at http://www.infotechemployment. com for $25.00 per individual U.S. State List. The State List also comes with "IT Staffing Firms" list Free.

More about these Companies.

Companies in the growing information professional services sector are no ordinary companies. These are companies winning new business as shown by their active contracts and are in the special business of supplying IT services and staff. Forget scouting individual jobs on Internet job boards. Contacting these companies directly will put you in touch with representatives hiring for multiple companies.

8 Reasons to Connect with IT Service Providers

- ☐ You can meet representatives of multiple companies, saving several weeks of research and interviewing.
- ☐ Introduce yourself. Even with today's technology, the only way to get hired is to meet someone.
- ☐ You will be able to "test your value in the market" and use the information to increase your income.
- ☐ Your income can grow significantly when a "bidding war" develops between two or more companies interested in you, as is often the case.
- ☐ Build your network of associates and contacts. There is a reason for the saying, "It's who you know."
- ☐ Place your resume now. And when they get ready to hire, they will come to you.
- ☐ Look at the vast "hidden" marketplace. These companies don't pay hefty fees to advertise on Internet bulletin boards.
- ☐ Use sources for serious professionals from senior-level to entry-level.

The Benefits

- ☐ The vast "hidden" marketplace is at your fingertips.
- ☐ These companies are specializing in hiring IT staff for computer jobs and tech jobs for their Clients-- with hiring authority.
- ☐ These are Contacts & links to companies with existing, current State, Federal, Corporate contracts to hire IT staff - companies with jobs.
- ☐ This is a Proven Method to find Quality Employment.
- ☐ You are in control.

What Jobs Are Available in the Growing IT Professional Services Sector

- ☐ **Tech Job Titles (Chart I)**
- ☐ **Tech Skill Sets (Chart I)**

"Tech Job Titles – Tech Skill Sets" is an excellent chart, put together by the editors of Information Technology *Jobs in America*, to show you an array of current tech job titles covering all aspects of technology within an organization. An array of Skill Sets accompanies the Job Titles. Employers increasingly want a bundle of skill sets. The Skills Set chart will help you think about your abilities and present your array on your Resume.

IT Job Classifications for Hirees (Chart II)

IT Job Classifications are used by IT Service Providers and IT Staffing Companies to rate hirees as to level of experience and expertise and pay. Typically, IT Service Providers have offered their clients hourly or annual rates for staff based on several levels of expertise and experience (regardless of software used or skill required). IT Service Providers will then position according to their skill, and pay them according to the job classification rate.

To see sample IT Job Classifications and their position descriptions and rates, see Chart II included here - IT Job Classifications. These are the IT Job Classifications developed by one client organization hiring from IT Service Providers. Twenty-three (23) actual companies agreed to supply tech staff, according to the job classifications, at the hourly rates shown on the Chart. Note, that typically the rate offered by the IT Service Provider is NOT the rate the employee will be paid. The employee will be paid 35-65% the contracted hourly rate. These IT Job Classifications show how IT Service Providers and Staffing Firms typically classify tech jobs to determine position and pay.

The Job Package or Rates of Employment

The Job Package with IT Service Providers and IT Staffing Companies will depend on several variables. You may be hired contract, contract-to-permanent, or permanent. You will negotiate your job package with the particular IT Service Provider or Staffing Company.

To give you some idea of sample Salaries, you may look at the real sample Hourly Rates agreed to by twenty-three IT Service Providers. Under their contract with the client organization, they will offer employees, under the respective job classifications, at the hourly rates published.

Completing the Contact, Application and Hiring Process

After you identify your companies, and prepare your Prospect List, you are ready to complete the contact by sending your Resume and making telephone contact.

A growing number of IT professionals intuitively realize the importance of a well-written IT resume in their job search. To balance skills representation and the uniqueness of your work experience, write the right resume. You will win because of the right skills, the right resume, and the quality of your contacts.

Professional tech job resume writers know that increasingly employers are looking for Tech Job Titles and Tech Job Skill Sets. Up front, the reviewer wants to know your IT Title - Key Qualifications - Skill Sets - Experience and Education.

Here is a sample of IT Titles:

- ☐ **Applications Developer/Programmer Mainframe**
- ☐ **Systems Manager Mainframe**
- ☐ **Applications Developer/Programmer Mid-Range**
- ☐ **Systems Manager Mid-Range**
- ☐ **Applications Developer PC- Systems Manager PC**
- ☐ **Business Process Analyst (BPA) &**
- ☐ **Business Process Re-Engineering Analyst**
- ☐ **C++ Programmer**
- ☐ **Computer Aided Design & Drafting Specialist (CADD)**
- ☐ **Computer Animation Designer**
- ☐ **Computer Graphics Designer**
- ☐ **Computer Programmer**
- ☐ **Computer Software Engineer/Computer Software Programmer**
- ☐ **Computer Systems Engineer/Computer Software Programmer**
- ☐ **Database Administrator/Programmer/Specialist**
- ☐ **Data Conversion Specialist**
- ☐ **Desktop Asset Manager/Specialist**
- ☐ **Desktop Support Specialist**
- ☐ **Electronic Commerce (EC) & Electronic**
- ☐ **Data Interchange (EDI) Developer**
- ☐ **Director of IT/IT Manager**
- ☐ **Documentation Specialist**
- ☐ **E-Commerce Manager/Director of E-Business**
- ☐ **Electronic Output Manager**
- ☐ **Enterprise Resource Planning (ERP) Consultant**
- ☐ **Geographic Information Systems (GIS) Systems Analyst/Manager**
- ☐ **Help Desk Analyst/Manager**
- ☐ **Imaging Services Analyst/Manager/Director**
- ☐ **Information Security Analyst/Manager/Director**

☐ **Interactive Voice Response (IVR) Application Developer**

☐ **Internet/Intranet Applications Developer/Programmer**

☐ **IT Administrative Support Specialist**

☐ **IT Management & Planning: CIO/CTO/Development Director/**

☐ **IT Policies & Procedures Director/Specialist/Analyst**

☐ **IT Procurement & Contracting Specialist/Manager**

☐ **IT Trainer**

☐ **Java Programmer**

☐ **JavaScript Programmer**

☐ **Local Area Network Services (LANs) Administrator/Technician**

☐ **Network Architect//Administrator**

☐ **Network Engineer**

☐ **Operations/Data Center Specialist/Director**

☐ **Oracle Database Programmer**

☐ **PeopleSoft Programmer**

☐ **Point-Of-Sale Systems (POS)**

☐ **Programmer/Developer**

☐ **Quality Assurance Specialist**

☐ **Sales: Technical Sales Representative**

☐ **SAP Specialist**

☐ **Security Administrator/Specialist/Technician**

☐ **Software Engineer**

☐ **Software Programmer**

☐ **Sun Solaris Systems Engineer**

☐ **Systems Analyst**

☐ **Systems Integration Director/Specialist**

☐ **Technical Trainer**

☐ **Tape Librarian**

☐ **Technical Writer**

- ☐ **Technology Procurement Specialist**

- ☐ **Telecommunications Engineer/Director/Specialist/Analyst**

- ☐ **Web Designer/Site Designer**

- ☐ **Web Developer/Programmer/Content Editor**

- ☐ **Webmaster**

- ☐ **Wide Area Network (WAN) Administrator/Specialist**

- ☐ **Workflow Management Services**

The Scannable E-Resume

Positioning yourself with the right title sets the stage. Then note and write on your Resume the skill sets you bring to the job. IT Skill Sets & Job Titles go hand in hand. You should bring all your skill sets to bear in your resume. You may be more comfortable with one skill than another. However, familiarity with the fundamentals of several skills indicates you are a ready learner and can adapt to new situations and products.

After you make initial contact with your companies and they ask to see your resume, ask them what skill sets you should highlight. Send them your resume and give them permission to interview you to customize your resume to the client they want to show it to.

Preparing the E-Resume

To e-Mail your Resume to company Contacts, you need to prepare the e-Resume and the e-Mail body. **The Scannable E-Resume fundamentals are as follows:**

☐ **Make it Scannable.**
☐ **Use ASCII Text formatting only, only Tabs and Spaces.**
☐ **Tabs & Spaces are the only formatting elements allowed in ASCII.**
☐ **Use a simple Font, no Borders, no Columns, no Underlining, no Bold face, no Italics**
☐ **The Font size should be between 12-14 points.**
☐ **Start your Resume with Skills-Abilities-Accomplishments, rather than Objective, Experience or Education**
☐ **Send the e-Resume in the e-Mail Body, AND as an e-Mail Attachment.**
  Include: Name, Address, Telephone, E-Mail
  Skills-Abilities-Accomplishments (Summary)
  Objective (Optional)
  IT Title – IT Position & Level
  Key Qualifications
  Keyword Skill Sets
  Experience and Education.
  Vendor Training - Company Sponsored Training
  Certifications
  Past 3-8 Years Experience
☐ **The Body of the e-Mail fundamentals:**
☐ **Copy-Paste your e-Resume into the Body of the e-Mail, in ASCII format**
☐ **List your Key Experience in the e-Mail Subject: field (such as "Resume Demonstrating 6 Years Database Experience"**
☐ **Start your Resume with Skills-Abilities-Accomplishments, rather than Objective, Experience or Education**
☐ **After you Copy-Paste your e-Resume in the e-Mail Body, Copy-Paste your Cover Letter, also in ASCII Text Format.**

REFERENCES

Info Tech Employment, Editors, <u>Computer Jobs with the Growing Information Technology Professional Services Sector</u>, William Briggs Publishing, 2007, http://www.infotechemployment.com.

Info Tech Employment, Editors, <u>IT Jobs-IT Prospects- Companies-Contacts-Links: Get Hired by Companies Winning New Business and Requiring New Staff</u> (2007), William Briggs Publishing, 2006, http://www.infotechemployment.com.

Registered Contract between 23 Companies and Client Company, 2006 from one Large U.S. Municipality, Published as Registered Contract in Municipal Government Public Records, by Info Tech Employment, Editors, <u>IT Jobs-IT Prospects- Companies-Contacts-Links: Get Hired by Companies Winning New Business and Requiring New Staff</u> (2007), William Briggs Publishing, 2006, http://www.infotechemployment.com.

Chapter Three
Information Technology Jobs in Government
U.S. Federal - State - City

Why You Want One – How to Get One

To put the U.S. job market into perspective, we are now in a Global Economy. This creates shifts in industries and markets. As industries compete and as markets open and fold, downsizing, outsourcing and restructuring are common. Government Jobs in Technology may be a good choice for you -- if you want to move with the industry for a steady career, and work in delivering the promise of e-government throughout the United States.

The individual with tech skills who wants to work in information technology, information systems or part of the technology endeavor in an organization has excellent employment opportunities and choices. You may work as 1) Contract labor, 2) Contract Labor-hired to a Permanent Position; 3) Full time Employee in business or industry, or 4) Full Time Employee in City, State or Federal Government.

Only the last choice, Full Time Employee in City, State or Federal Government, is an employment choice without the risks and upsets commonly caused by corporate downsizing, outsourcing and restructuring.

Contract Labor is hired on an as "needed basis" by a hiring agent for a company or government agency. The employee will be placed for a fixed term at an hourly rate. This type of work is often good for 1) the person entering the field, 2) the person wanting to see many types of work situations before settling down, 3) the person who wants to work in the Information Technology Professional Services sector on a regular and continuing basis (Info Tech Employment, 2007).

We are now in a global economy with shifts in industries and markets.

Contract Labor hired to Permanent employment often results 1) when an employer wants to hire an employee full time or 2) when an employer no longer wants to or is unable to (due to changes in hiring policy) pay the employee on a consultant basis and must move the employee to full time status.

A government job in technology with job permanence over a 25-year career, a higher class of salaries in IT, and built-in pension may be the right choice for you.

Full Time Employment at a Business or Industry occurs as businesses and industries rely increasingly on information technology, create a data center or infrastructure, and hire staff to handle the technology needs of the organization. Almost all businesses and industries have need for information technology and support personnel. Jobs are easily found. However, the nature of business and industry is often unstable for the individual employee. Downsizing, Outsourcing, Obsolescence and Restructuring often spells the "DOOR" for the individual employee.

Full Time, Permanent Employment in Government – U.S. Federal-City or State – adds a new word to the mix. *"Permanent"* generally means that once an employee is hired competitively and passes a probationary performance period, they are considered a Career Employee. They will be permitted to perform their job, or a similar job in another agency should there be a restructuring, for the lifetime of their career. (This is not the place for explaining the nature of the Career Civil Service in Federal-State and City governments. See the References provided in the bibliography for more information).   A 'Full Time Permanent Employment in Government' will not suffer the same effects of downsizing and outsourcing as a non-permanent government employee, and is not subject to the same downsizing, outsourcing, and restructuring as in business or industry. The Full Time Permanent Employee in Government will not lose his/her job under most circumstances.

**Top 10 Reasons To Get a Government Job
In Technology**

1. In almost all cases, **Experience is an acceptable substitute for
   Education** in obtaining the government job in technology.

2. The **Career Ladder for the Technology Job career growth series of jobs
   allows you to move from position to position, agency to agency,
   department to department to achieve Promotion and Advancement**

3. Over the long run, **you will make more money with a government
   job in technology than with private employment** with its expected
   periods of unemployment and transition.

4. Government jobs in technology offer **on-the-job training. As**
   government transitions to new equipment and software, agencies
   provide training for its career employees

5. City, State, and Federal jobs typically offer, on average, a 2.2%
   5% raise **per year.** This raise may not seem a lot. However, these raises
   are **compounded**. They can be **counted on** by permanent employees.
   A "Survey of IT Jobs in U.S. States & Major U.S. Cities 2006-2007"
   conducted by Info Tech Employment shows that most U.S. States and
   Major Cities offer between 10-35 Civil Service Information Technology
   Job Titles. The Salaries for IT Job Titles are higher than for many trade,
   labor and administrative titles. The Average Raise per Year for IT Job
   Titles, according to the Survey, is 2.25%, with a cumulative 5-Year Raise
   of 11.25%, and a Compounded Raise of 11.75% (Info Tech Employment,
   Survey, 2007, http://www.infotechemployment.com.)   In addition,
   many States and Major Cities have Service in Job and Service in Title
   Longevity Increases, at 5 years, and at 10 years. These Longevity
   Increases, once earned, continue to be compounded as part of the
   Salary, and paid over the career of the employee. Over the course
   of a career history, these raises and longevity in title increases add
   up. A government employee, whose job skills will be enhanced with
   training along the road, will experience an equal or better salary than an

employee in private business. The government employee will not lose
income due to unemployment. The government employee will not have
to accept a job at a lower wage in a job transition, lose a job due to
outdated skills, or suffer layoffs due to downsizing or restructuring.

6. Government Jobs come with a **built-in pension** that the Employer
pays for. The **Pension** is equivalent in most cases to ½ salary of final
3 year salary average times number of years of employment. The
Average Retirement

Pension Percentage among the 50 U.S. States and Major U.S. Cities, found
in the Survey, was found to be between 1.5%-2% . Using the figures
gathered in Info Tech Employment Survey, a starting
salary of $55,000 in an Information Technology job, a 2.25% raise per
year yields an 11.75% compounded raise over 5 years (or $61,475.). The
20-Year Retirement Pension for a career employee at a starting salary
of $55,000 (without Longevity added in) is an estimated $27,369. The 25-
Year Retirement Pension for a career employee at $55,000 (without
Longevity) is estimated at $45,876. The 30-year Retirement Pension
for a career employee at $55,000 (without Longevity added in) is
estimated at $61,530. The Career Pension is in addition to Social Security
Benefits. The Estimated Pension amount is in today's dollars.

7. **Learning on the job and training comes with the territory**. You will
supplement your skills and move with the industry as you work with
others in the information technology infrastructure and endeavor

8. While the wait on a list call may seem long, tedious and time wasted,
in reality it is time well spent. **Good employment is on the other end of a
list call wait**.

9. **Health and Medical Benefits** continue to be a part of government jobs.
It is estimated that the Health and Medical Benefits package for you and
your family, on average, supplements your salary by 33%.

In other words, if you were to pay for your health and medical benefits
out of pocket, it would cost you an additional 33% of your salary. Or, to
put it another way, your salary is, in effect, worth 33% more than base
salary because your employer, the government agency, is paying for your
benefits. A $55,000 salary is in effect worth $55,000 x 33% ($18,150) or
$73,150.

10. **Paid Vacation Time & Sick Time** continues to be equal to or higher than
that provided in private industry.

Financial facts

To put the U.S. job market and your career into further perspective, here are some further facts.   Your career and personal finances will benefit greatly over a 25 year work history by fewer or zero bouts of unemployment. Your career and personal finances can suffer greatly over a 25 year career life, by any bouts of unemployment.

You will benefit from a Health and Benefits package offered by a government employer. Most companies will stop offering significant benefits packages because they won't be able to afford them.

That means a government salary is, in effect, increased by 25-35%, the value of the health and benefits package paid by the government employer. It means, to the contrary, a salary in private industry, is decreased by as much as 25-35% because the employee will have to spend an additional 25-35% of salary out of their own pocket for health coverage for the employee and his or her family.

Your career as a government employee will provide an employer-sponsored and paid Pension. Employer-sponsored and paid for Pension Plans in private business and industry have almost all disappeared in the past 50 years. They have been replaced by 401K plans, where the employee saves their own money, and in some, not all cases, the employer makes a partial match to the funds.

The Government employer sponsored and paid for **Pension Benefit Payout can be equal to half the final average salary**, of the employee's final three work years. In recent years, many government paid-for Pension Plans have stopped requiring the employee to make a contribution to their pension from out of their annual salary. (For more Pension Benefit Projections for Technology Job Titles in Government, see Chapter Three).

Benefits in Brief

These are the Benefits in Brief, discussed in greater detail in Chapter Three in the Section, The Job Package.

- **Pay**
- **Permanence**
- **Annual Raises**
- **Longevity Increases**
- **Pension Plan**
- **Security**
- **Union Representation**
- **Health & Benefits Package**
- **Vacation**
- **Sick Days**
- **Flex Time**
- **Long Term & Short Term Disability**
- **Career Ladder**
- **Training and Career Development**

The New Face of Government

The New Civil Service and
Public Unionism for Technology Jobs

Beginning in the 1980's, a new Civil Service took shape. Dramatic downsizing in U.S. Federal, State, and City government, from peak 1960's workforce levels, occurred. Business-process engineering reshaped government departments, job functions, and titles, focusing services on business processes. Productivity gains brought about by the technology itself reshaped workforce levels and government processes.

The new Civil Service retains its seminal historic purpose – to provide a workforce hired by merit rather than by personal patronage. It continues to ensure the entrance of qualified workers for new industries into government.

Yet the face of the Civil Service, especially for the technology employee, has changed. The Civil Service is *leaner* and *greener*. It is characterized by a reduction of clerical level jobs, the creation of a new class of employees with higher salaries, the creation of new Civil Service titles to cover computer and emerging technology jobs; and the incorporation of technology into all phases of government operations and business processes.

Civil service designates the body of people employed in the civil administration of governments. It excludes elected officials, as well as the military, and encompasses the vast bulk of those who see to the daily functioning of the public sector, from the municipal level to the national level. In recent times, the term Civil Service has come to mean not just the strata of officials who administer government, but a set of standards by which they are selected: it reflects the idea that government functions best when it is staffed based on merit and not political patronage. Most civil servants throughout the world today are chosen based on examinations or experience and education papers as a substitute for multiple choice examinations (AFSCME, CWA Local 1180, 2006).

Example: *New York Civil Service Law*

In New York State, the merit system of Civil Service is enshrined in the State Constitution. Article V, section 6 of the Constitution states:

Appointments and promotions in the civil service of the State and all of the civil divisions thereof, including cities and villages, shall be made according to merit and fitness to be ascertained, as far as practicable, by examination which, as far as practicable, shall be competitive.

The state's Civil Service Law implements this mandate of the State Constitution. It applies to state as well as municipal employment. Municipalities each have their own rules to implement the state Civil Service Law. In New York City, those rules are set by the New York City Civil Service Commission, and administered by the Department of Citywide Administrative Services (DCAS) (AFSCME, CWA Local 1180, 2006).

Civil Service and Civil Service Employees

The bulk of Civil Service employees work in Civil Service titles subject to examinations in respective States and Cities (or Experience and Education summary papers as a substitute for exam). The Federal Government requires an Application that will be graded to see if a candidate meets the job requirements; the best candidate based on this review, will be offered a job interview.

In almost all cases, experience is an acceptable substitute for formal education for Civil Service jobs. The opportunity to describe experience and education is provided on all job and exam or experience and education applications

The Union Locals of the State, City or Federal government represent both workers who are "permanent," i.e., who have passed the Civil Service test for the title they are serving in, and workers who are "provisional," i.e., who have not passed the civil service test for the title they are serving in and were appointed provisionally to their job.

When a Civil Service exam or qualification by experience and education paper is given, the exam or qualification requirements are reviewed and graded. People who pass and have the requirements are certified as Qualified and placed on a Certified List. Once the list is established afterwards, City or State agencies hire from it. The list consists of all those who passed the test, ranked by their scores. Civil Service Law in most U.S. States and Cities requires agencies to utilize the list when they are hiring for that title, and requires them to consider the top three scorers remaining on this list; this is known as the "one-in-three rule." Once a list is established, it remains in effect for one year, and can be extended for up to three additional years. (For more information, see Completing the Application & Hiring Process.)

Provisional employees have no tenure rights. They may be initially appointed to their jobs if there is no list in effect at the time, but when a list is established following a test, agencies are required to hire from the list, and provisionals may lose their jobs as permanent civil servants are hired off the list.

There are two types of exams: "promotional exams" are open to those who hold a permanent Civil Service title in the same promotional line (e.g., someone who has a Clerical Associate title would be eligible to take the Principal Administrative Associate promotional exam); while "open competitive exams" are open to anyone regardless of civil service title (there are still educational and other requirements). Local Unions urge eligible provisional members to take a promotional exam for the title in which they are serving as soon as possible. They urge those without any Civil Service title to take an open competitive exam for the Civil Service title in direct line for promotion into their Local Union title. Department of Citywide Administrative Services (DCAS) (AFSCME, CWA Local 1180, 2006). (For more information, see Completing the Application & Hiring Process.)

The Historic Roots

A Brief History of Civil Service

The first use of examinations to select civil officials was in China during the Han dynasty (206 B.C.E. - 220 C.E.). In the west, the selection of civil administrators based on merit did not begin until the rise of national states replaced the feudal order. In the mid-17th century, Prussia instituted a Civil Service on a competitive basis. Similar reforms followed in France, where they became the basis for the Napoleonic reforms at the beginning of the 19th century.

In the United States, as early as 1853 Congress set to fight the forces of corruption, waste and ineptness in hiring by setting a salary scale for four types of clerks in the Washington offices of the Treasury, War, Navy and Department of the Interior, and required major departments to establish examining boards to hold "pass examinations" for applicants. In 1868, during Andrew Johnson's administration, a joint committee of Congress recommended the introduction of competitive examinations and other reforms. The first Civil Service Commission was established by Congress in 1871, authorizing the President to regulate the "admission of persons into the Civil Service. A board quickly adopted rules classifying all positions according to the duties to be performed and grades for purposes of promotion, setting up competitive examinations. In 1882 The U.S. Civil Service Commission was formed. The first civil service reform association was formed in New York City in 1877, and in 1883 New York City and Brooklyn became the first cities in the nation to adopt Civil Service regulations. The national civil service movement was inspired by the New York examples, and the 1883 Pendleton Act reestablished a federal Civil Service Commission, and this one lasted (Liston, 1967).

The Civil Service was started nationally in the Theodore Roosevelt era. He insisted that exams be practical and test the actual duties performed. The Retirement Act of 1920 and the Classification Act of 1923 established the principle of equal pay for equal work. In 1938 President Roosevelt issued two executive orders stating that all positions which were not excepted by law from the competitive service were in the competitive service. The second order established Divisions of Personnel in the executive departments and agencies. The sense of security and well being Civil Servants enjoy today is largely due to the gains made by unions in the post depression years through WWII. (Liston, 1967, 38). By 1950, 45 States had Civil Service systems to hire for State and City jobs.

Public Employee Unionism expanded membership of Civil Servants in the 1950's. The American Federation of State, County and Municipal Employees (AFSCME), the American Federation of Teachers (AFT), and other unions of firefighters, policemen, nurses, civil servants and post office workers swelled the ranks of the public employee unions from under 400,000 in 1955 to over 4 million by the early 1970's.

AFSCME, a union for small groups of technical and professional workers, became one of the AFL/CIO's largest affiliates. It grew into a union of gray and new white collar workers, encompassing industrial trades, social service workers, clerical workers, and the class of information technology workers (Zieger, 1994, 164).

The breakthrough of Public Employee Unionism into the 1960's prepared a climate ripe for the representation of emerging technology workers by the public unions in the 1970's, 1980's, and 1990's.

As Personnel Departments identified new workforce demands and created job titles and classifications in the 1970s-1990's, the AFSCME/AFL/CIO unions spread their wings to represent the workers in the titles. The various Civil Service Commissions, Departments of Personnel and Public Employee Unions worked to incorporate new computer and emerging technology jobs titles and examinations into the government Civil Service.

Ensuring a Qualified Workforce for New Technologies
Civil Service Job Titles for Technology Jobs

The role of labor is essential in the operation of government. As new needs develop, business and government need to hire new staff. In business, companies hire competitively by advertising job openings, searching college placement and employment offices and hiring companies specializing in IT or information technology to provide them the expert staff they need.   In government, labor is hired either open competitively through the Civil Service exam process, or contractually by hiring subcontractors in IT or information technology to provide the expert labor.

Since the mid-1970's, the need for an information technology workforce has changed the landscape of State, Municipal and Federal U.S. government. New workforce needs have necessitated new job titles, job classifications, on-the-job education, training, hiring, and pay scales.

Developing New Job Titles for Emerging Technologies

First generation technology workers often worked under non-technology job titles. As late as 2005, many government career manuals failed to bring to light the new information technology sector or mention information technology as a viable source of employment. Initially, the newness of the industry, the relative unfamiliarity with the nature or complexity of the work, and the rapidly changing face of emerging technology, created a particular climate in which computer job and information technology job titles were developed.

During the 1980's, Federal, State, and City Personnel and Administrative Services Departments created task forces to create job titles and job descriptions that would ensure the movement of qualified workers into jobs needed for the future. The job descriptions could neither be too specific, as related to a specific hardware or software, nor too generic, because that would leave the door open to people with no training or experience. Often training to operate specific hardware and software was required. To accommodate this, Certification, Education and Experience requirements, with particular vendor products, were included in many job descriptions. These jobs titles have been expanded and refined, as new needs have been identified and new job titles required.

Public Unionism for Technology Jobs

The sense of security and well being Civil Servants enjoy today is largely due to the gains made by Public Unions in the post depression years through WWII. (Liston, 1967, 38). Affluent workers and stable unions characterized the 1950's and 1960's. (Zieger, 1994, 164).

"Aggressive organizing by such unions as the American Federation of State, City & Municipal Employees (AFSCME), the American Federation of Teachers (AFT), and other unions of firefighters, policemen, nurses, civil servants, and postal employees... swelled union membership among government workers from under 400,000 in 1955 to over 4 million by the early 1970's," according to Robert Zieger in American Workers, American Unions. Public sector unionism grew through through the 1960's and 1970's. While the microchip revolution permitted private sector corporate employers to relocate in low-wage non-union countries like Malaysia, the Carribean, China and India, one of the biggest buyers of the new microchip equipment was government – spending money on a new trained workforce to use the equipment. Despite problems for unions in the private sector in the 1980's and 1990's, unions in the public sector continued to provide the stable workforce the Federal, State and Local governments needed." (Zieger, 1994).

Between 1950 and 1980, the prosperity and growth of gross national product led to "big government", both in terms of the payrolls of federal, state and local governments, and the programs and constituents government supported in a new welfare state. By the 1980's the cost of this government to the American taxpayer was deemed too high.

New technology enabled Federal, State and Municipal government to "downsize," to trim payrolls. It enabled Federal, State and Municipal governments to reduce the cost of social programs with legislated "welfare reform." Welfare reform coincided with new technologies. New technologies were used by State and Local social services agencies to develop job opportunity databases in conjunction with American businesses. Information technology systems continue to be used by social service workers to identify job opportunities for welfare clients and to help them schedule interviews and start to work.

The stable unions maintained their stability in government through these years. They supported reduction of workforce through the attrition of older workers. They furthered   the "re-engineering of government" by developing of new Civil Service job titles and salary bases with Departments of Personnel to accommodate a new class of technological workers.

The breakthrough in public employee unionism from the 1950's and 1960's laid the ground to benefit the new class of educated and skilled information technology professionals.

Growth in membership by representing these new titles balanced losses in union membership brought about by reduction of payrolls elsewhere. The unions continue to serve as a channel for economic gain and equality of treatment among minorities, immigrants and highly educated and skilled professionals. Collective bargaining and coverage of information technology professionals has created a high standard of living, rather than a substandard living, for a new class of educated and skilled technology professionals.

Personnel Departments identified new workforce demands and created job titles and classifications in the 1980s-1990's. New Civil Service job titles, with union representation, are an ardent reminder to government workers or Americans that we too will share in the fruits of the capitalistic system, and the productivity gains brought by technology.

Organized labor's achievements to organize the workforce in technology jobs can be seen in:

  □ the creation of Union Locals to represent information technology jobs,
  □ the creation and definition of job titles to reflect the new skills required
     for information technology jobs,
  □the creation of experience and education exams to determine the
     qualifications of job candidates, and
  □workplace safety and security guidelines and measures for workers
     who operate video display terminal equipment and other high tech
     equipment.

While the zeal in organized labor of the 1930's and 1940's waned during the 1960's and 1970's, when there was more job security and less limitation to obtaining a job, the concerns of that zeal have been raised again with the current generation.

International outsourcing, corporate mergers, and reorganizations are driving up the desirability of government jobs with union protection and benefits. More people want good government jobs. The high cost of union negotiated government job benefits makes the nature of union-management negotiations as much "about the money" as it was prior to WWII.   Labor and Management today are locking heads on sticking points such as who pays what share of medical benefits, salaries, benefits for new employees, and other tradeoffs that would reduce the union benefit package and reduce the cost of pensions.

In the 1990's, as an alternative to all-Union Civil Service staff with information technology staff reaping full benefits and paid pensions, many Federal, State and Local governments brought in consultants. The injunction in many State and City administrations was to "jump start" new technology applications and build infrastructure and applications fast with expert trained staff, and to build a core trained information technology workforce in Civil Service. Management now had a choice of hiring options: they could hire contract, contract-to-permanent, or full time permanent for an in-house staff, and use a combination of all three employment methods. Government jobs in technology have grown, both those filled by third-party providers and those filled through Competitive Civil Service for a Career Civil Service workforce in emerging technologies. The benefits to the information technology jobseeker have been and will continue to be considerable.

Government Jobs in Technology: Who Is Qualified?

A Higher Educated Workforce

Since there was a limited supply of candidates coming out of college with computer science degrees in the 1970's and 1980's, at the outset of the technology boom personnel departments looked to candidates with higher education, with their proven ability to learn. Many people moved into information technology with degrees in English, Math, Engineering, and Business. With their abilities to think critically and research, new staff learned software packages, performed systems analyses, and built information technology infrastructures and systems.

The demand for people with higher education, to research, implement and maintain new technology, has created a "new division of labor". In their book, The New Division of Labor: How Computers are Creating the Next Job Market, Frank Levy and Richard Murnane describe how the increased use of computers corresponds to an increased demand for a higher skilled workforce. (Levy and Murnane, 2004, 3-34) "Expert thinking" is required to know a technology, a product, a process, and to interpret data or situations and solve problems. "Critical reasoning" is required to understand how the parts fit together and to assess what needs to be done. "Complex communication skills" are required to communicate with vendors, clients, and team members within the organization. Rapid technology change raises the value of verbal and quantitative literacy.

"This dynamic, repeated in many workplaces, has contributed to the extraordinary growth over the past twenty-give years in the earnings gap between college graduates and high school graduates. In 1979, the average thirty-year old man with a bachelor's degree earned just 17 percent more than a thirty-year old man with a high school diploma. Today, the equivalent college to high school wage gap exceeds 50 percent, and the gap for women is larger. Employers judge that college graduates are more likely than high school graduates to have the skills needed to do the jobs requiring expert thinking and complex communication....These skills include the ability to bring facts to bear in problem-solving, the ability to judge when one problem-solving strategy is not working and another should be tried, and the ability to engage in complex communication with others" (Levy and Murnane, 2004, 3-34).

Computers are creating jobs even as they destroy jobs. Since the 1970's, companies that invested heavily in computers have shifted their workforces away from high school graduates and upward toward college graduates. (Levy and Murnane, 2004, 3-34).

The same trend has been seen in government. Clerical jobs have been reduced. Clerical functions such as timekeeping and payroll are now automated. Computers now substitute for and complement some work. Computers also take over various rules-based operations, where the operation can be automated. Middle manager and supervisory positions have been reduced and redefined, because the need to maintain an army of clerks has disappeared.

However, the new technologies open doors. They require a higher skilled workforce that can bring "expert thinking" and "complex communication skills" to the job. A proportionately smaller and higher paid class of employee, a "new division of labor", has been created in U.S. Federal, State and Municipal government, to research, develop, implement and maintain computer infrastructure and systems. In addition, managers and analysts are required to re-engineer government processes to a service delivery model utilizing the emerging technologies. Managerial and analyst tasks include systems analysis, data analysis, data security, project management, system management, and information quality assurance and quality control. These functions have redefined many job titles, now classified as information technology job titles.

Experience Is an Acceptable Substitute for Formal Education

Government jobs in technology require teamwork, expert communication, and critical thinking— troubleshooting, making decisions, developing systems that are business-driven, and building and maintaining computer infrastructures at all levels of government. These government jobs in technology will be required throughout the decade and beyond. Because demand exceeds supply, government jobs in technology are available to people with experience, as an acceptable substitute for formal education, in almost all cases. The President of the Association for Computing Machinery reported recently that the number of American college students majoring in computer science is dwindling. David A. Patterson cited a survey from last year that found only 1 in 75 college students majored in computer science in 2005, compared to 1 in 30 in 2000 (ACM, 2006).

Government jobs in technology allow experience to substitute for formal college education in nearly all cases. Because of high demand, many jobseekers are moving into government by bringing experience, vendor-sponsored training or vendor product certifications. Because technology is changing so rapidly, it is difficult for college students to learn all products or new technologies. College students majoring in computer science and management information systems will bring principles of information technology and a mind-set capable of life-long learning to their computer jobs. Government jobs in technology will continue to go to people with a computer science or management information systems education. They will bring their educational success to their computer careers. Jobs will also go to people who bring experience as an acceptable substitute for formal college training.

Now, a survey from the Society for Information Management (SIM) indicates that getting the best possible people on the payroll will become the challenge in coming years. In "The Information Technology Workforce: Trends and Implications 2005-2008," authors say that factors such as the shift from IT services to business-process services, imminent baby-boomer retirements and declining IT-focused enrollments in U.S. and European universities will change the IT employment landscape between now and 2008 (SIM, 2006).

Core Skills Include Business-Process Understanding –
Critical Thinking – Communication

Building a government career in technology requires technical skills, as well as business skills. Employers seek employees who understand business processes. Jobseekers with business skills and excellent communication skills will be highly prized. The business and soft skills play a key role. The soft skills, such as oral and written communication, team working, critical/analytical thinking, problem solving, and adaptability, are cardinal. Business skills, such as project management, customer relations, needs analysis, and understanding business-driven decisions and the value of cost-benefit analysis come into high play.

IT professionals moving into government need to acquire more knowledge of the business side of IT in order to advance their careers. Technical aptitude will always be a prerequisite for entry into the IT profession, but business skills account for five of the top 10 critical skills that organizations will require for their in-house staffs over the next three years.

The need to acquire business knowledge in addition to technical proficiency has been a recurring theme for IT solution providers during the past few years, and it's especially true for those who buy technology solutions.

"It's one thing to talk about the bells and whistles and what a technology can do, but you have to make a business case for it to the executive and management level to move forward," says Tony Vasco, vice president of the security division for Convergent, a systems integrator in Schaumburg, Ill, as reported in March 2006 VAR*Business*. (VarBusiness, 2006).

A successful government career in technology requires working well individually and as a team member, embracing knowledge about emerging technologies, demonstrating troubleshooting ability, and the ability to work to facilitate the core functions and services of government.

Professional education is one corner stone. A technical postsecondary education is strongly recommended. A four-year degree in Computer Science, Computer Engineering, Information Technology, or Management Information Systems makes a professional highly qualified. Postgraduate degree programs qualify an applicant to negotiate for a higher pay level.

Vendor-related certification, such as the Sun Certified Java Programmer Certification or Microsoft's MCSE certification and the IT certificate programs offered by higher educational institutions also qualify an applicant, especially for vendor-specific, product-specific computer jobs. Experience transferred from industry to government carries a great deal of weight on government job applications and experience and education papers.

Drawing Graduates
from Various College Degree Programs & Majors

English, Math, Computer Science, Business Administration, Management Information Systems, Public Administration, and other college degree programs and majors are suitable B.A. and M.A. majors to meet an education requirement for most government jobs in technology. While a computer science degree, associate tegree, technical college degree or certification is desirable, it is not necessary to have a computer science degree or major to get a government job in technology. Applicants are usually credited as meeting the education requirement with a high school diploma and/or 4-year college degree. Job requirements may give additional credit for a specific college major, a certain number of courses in a technical skill, or post graduate work. As an acceptable substitute for the formal education requirement, a certain amount of experience is specified in the open competitive test filing or job announcement.

Government Agencies
Attracting & Retaining Experienced IT Workers

By 2015, nearly one in three workers in the United States will be over the age of 50 (BLS, 2006). As the relative proportion of younger workers declines, attracting and retaining experienced and reliable workers will become a core business strategy for all employers. There are good opportunities in government for experienced employees to get new computer jobs, to change agencies, or to change divisions and obtain job upgrade promotions.

Climate Favorable for Entry Level & Experienced Personnel

There will be more government jobs in technology available than supply over the next decade. Demand will be exceeding supply, for several reasons. An aging workforce is retiring, making it an optimum time for entry-level people to move into information technology. Entry level computer jobs are available, as well as advanced positions. There are good opportunities in government for experienced employees to get new computer jobs, to change agencies, or to change divisions and obtain job upgrade promotions.

Lucrative Pay

Government jobs in technology are one of the most lucrative careers today. With raises and longevity increases, the salaries will outpace increases in inflation. Starting computer job salaries will grow about 5% this year over, last year's base, according to *InformationWeek*. (InformationWeek, 2006) While minimum wage in the U.S. is around $7.00 an hour, most computer jobs in median salary ranges pay an annual $15-$35. per hour, with an additional 33% vacation, and health care benefit package, making the job package equivalent to $45-75 per hour.

Students have always poured into the most lucrative and promising careers. As IT salaries continue to be generously met by government employers seeking to meet demand, college students will see the wisdom of that 4-year degree in IT or gaining on-the-job experience in emerging technology. IT is a viable long-term career path. A four-year degree in programming or engineering will yield the graduate over 50% more in higher wages during his or her lifetime, than that earned by the high school graduate. Whether someone qualifies for a government job in technology through a college degree or through on-the-job experience, the salaries are lucrative. For detailed information on Pay and Benefits see The Job Package .

Types of Civil Service Technology Jobs –
Technical & Non-Technical

There are many types of technology jobs – technical and non-technical. Electronic data processing, programming, information technology, IT, management information systems and telecommunications all refer to departments and activities related to technology. Other departments and Program Areas in Federal, State and City government, besides the Information Technology Departments, also have technology jobs, both technical and non-technical.(Info Tech Employment, 2007).

Information technology has become so integral to American business and government that it has created new occupations to provide auxiliary support to the IT infrastructure and endeavor.

IT Procurement Jobs have grown up to manage the creation of RFPs (Requests for Proposals), Bid Analysis, Purchase and Maintenance Contracts, Personnel Contracting and the management of contracts. These jobs require special knowledge of the IT industry and the procurement field. People may enter an IT procurement job from another department and learn-as-you-go. Or they may be hired as a computer programmer or systems engineer to facilitate the procurement function for the hardware and software requirements. Computer Project managers often manage IT procurement contracts for staff and services. There is usually continuous communication between staff holding IT procurement jobs and technical staff delineating hardware and software contracts and outlining staffing needs.

IT Training Jobs exist both within an organization and with the numerous information technology training suppliers. Companies and government agencies contract for information technology training on new software and hardware or train trainers in Civil Service titles to train staff. They may also contract for on-site or off-site information technology training for their employees. People may enter an information technology training job with a liberal arts or other degree or with hands-on business or training experience. IT trainers who work for a software or hardware vendor will be expected to know their product. IT trainers who train on software use will expand their tech jobs horizons by knowing may software products used in the workplace. Information technology training will be an integral part of any organization's employee development program. Both specialized information technology training and generic information technology training will ensure a modern organization where employees are conversant with software and the ability to handle information.

IT Project Management jobs, utilizing project management software such as Microsoft Project, Crystal Reports, Network Associates Magic, and Visio, are required in many departments. They are especially integral to the IT and Telecommunications departments of an organization. Project managers and systems analysts using project management software create project plans outlining system development life cycles and timelines. They gather statistics of call centers, tech support centers and organization groups to analyze IT operations. They use drawing and visualization software to map IT center server configurations. IT project management jobs usually do not require a degree in computer science. They require project management software skills, an ability to understand the parts of an organization and IT operation, and good communication skills.

IT Security jobs may fall under the web development group of an organization, under the telecommunications department, or in tech support. Information technology security jobs may reside in a separate security department responsible for facility and data security. IT service providers and outsourcers often hire IT staff to do security planning for their clients. Outsourcers may perform the access control function for their clients. Access control managers and access control specialists carry out access control functions for computer users, workgroups, and applications. Security specialist jobs exist for network engineers to establish secure network connections, decide on proxy servers to control content, and to determine firewall requirements. Systems analysts jobs are required to determine security requirements for safe electronic file transmissions, electronic file payment systems, HIPPA data release requirements and e-commerce systems.

While some tech jobs are clearly "technical" in nature, requiring math experience, there are so many non-technical tech jobs that no one should consider themselves out of the running for information technology employment. Skills are transferable from one agency to another and from one business process to another (Info Tech Employment, 2006). (For a complete list of **Types of Technology Jobs – Technical and Non-Technical** see the **IT Skills Set & Job Titles Chart** I in Chapter Two.)

The greatest benefits to technology jobs in government include excellent pay, exciting work challenges, opportunity for continued learning, opportunity for career advancement, and growth with the technology industry.

The Top 8 Fastest Growing Jobs according to the U.S. Bureau of Labor Statistics

- ☐ Computer software engineers, applications
- ☐ Computer Support Specialists
- ☐ Computer Software Engineers, Systems Software
- ☐ Network and Computer Systems Administrators
- ☐ Network Systems and Data Communications Analysts
- ☐ Desktop Publishers
- ☐ Database Administrators
- ☐ Computer Systems Analysts

Technology In Government

The Computer Revolution

The computer revolution originated largely in the United States. Much of the funding for early computer science, for the development of high speed computing, and for the development of the Internet, has come from the United States Government (NRC, FAR, 1999). It is fitting that benefits of the computer revolution accrue to the U.S. Federal, State and Municipal governments in delivering services to citizens, to U.S. citizens, and to the U.S. economy in productivity gains, economic gains, job growth, and the growth of the computing industry.

As this Chapter will show, the utilization of technology in government at the Federal, State and City levels is a continuing story, one that affects all levels and processes of government. It goes back at least 150 years.

The utilization of technology in U.S. Federal, State and City government has created manifold opportunities for U.S. workers in job creation and job growth. The Civil Service and U.S. Public Unionism have responded to the need by government for employees with new trades in emerging technologies. (See Chapter II, The New Civil Service)

The computer revolution has transformed the U.S. economy in the past 50 years. U.S. firms have led the computer revolution. Companies such as International Business Machines (IBM), Intel, Microsoft, Sun Microsystems, and Hewlett-Packard have led global international markets in computing technology. Other companies, such as Cisco Systems, and Lucent Technologies have led advances in the data communications field.

A true information technology infrastructure is in place today for use by business and government, transforming the way business and governance is conducted. Industries, from manufacturing to banking to services such as airlines operate at current levels of activity because of computing power and communications systems. Government has transformed its most basic functions with the computer. It has reached new levels of productivity 1) in the storage and dissemination of information, 2) in the management and use of information to govern, and 3) in the dispersal and collection of the government 'treasure', monies, revenues, taxes, food stamps, social services, other tangible and non-tangible public services (Margetts, 1999, 3-20).

History as a Background

Telegraph-Telephone-Typewriter

History serves as a background to this revolution. Samuel F.B. Morse opened the first long-distance telegraph line, connecting Washington and Baltimore in 1844. The Western Union Telegraph Company started telecommunications. By the end of the Civil War, telegraph lines extended over most of the U.S., ranging to the far Western states.

The telephone, under Alexander Graham Bell's patent in 1876, grew from a communications luxury to a communications standard. The growth of telephone networks provided universal access to Americans and abroad, and established a telephone network infrastructure that would extend throughout the U.S.

The typewriter and transcription device changed the way information was recorded, documents prepared and business conducted. Thousands of new workers between WWI and WWII entered the workforce with typing skills to employ in business (Relyea & Hogue, 2004, 18).

The Revolution

Mainframe-Minicomputer-Personal Computer
Local Area Networks-Wide-Area Networks

The electronic computer was first developed to be a better computational device. It was soon perfected to sort, file, edit and process information. The "mechanical differential analyzer" built at the Massachusetts Institute of Technology in 1930 led to first generation machines, using vacuum-tube circuits, in the 1950's, and second generation machines using transistors in the 1960's (Margetts, 1999, 1-2).

Third generation computing machines used integrated circuits. The 1960's brought the development of large mainframe computers, centralized computer systems, with the main processors held at regional computing centers, connected to "dumb" terminals without actual processing power (Margetts, 1999, 2).

Throughout the 1960's and 1970's, Cobol and Fortran programmers developed diverse business and scientific applications for Mainframes, utilizing the computer's electronic data processing (EDP) ability to process volumes of information based on lengthy tables, and to make high speed extended calculations based on programming instructions.

The 1970's was an era where terminals spread across departments, with a growing workforce transferring office skills to office automation and working at the new nexus where word processing met data processing.

With fourth generation machines (mid-1970's), using very large integrated circuits, multiprocessors, digital networks and less costly memory chips, the development of minicomputers (1980's) became possible. Manufacturers like Digital Computer Corporation and SUN Microsystems worked on creating faster, less-expensive computers with 64-bit processing power throughout the 1970's.

The widespread release of the Personal Computer after 1985, with local processing ability, and the release of the Microsoft Windows Operating System and Microsoft's Office Software, made computer data processing and automated word processing within reach of every desk. With its graphical user interface and desktop icons, the Microsoft Windows Operating System and Microsoft's Office Software made it possible for non-programmers to understand and access computer applications.

The personal computer, with local storage power and connectivity potential over LANS and WANS to larger mainframe and minicomputer processors, changed the office and electronic data processing landscape. Private and public telecommunications networks played an important role in this development (Margetts, 1999, 2). High-speed telecommunications with packet switching made digital networks possible. Within organizations, digital computer networks started to serve as the opportunity for Voice Over IP where telephone data could ride on top of computer networks.

During the 1980's, minicomputers, with 64-bit processing, led to the emergence of high-performance personal computers, with graphic user interface, and the creation of Local Area Networks (LANs) and Wide Area Networks (WANs). High-speed telecommunications with packet switching made digital networks possible. Software manufacturers developed new business-oriented software tools.

Database technologies were refined from large database repositories, accessed by 1st generation database languages , to 2nd, 3rd and 4th generation database developer tools like PowerBuilder, FoxPro and Oracle, with multi-layered object structuring ability for greater ease of processing and access to data.

By the 1990's, the capacity of personal computers, computer workstations, linked to Local Area Networks (LANs) (linking locations within a building) and Wide Area Networks (WANs) (linking remote locations), expanded the communications and processing capabilities of an organization's computer processors.

A true information technology infrastructure, for use by business and government, was in place by the beginning of the new Millenium (2000), with the advent of the Internet and the widespread use of the World Wide Web.

Network Computing - The Internet – World Wide Web -- e-Mail

Approximately 15 years after the first computers became operational, researchers began to realize that an interconnected network of computers could provide greatly expanded service power. During the 1960's, a number of researchers began to investigate the technologies that would form the basis for network computing.

The basis for network computing started with the U.S. government's Defense Advanced Research Projects Agency (DARPA). DARPA funded development of a packet-switched network with routers, called the ARPANET. Packet-switching is a technique of breaking-up a conversation into small independent digital units, each of which carries the address of the destination and is routed through the network independently. Specialized computers at the branching points in a network can vary the route taken by packets on a moment-by-moment basis in response to network congestion or link failure (NRC, FAR, 1999, 171).

The U.S. had a communications network, the public switched telephone network (PSTN) as early as 1962 (NRC, FAR, 1999). However, the switching network of the telephone was not used. ARPANET created the first computer network (NRC, FAR, 171). Out of the ARPANET computer network project, came the Transmission Control Protocol/ Internet Protocol (TCP/IP), as well as the File Transfer Protocol (FTP).

FTP allows users to move files to their own workstations and work with them as local files. TCP/IP was designed to connect multiple networks to form an Internet and is used today as the Internet's basic packet transport protocol. Ethernet was developed at Xerox for Local Area Networks (LAN's) within a building or local area.

The DARPA research subsequently supported the creation of the protocols used for interconnecting networks across the Internet, including domain names, and e-mail. While Electronic Mail (e-Mail) started in 1965 as a way for multiple users of a time-sharing mainframe computer to communicate, it emerged after the creation of the ARPANET in 1969 as "network email." It was popularized as work group collaboration software by vendors such as Wang, Lotus, IBM, and Microsoft. These systems often provided enhanced e-mail features (such as file attachments, Rich Text Format, and delivery confirmation). These systems communicated with other, non-like, systems via specialized e-mail gateways which translated one vendor's e-mail format into a form understandable by another vendor. The CCITT developed the X.400 standard in the 1980s to allow different e-mail systems to interoperate. A much simpler protocol called the Simple Mail Transfer Protocol (SMTP) was soon developed which has become the de facto standard for e-mail transfer on the Internet. With the widespread use of personal computers connected to the Internet, interoperability via SMTP-based Internet e-mail has become a pivotal feature in all e-mail systems (NRC, FAR, 1999, 6, 180).

The World Wide Web and browser technology currently used to navigate the Internet were invented by Timothy Berners-Lee and Robert Cailliau at CERN, the high-energy physics laboratory in Geneva Switzerland, and Marc Anderson, then a student at the NSF-sponsored National Center for Supercomputing Applications at the University of Illinois at Urbana-Champaign (NRC, FAR, 1999, 6,180).

The Web capitalized on the widespread telephone infrastructure already in existence, which provided the underlying physical infrastructure to carry digital packet-switched data (NRC, FAR, 1999, 6, 159-165, 181). The U.S. National Research Council provides a complete history of the development of the Internet and World Wide Web (WWW) in Funding a Revolution: Government Support for Computing Research.

Al Gore, the U.S. Vice President, who first coined the term "Information Superhighway," announced in 1977 "With computers and telecommunications, we need not do things as we have in the past. We can design a customer-driven electronic government that operates in ways, that, 10 years ago, the most visionary planner could not have imagined" (NRC, FAR, 1993, 121-122).

The Internet is a federation of commercial service providers, local educational networks, and private corporate networks, exchanging packets using TCP/IP and other protocols. The Internet, developed from the U.S. federally-funded research in computer networking (Corbett, 2004, 346; Margetts, 1999, xiii; NRC, FAR, 1999, 8-9, 169) complemented developments in private industry by computer and telecommunications manufacturers.

The Internet grew through the 1980's and 1990's to take its central place today in national and global communications. The Internet, capitalizing on a loose confederation of inter-connected computer networks being built by organizations, government, and businesses (with servers residing at the location of the individual user or organization), permits organizations and institutions to put information they want to transmit to the public on web servers to make it available to the public over the Internet. With the Internet and the World Wide Web (WWW), electronic mail, file transfer, and on-line interactive processing became possible for the first time, permitting national and global communications, e-commerce, and electronic data processing, in interactive real time.

Other developments in computing research have made Information Technology (IT) possible for use in government as it exists today. These developments have been transferred into industry, into software and hardware products, and into the information systems and IT infrastructures built by business and government. These IT infrastructures make the re-engineering of business and government processes possible.

Relational Databases – Data Warehouse

Relational databases developed through serendipitous competition and cooperation between industry leaders, independent, and government-funded researchers.

COBOL (Computer Operated Business Oriented Language) was the programming language developed for use by IBM Mainframe computers to process data, prior to 4th generation database developer tools, such as FoxPro, PowerBuilder, Informix, Sybase, Microsoft Access, and Oracle Database developer tools.

In 1970 E.F. Codd proposed "The Relational Model" whereby information was not tied to the machine language processing. He criticized existing models for confusing the abstract description of information structure with descriptions of physical access mechanisms. He wrote, "It provides a means of describing data [through algorhythms] with its natural structure only—that is, without superimposing any additional structure for machine representation purposes.(Codd, 1970' In other words, the relational model consisted of 1) data independence from hardware and storage implementation, and 2) automatic navigation for accessing data" (NRC, FAR, 162).

A relational database contains multiple tables. Relationships between tables are not defined explicitly; instead, 'keys' are used to match up and link rows of data in different tables. A key that has an external, real-world meaning (such as a client's name, a car's license plate number, a social security number), is sometimes called a "natural" key. If no natural key is suitable (numerous people named Smith), an arbitrary key can be assigned (such as by giving employees ID numbers or work order request numbers). Most databases have both generated and natural keys, because generated keys can be used internally to create links between rows that cannot break, while natural keys can be used, less reliably, for searches and for integration with other databases.

A relational model is a way of structuring data, as well as a set of operations that can be performed on the data. The relational model, defines a set of operations that can be performed on the data. These include project (the process of eliminating some of the columns), restrict (the process of eliminating some of the rows), union (a way of combining two tables with similar structures), difference (which lists the rows in one table that are not found in the other), intersect (which lists the rows found in both tables), and product (mentioned above, which combines each row of one table with each row of the other).

The Structured Query Language (SQL) is the primary interface to these operations. Relational databases with SQL allow programmers to write queries that were not predeveloped. As a result, relational databases can be used to develop applications customized to a business or government need. The database data structure and operations, can be modified over decades as new relations present themselves, thus presenting a long-term solution for information storage, processing and retrieval.

Today in E-Commerce and E-Government, information databases, client-customer-citizen databases, and service-product databases, function at a speed and detail due to the relational database model and query languages. Relational databases allow analysts in government to specify the relations they want to exist between pieces of data and the processes and functions they want to perform with the data.

As developed by industry leaders Informix, Sybase, and Oracle Computer Corporation, relational databases can be used with Client/Server technology to create a seamless interactive process whereby data is referenced from a single or multiple databases, transactions made, and results stored or delivered to end-users through graphical user interfaces or web browsers.

Data warehousing is a technology architecture designed to organize disparate data sources into a single repository. It provides access, for example, to historical data on citizens, clients, trend data, data from different databases. A data warehouse is an informational database, intended to enable a discovery-oriented approach to database querying (Inmon, 2002). The Environmental Protection Agency's "EnviroFacts" data warehouse (http://www.epa.gov/enviro) is an example of a data warehouse that is used for the purpose of providing public access to government data. (Harper, 2004, 239.)

Relational databases are used in many applications. They are the preferred method of storage for large multi-user applications, applications that will change over time, and applications where different databases will be accessed to produce the required information.

Cryptography- Data Security-Information Privacy

Information Privacy and Data Security have become essential components of the computer revolution. Developments in cryptography-data encryption techniques and data security have ensured information privacy and freedom from data corruption or misuse in business, e-commerce and e-government (Anderson, 2001; Kirschbaum, 2006).

Privacy issues exist wherever uniquely identifiable data relating to a person or persons are collected and stored, in digital form or otherwise. The Right to Privacy, guaranteed under the U.S. Constitution, extends to data and is especially critical to cover financial information, health information, and criminal justice information. The challenge in data privacy is to share information between authorized parties and information shareholders while protecting personally identifiable information from disclosure. Developments in cryptography and data security have made possible computer and network software products that keep data safe from unauthorized use or corruption, in storage, processing and transit.

Essentially, cryptographic techniques involve transforming information, scrambling it so it becomes unreadable during transmission. The intended recipient can unscramble the message, but eavesdroppers cannot. Cryptography makes extensive use of discrete mathematics, including topics from number theory, information theory, computational complexity, and statistics. The principles have been formalized and incorporated into computer products by computer and network software manufacturers.

In 1972 the U.S. National Bureau of Standards (renamed the NIST (National Institute of Standards and Technology (NIST) identified a need for a government-wide standard for encrypting unclassified, sensitive information. The National Bureau of Standards and the National Security Agency solicited proposals for a cipher that would be suitable to encrypt unclassified, sensitive information. IBM submitted a cipher developed during the period 1973–1974 based on an earlier algorithm, Horst Feistel's Lucifer cipher. The Data Encryption Standard (DES) was approved as a federal standard in November 1976, and published on 15 January 1977 as FIPS PUB 46, authorized for use on all unclassified data. It was subsequently reaffirmed as the standard in 1983, 1988 (revised as FIPS-46-1), 1993 (FIPS-46-2), and again in 1998 (FIPS-46-3), the latter prescribing "Triple DES". On 26 May 2002, DES was superseded by AES, the Advanced Encryption Standard, following a public competition). DES and AES are in widespread use in computer and network security software products (NRC, FAR, 1999, 193; Kirschbaum, 2006).

Multi-Platform – Cross Platform Resource Sharing Operating Systems

Sun Solaris, Unix, Linux

Client-server technologies, coupled with LAN and WAN networks are the success story of the 21st Century. Many software programmers and network programmers in many business, scientific and technical settings will be using Unix-based operating systems such as Sun Solaris, IBM AIX and Linux. The creation of high-speed servers with the UNIX operating system now allows programmers to do things they couldn't do previously. The UNIX operating system was designed to let a number of programmers access the computer at the same time and share its resources. In addition, it provides an environment so powerful that many telecommunications switches and transmission systems are controlled by administration and maintenance systems based on UNIX. IT professionals now learn and use Unix-based operating systems such as Sun Solaris, IBM AIX and Linux (Info Tech Employment, IT Jobs, 2006). The features that made UNIX highly suitable for government applications are:

- ☐ Multitasking capability
- ☐ Multiuser capability
- ☐ Portability
- ☐ UNIX programs
- ☐ Library of application software

While initially designed for medium-sized minicomputers, the UNIX-based operating systems have been rolled out to mainframes and personal computers. Sun Solaris, IBM AIX5L, and Linux are Unix-based operating systems. They allow users to:

☐ easily share printers and files across any network
☐ break down barriers between platforms to make resource sharing easy
☐ provide Windows file and print services
☐ integrate web and hosting services
☐ painlessly manage network access
☐ develop enterprise applications
☐ manage storage
☐ accelerate and extend the network
☐ secure the network
☐ enable desktop environments
(Sun Microsystems, 2006)

Multi Platform & Component Programming Software - JAVA Software
Java, JavaScript, Visual Basic Programming Software

Java and Java Script allow other possibilities for government computing. These programming languages and scripts created new possibilities in the computer industry when client-server technology mounted, creating the need for Java, Java Script and Visual Basic Programmers able to do Graphical User Interface (GUI) interfaces and direct to web scripting.

Java (not to be confused with JavaScript) is the programming language developed by Sun Microsystems that enables programmers to build an application for one platform and run it on another. For example, building applications for small handheld devices or a mission-critical enterprise-wide application becomes possible with Sun's Java. The Java programming language is a robust and versatile programming language, enabling developers to:

☐ Write software on one platform and run it on another.
☐ Create programs to run within a web browser.
☐ Develop server-side applications for online forums, stores, polls,
  processing HTML forms, and more.
☐ Write applications for cell phones, two-way pagers, and other
  consumer devices. (Sun Microsystems 2006)

JavaScript is not Java. JavaScript was developed by Brendan Eich at Netscape. Because of its linkage to web browsers, it instantly became popular. It is well suited to client programming. Government programmers may now use Sun Microsystem's Java application development product, with knowledge of the JavaScript programming language to script direct to web. Java Programming JavaScript also utilize related Web development scripting languages, such as HTML, CGI, Perl, CSS, ASP, and PHP. In addition, Java and JavaScript programming interfaces with Macromedia Flash, DREAMWEAVER, Adobe Photoshop, and FrontPage. Working with the Java and Windows, UNIX, and LINUX platforms, government technology staff may develop Web or Java/J2EE-based applications with JSP, SERVLETS, Java, and EJB (Info Tech Employment, IT Jobs, 2006).

Speech Recognition-Interactive Voice Response Software

Speech recognition technologies allow government to improve productivity and increase ease of use for the public in a wide variety of computer-telephony applications..

Building on work conducted with industry and federal funding, several companies, including IBM, Dragon Systems, and Lucent Technologies introduced in the 1990's robust continuous speech recognition software for use with personal computers NRC, FAR, 1999, 205). Automatic speech recognition, computer speech recognition, or voice recognition allow the human voice to be digitized and the patterns transformed into words. Commercial systems for speech recognition have been available off-the-shelf since the 1990s (Rabiner, 1998).

Speech recognition software is used for automatic transcription, important in legal proceedings and 911 call centers. Speech recognition has allowed government to extend the speech recognition capabilities to people with disabilities who have difficulty interacting with their computers through a keyboard to do their job.

In telephone technology, voice recognition or speech recognition technology is used increasingly with Interactive Voice Response (IVR) computer-telephone systems to speed caller transactions and provide information from relational databases. Speech recognition in combination with Interactive Voice Response (IVR) systems, and relational databases now deliver customized information and perform customized transactions to deliver individualized services.

Customer service call routing, financial account information, directory assistance, services assistance and info-lines all rely on sophisticated speech recognition, telephony and computer technologies in conjunction with relational databases

Computer Graphics –
Geographic Information Systems (GIS)

Computer graphics enable scientific visualizations, computer-aided design programs, biomedical imaging, geographic information systems (GIS), art and publishing graphics, and computer animation.

The earliest use of a computer-generated graphical display on a cathode ray tube (CRT) was in Project Whirlwind, a project sponsored by the U.S. Navy to develop a general purpose flight simulator (NRC, FAR, 1999, 228). These and other early projects convinced the National Science Foundation, the National Institutes of Health and the National Aeronautics and Space Administration to make investments in computer graphics research throughout the 1950's and 1960's. The payoffs of these investments were enormous. Research in computer graphics was established in universities. Graduates seeded the industry pool.

In the 1960's from MIT's Lincoln Laboratory Ivan Sutherland developed a graphics program called Sketchpad as his dissertation. Sketchpad was an interactive design tool for the creation, manipulation, and display of geometric objects in two-dimensional space (2D) or three-dimensional (3D) space. Sutherland moved to the University of Utah and students of the Utah program developed an area search method, a scan-line method, a hardware system, and a method of continuous shading. The work of these individuals laid the groundwork for a variety of graphics fields, including surface rendering, simulations, computer graphics, graphical user interface design, and early steps toward virtual reality. "No less than 11 commercial firms, several of which ship more than $100 million in products annually, trace their origins to the Utah program" (NRC, FAR, 1999, 232).

Developments in graphics hardware and RISC technology (reduced-instruction set computing) enhanced graphics capabilities and reduced costs. Reduced instruction set computing (RISC) optimized the flow of instructions through the processing unit. The development of computer workstations using powerful 32-bit or 64-bit microprocessors enabled local processing.

With the birth of workstation computers (like LISP machines, Paintbox computers and Silicon Graphics workstations and others) came 3D computer graphics, based on vector graphics. Instead of the computer storing information about points, lines, and curves on a 2-dimensional plane, the computer stores the location of points, lines, and, typically, faces (to construct a polygon) in 3-dimensional space. Vector graphics store precise geometric data, topology and style such as: coordinate positions of points, the connections between points (to form lines or paths), and the color, thickness, and possible fill of the shapes. Most vector graphic systems can also use primitives of standard shapes such as circles, rectangles, etc. In most cases, a vector graphic image has to be converted to a raster image to be viewed.

Raster graphics is a uniform 2-dimensional grid of pixels. Each pixel has a specific value such as, for instance, brightness, color, transparency, or a combination of such values. A raster image has a finite resolution of a specific number of rows and columns. Standard computer displays shows a raster image of resolutions such as 1280(columns) x 1024(rows) of pixels. Today, raster and vector graphics are often combined in compound file formats (.PDF, .SWF)

Companies such as Silicon Graphics, Evans & Sutherland, HP, Sun Microsystems, IBM and others brought RISC computing to market. Adobe Software, its subsidiary Macromedia, Quark xPress and other companies have brought vector and raster graphics to the graphics design, publishing, e-publishing, and computer animation fields (NRC, FAR, 1999, 8, 238).

Computer graphics enable scientific visualizations, computer-aided design programs, biomedical imaging, geographic information systems (GIS), art and publishing graphics, and computer animation.

Geographic Information Systems (GIS)

Geographical Information Science is a specialized area of Information Technology. It is the science underlying the applications and systems, taught as a degree program by several universities.

Geographic Information Systems (GIS) combine computer graphics capabilities and relational database capabilities to create, store, analyze and manage spatial data and associated attributes. Graphic display techniques such as shading and altitude in a GIS can make relationships among map elements visible, heightening one's ability to extract and analyze information.

Development of GIS open source software continues to evolve, especially for web and web service oriented applications, with the broad use of non-proprietary and open data formats such as the Shape File format for vector data and the Geotiff format for raster data, as well as the adoption of Open Geospatial Consortium (OGC) protocols such as Web Mapping Service (WMS) and Web Feature Service (WFS). Open source GIS software includes GRASS GIS, Quantum GIS, MapServer, GDAL/OGR, PostGIS, uDig, among others.

Notable industry proprietary GIS software includes:
Autodesk –AutoCAD; Caliper – Maptitude and TransCAD; CARIS (Computer Aided Resource Information System) – GIS systems for hydrography and cadastral systems; ENVI by ITT Industries; ERDAS IMAGINE – by Leica Geosystems; ESRI –ArcView, ArcGIS, ArcSDE, ArcIMS, and ArcWeb services; KMLer - Google Earth extension package for arcGIS; Genamap; Giselle – by Cosylab; Google Earth; IDRISI – by Clark Labs; Intergraph – GeoMedia; Manifold System; MapInfo – MapInfo Professional and MapXtreme; MetaCarta; Oracle Spatial; SAS/GIS; Smallworld by General Electric, for public utilities and other related industries, and others

Geographic Positioning Systems are being developed for voice-over IP telephony to be able to identify the location of incoming calls for emergency services. GPS devices integrated with everyday objects (Cell phones, PDA's, Laptops) will facilitate other government services.

GIS work includes:

- Data Capture: the most common method of data creation is digitization)
- Data Representation: GIS data represents real world objects (roads, l and use, elevation) as discrete objects (a house) and continuous fields
- Relating information from different sources
- Data manipulation Projections, coordinate systems and registration
- Spatial analysis with GIS
- Data modeling: A rainfall contour map
- Topological modeling
- Data output and cartography: the design and production of maps, or visual representations of spatial data.
- Data Analysis, Problem Solving & Interpretation

GIS Specialists are required by industry and government. GIS Specialists are required for:

- Sustainable Development - Zoning - Urban Planning
- Natural Resources - Parks & Recreation
- Natural Resources - Environmental Protection
- Real Estate - Taxation & Revenue
- Safety & Security - Defense and Homeland Security
- Public Health – Disease Control & Departments of Health

☐ Crime Mapping - Police
☐ Human Services Delivery – Social Services
☐ Transportation Development
☐ Emergency Services – 911 Location
☐ Government Services – Citizen Location-based Mapping

GIS Specialists work with agency management to perform scientific investigations, resource management, asset management, Environmental Impact Assessments, development planning, cartography, and GIS analysis on an as-needed basis. GIS Specialists perform data analysis, problem solving and interpretation (Chang, 2005).

Computers in Federal - State - City Government

Between 1950 and 1980, the prosperity and growth of gross national product led to "big government", both in terms of the payrolls of Federal, State and local governments, and the programs and constituents government supported in a new welfare state. By the 1980's the cost of this government to the American taxpayer was deemed too high.

New technology enabled Federal, State and Municipal government to "downsize," to trim payrolls. It enabled Federal, State and Municipal governments to reduce the cost of social programs with legislated "welfare reform." Welfare reform coincided with new technologies. New technologies were used by State and Local social services agencies to develop job opportunity databases in conjunction with American businesses. Information technology systems continue to be used by social service workers to identify job opportunities for welfare clients and to help them schedule interviews and start to work.

Beginning in the 1980's, dramatic downsizing in U.S. Federal, State, and City government, from peak 1960's workforce levels, occurred. Business-process engineering reshaped government departments, job functions, and titles, focusing services on business processes. Productivity gains brought about by the technology itself reshaped workforce levels and government processes.

The changing shape of government coincided with the computer revolution and was facilitated by it. Technology helped government re-engineer and re-shape itself. Government helped technology come into the fabric of government and business processes.

A New Government Workforce

Downsizing & Change in Shape
Changing Pay Scales & Education Requirements

A new government workforce has taken shape because of computers in Federal, State and Municipal government. The workforce is *leaner* and *greener*. It is characterized by a reduction of clerical level jobs, the creation of a new class of employees with higher salaries, the creation of new Civil Service titles to cover computer and emerging technology jobs; and the incorporation of technology into all phases of government operations and business processes.

As the need for clerical workers has disappeared, as well as the need for middle managers to manage staff, salaries have been redirected to tech job workers. Pay Scales have changed. Savings from reduction of workforce and downsizing have been rolled into computer tech job salaries.

Staffing Requirements for Government

The staffing directions in government are driven by workforce requirements. They reflect the trends that drive hiring by corporations and IT service providers. (For more information, see Chapter III, Section II, The New Face of Government, for a full description of these forces that drive hiring.)

New Players - New Partnerships

Application of business principles to e-government has brought with it the cost-saving techniques of relying on expertise by hiring third-party vendors rather than retaining an in-house staff. Challenges involve 1) defining responsibilities that cannot go to third party vendors, 2) utilizing the available hiring strategies for building and retaining specialized staff; 3) assessing projects on the basis of development and maintenance needs and determining staffing requirements accordingly (Richardson, 2004, x; 200-217; Franzel and Coursey, 2004, 63-77).

Modified Processes
Re-Engineering Government & E-Government

New technology enabled Federal, State and Municipal government to "downsize," to trim payrolls by capitalizing on the productivity gains offered by automation and technology. Throughout the 1970's office automation created productivity gains in government.

In the 1980's with the possibilities afforded by LANS, WANS, the Internet, and the co-joining of electronic data processing and computer communications technologies, a digital government became possible to further automate government processes.

"Electronic government or E-government, can be defined as the 'use of technology, particularly web-based Internet applications, to enhance the access to and delivery of government information and service to citizens, business partners, employees, other agencies and government entities (McClure, 2000) The "Promise of e-Government" is described by David Garson as an attempt "to bring the e-business model into the public sector." (Garson, 1999). To bring about the promise, "reinventing government" and "reengineering government" has become central and co-creative.

In 1993, Vice President Al Gore's National Performance Review (NPR), he emphasized the need of 1) making government more business-like, including more reliance on markets and public-private technology, 2) using technology to replace existing processes, and 3)achieving cost-savings by shrinking the overall size of government. (Fletcher, 1999). In 1997 Vice President Al Gore coined the term "information superhighway." Re-engineering government departments to improve productivity involves modifying processes: 1) delivering services using digital government; 2) cost saving using online processes with the realignment of staffing, and 3) creating a new class of employee to develop and maintain technology systems.

The Functions of Technology in Government
E-Government - Digital Government

In *The Tools of Government* Christopher Hood (1983) explained the functions of government as:

- □ **Node** – being in the middle of an information or social network
- □ **Treasure** – being the holder and distributor of social and monetary goods
- □ **Authority** – being the administrator of Laws; possessing Legal and Official power;
- □ **Organization** – a group of people with skills to deliver and administer the resources of government.

Technology is used in government in parallel ways as:

- □ **Information Node** - to deliver and gather information
- □ **Governance Tool** - to implement policy and uphold the law by data processing/decision-processing systems,
- □ **Treasure Tool** - to distribute goods and services, including monies and goods, electronically
- □ **Organizational Tool** – to facilitate the delivery of services within the organization (Margetts, 1999).

New technologies are used in:

- □ **E-Governance** - to sustain policies and regulatory systems and administer goods and services based on the Law
- □ **E-Management** - to use information, the information technology infrastructure, and IT processes to enhance the management of government
- □ **e-Democracy** - to interact with citizens in support of the democratic process
- □ **E-Commerce** - to conduct the business of government with citizens, business partners, vendors and other government agencies using information technology (Richardson, 1999, 214)

Services are delivered by:

- □   **Information Access and Delivery**

☐ **Document Access and Download**
☐ **Application Processing – Services - e-Permits - Licensing**
☐ **E-Commerce Applications**
☐ **Communication with Officials and Agencies**
☐ **Multimedia Streaming and Playback**
☐ **Online Databases**
☐ **Online Mapping/GIS applications**
   (Stowers, 1999, 175)

Further, the use of technology in government delivers goods and services:
☐ **Government to Citizen**
☐ **Government to Business**
☐ **Government to Government** (Margetts, 1999).

Managing Technology in Government

Players - Departments - Information Stakeholders

Managing Technology in Government involves many players and departments. It creates jobs both within information technology departments and within program area departments. There are clear divisions of responsibility across agencies and departments. All players or stakeholders in government need to understand where management responsibility lies – for governance, for service identification and implementation, for service delivery, and for information technology systems and services to departments.

Typically, agencies and departments are responsible for programmatic duties. Human Services Agencies, for example, are responsible for following the Law to deliver social services mandated by Federal, State and Municipal Law, and for creating the processes for the delivery of services. The program areas within Human Services, for example, – child welfare, medical assistance, income support, emergency assistance, job training and placement –identify the programs to carry out their responsibilities in these areas. They establish the processes, and when required, they work with information technology department to program the processes, create data processing applications, and operate the information technology systems required.

IT departments, either within departments and agencies, within Federal government, States and Cities, are responsible for the digital storage, processing and archiving of information and the computer systems and infrastructure that are necessary to carry out e-government processes. Information Technology departments also provide services to programmatic areas in helping design and program information technology systems required.

Information Technology Stakeholders

Technology in government cuts across departments and agencies. IT jobs can be in departments that are directly responsible for collecting information and implementing services, known commonly as Program Areas. Or, government jobs in technology can be in management information systems department, department of information technology departments, or computer centers, responsible for the digital storage, processing and archiving of information and the computer systems and infrastructure that is necessary to carry out e-government processes.

Data Stewardship

"Data Stewardship is an organizational commitment to ensure that identifiable information is collected, maintained, used, and disseminated in a way that:

☐ **Respects Privacy**
☐ **Ensures Confidentiality and Security, Reduced Reporting Burden, and**
☐ **Promotes Access to Data for Public Policy."**
(Mullen, 1999, 145).

Data Stewardship operates on principles determined by roles and responsibilities in the management of information. These considerations are primary:

☐ **Information is an Asset**
☐ **Shared Accountability**
☐ **Multiple Stakeholders**
☐ **Owners of Information**
☐ **Users of Information**
☐ **Subjects of Information**
☐ **The Organization**
☐ **The Constituency**
☐ **The Law**

Legislation to Provide a Policy Foundation for Technology in Government

A policy foundation has been created over the last 30 years, with the growth of technology, to forward information technology in government in the U.S. and to govern the use of technology in government and build in the controls necessary to make technology use comply with principals of U.S. Law and values.

The Privacy Act of 1974, the Computer Security Act of 1987, the Paperwork Reduction Act of 1995, the Supreme Court decision that it is illegal for government to sell citizen information such as driver license information; the Clinger-Cohen Act (originally named the Information Technology Management Reform Act of 1996) establishing a Chief Information Officer (CI) in every federal agency the Electronic Freedom of Information Amendments of 1996; and President Clinton's Executive Order 13011 calling for interagency coordination of technology applications, all established a framework to support digital government. (Relyea and Hogue, 1999 vii, 16-33)

The Privacy Act of 1974 constrained the government's use of personally identifiable information. The original Paperwork Reduction Act of 1980 (PRA) was refined by the PRA of 1986, and 1995 to define requirements for the management of information including electronic information. It encourages Federal agencies to promote an electronic information management environment for recordkeeping, filing, and archiving.

Congress enacted the Computer Security Act of 1987 requiring each Federal agency to develop security plans for its computer systems. The act subjected the plans to the review of the National Institute of Standards and Technology, which subsequently supported development of the Data Encryption Standard (DES). With the growth of the Internet and computer storage systems the government's ability to collect, analyze or disclose personal information about citizens and residents has dramatically increased. Policies have been put in place to protect personal privacy, ensuring confidentiality of information collected or transmitted, and implement security controls (Mullen, 1999, ix, 134-148)

In 1996, the Clinger-Cohen Act, mandated a Chief Information Officer at reach Federal agency, responsible for the acquisition, implementation and maintenance of information technology for "performance-based and results-based management." (Relyea and Hogue, 1999, vii, 16-33).

President William Clinton issued Executive Order 13011 in 1996 to promote the Federal programs through a coordinated, interoperable, secure, and shared government-wide infrastructure supported by a diversity of private sector suppliers and cadre of IT professionals. Other policy directive and legislation have been passed by the U.S. Congress in subsequent years to foster the development and security of computer systems and the Internet for the public good. (Relyea and Hogue, 1999, vii, 16-33).

The amended e-Government Act of 2002, introduced by Senator Joseph Lieberman (D-CT) set up a policy framework for a government strategy to allow citizens to access their government information and services electronically, over the Internet. It also establishes the need for a Federal Chief Information Officer working out of the Office of Management and Budget and the Office of Electronic Government housed in OMB.

The "E-Government Strategy" released from the Executive Office of the President in 2002 under President George Bush calls for a citizen-centered, results-oriented and market-based e-government strategy. Cross-agency projects were identified and funded to deliver services: government to citizen, government to business, government to government, and intra-governmental to improve internal efficiency and accountability (Fletcher, 2004, 57.)

Policies affecting the implementation and initiatives in IT in the federal government have carried over to States and Cities. States and Cities have similarly reengineered government processes, following initiatives to reduce paperwork, to protect privacy, data and systems, and to use information properly, and to follow the principles of democracy.

Major Service Delivery Methods & Systems

The Web Portal Model – Internet & Intranets

The web portal model is being used as a technology framework in the U.S. Federal government to carry out the electronic government strategies set forth in the President's Management Agenda of 2002. A portal is a doorway for users to access the web. The development and use of a single point of entry to First.gov is the official Federal government web portal for all information and services delivered by the Federal executive agencies. Firstgov.gov is the official Internet portal to the U.S. Federal government. FirstGov.gov provides powerful search engine capabilities to search every word of every U.S. government document archived. It covers all three branches of U.S. Federal government. FirstGov. gov links to a number of other web portals providing specific information: www.students. gov; www.workers.gov; www.science.gov; www.consumers.gov; www.gsa.gov; www. USAjobs.gov and others.

The web portal model has been adopted by many Federal, State and City agencies. It is used for the delivery of services to U.S. citizens, to provide interactions with business, and to conduct business between other government agencies. FirstGov.gov; www. USAjobs.gov; www.irs.gov; www.nsf.gov and other portal sites all follow the portal model of delivering services and information to citizens (Fletcher, 2004, 52-86; Franzel, 2004, 69-77.) Today, all 50 U.S. States and most U.S. Cities have web portals as a single point of entry to State and City information and services.

Intranets are used within government agencies and departments to provide a private network for the exchange of data and information within the organization, closed to the public.

The Internet and the World Wide Web (WWW), electronic mail, file transfer, and on-line interactive processing permitting interoffice, local, national and global communications, e-commerce, and electronic data processing, in interactive real time.

Data Processing Applications

Data Processing Applications handle the processing of information. From large mainframe computers, to mid-range computers, to PC workstations, data processing applications gather information, legacy systems

Relational Databases & Data Warehouse

Today in E-Commerce and E-Government, information databases, client-customer-citizen databases, and service-product databases, function at a speed and detail due to the relational database model and query languages. Relational databases allow analysts in government to specify the relations they want to exist between pieces of data and the processes and functions they want to perform with the data.

As developed by industry leaders Informix, Sybase, and Oracle Computer Corporation, relational databases can be used with Client/Server technology to create a seamless interactive process whereby data is referenced from a single or multiple databases, transactions made, and results stored or delivered to end-users through graphical user interfaces or web browsers.

Relational databases are used in many applications. They are the preferred method of storage for large multi-user applications, applications that will change over time, and applications where different databases will be accessed to produce the required information.

Office Automation Applications

Office Automation applications handle business applications easily and locally, with the use of office automation software, such as Microsoft WORD, Excel, Access, PowerPoint, Microsoft Outlook, and Graphics software such as Quark xPress and Adobe Acrobat, InDesign, Photoshop, and other software products.

E-Procurement

The Internet is a tool for the procurement process used for 1) issuing bids, 2) publishing RFI's and RFPs; 3) reporting on contracts, 4) registration of vendors, 5) publishing service and product pricing schedules; 5)verification about vendor compliance on work laws, scofflaws and tax delinquencies; 6) electronic payment.

E-Commerce

E-Commerce, or the transacting of business electronically, between government and citizen, government and business and government and business, characterizes many software applications. When citizens e-File their IRS Tax Return, this is e-Commerce. When the U.S. Federal Government issues a refund and deposits in a citizen's Bank Account, this is e-Commerce.

Major e-Commerce systems include the U.S. Internal Revenue Service Tax Collection & Refund Systems, the U.S. Social Security Administration systems; State and City Property Tax and other Revenue Collection Systems, State and City Vendor Payment Systems, Social Service Benefits Systems; all Electronic File Transfer payment systems.

Geographic Information Systems

"GIS uses information and communication technology tools to store, analyze, query, manipulate, distribute and display data that has been spatially-referenced using addresses, political and administrative boundaries, or earth bound coordinate systems. GIS is used in a broad range of public sector applications, including, for example, land use and urban growth planning, legislative redistricting, crime tracking and law enforcement, benchmarking human services, emergency management, environmental monitoring, and public information services" (O'Looney, 2000, Gant & Ijams, 2004, 249.) A specific example is "Snow Fighter," a GIS application used by the City of Indianapolis to manage snow removal. A live-accident map in Tulsa allows citizens to see where traffic problems and accidents occur (Gant and Ijams, 2004, x, 248-262.) For more information on GIS, see Chapter III, Technology in Government.

Other Major Service Delivery Methods & Systems

As the information technology industry develops, there will be yet new methods to deliver services. Each method fills a purpose. The collection, handling, storage, transport, processing, delivery, access, and storage of information is handled by technologies from various software and hardware vendors.   The following methods and technologies, to name but a few, are called on in many different contexts to deliver services:

- ☐ **Content Managers**
- ☐ **Archiving & Storage Systems**
- ☐ **Records Management**
- ☐ **Data Cross Match Systems**
- ☐ **Forms Management Systems**
- ☐ **Data Engines**
- ☐ **Digital Print to Mail**

What Government Jobs in Information Technology Look Like

While it would be difficult to give a uniform picture of an information technology job in government, there are some characteristics that define IT jobs. IT jobs will involve:

- ☐ **Unique Agency & Department Missions**
- ☐ **Information Technology Functions**
- ☐ **Research & Planning into Business Processes**
- ☐ **Research & Planning into Emerging Technologies**
- ☐ **Building Systems**
- ☐ **Building & Maintaining Databases**
- ☐ **Building & Maintaining Internet and Intranet Website Portals**
- ☐ **New Players & Partnerships with Third-Party Vendors & Staff**
- ☐ **Maintaining Systems**
- ☐ **Building IT/IS Infrastructure**
- ☐ **Maintaining IT/IS Infrastructure**
- ☐ **IT Procurement & Management Analysis**
- ☐ **Management of Contractors & Vendors**
- ☐ **Constant Work**

REFERENCES

AFSCME, CWA Local 1180, 2006, http://www.cwa1180.org/civil/civil.shtml

Anderson Ross A., Security Engineering: A Guide to Building Dependable Distributed Systems, 2005.

Anderson, Ronald E., Ethics in Digital Government, in Digital Government, Principles and Best Practices, ed. Pavlichev, Alexei, and Garson, David, A., Idea Group Inc., 2004, 218-235

Association for Computing Machinery (ACM), http://www.acm.org/globalizationreport

Chang, K.S., Introduction to Geographic Information System, McGraw Hill, 3rd edition, 2005.

Corbett, Christopher, The Future of Digital Government, in Digital Government, Principles and Best Practices, ed. Pavlichev, Alexei, and Garson, David, A., Idea Group Inc., 2004, 344-367.

Fletcher, Patricia Diamond, Portals and Policy: Implications of Electronic Access to U.S. Federal Government Information and Services, in Digital Government, Principles and Best Practices, ed. Pavlichev, Alexei, and Garson, David, A., Idea Group Inc., 2004, 52-62.

Franzel, Joshua M. and Coursey, David H., Government Web Portals: Management Issues and the Approaches of Five States, in Digital Government, Principles and Best Practices, ed. Pavlichev, Alexei, and Garson, David, A., Idea Group Inc., 2004, 63-77.

Gant, Jon and Ijams, Donald S., Digital Government and Geographic Information Systems, in Digital Government, Principles and Best Practices, ed. Pavlichev, Alexei, and
Garson, David, A., Idea Group Inc., 2004, 248-262.

Garson, David A., The Promise of Digital Government, in Digital Government, Principles and Best Practices, ed. Pavlichev, Alexei, and Garson, David, A., Idea Group Inc., 2004, 2-15.

Gore, Al, quoted in Fletcher, Patricia Diamond, Portals and policy: Implications of Electronic Access to U.S. Federal Government Information and Services, in Digital Government, Principles and Best Practices, ed. Pavlichev, Alexei, and Garson, David, A., Idea Group Inc., 2004, 52-62.

Harper, Franklin Maxwell, Data Warehousing and the Organization of Governmental Databases, in Digital Government, Principles and Best Practices, ed. Pavlichev, Alexei, and Garson, David, A., Idea Group Inc., 2004, 236-247.

Hood,C., The Tools of Government, London, MacMillan, 1983.

Info Tech Employment, Editors, Computer Jobs with the Growing Information Technology Professional Services Sector, William Briggs Publishing, 2007, http://www.infotechemployment.com .

Info Tech Employment, Editors, IT Jobs-IT Prospects- Companies-Contacts-Links: Get Hired by Companies Winning New Business and Requiring New Staff (2007), William Briggs Publishing, 2006, http://www.infotechemployment.com .

Krysiak, Mark E.; Tucker, Carla; Spitzer, David; and Holland, Kevin, E-Procurement: State Government Learns from the Private Sector, in Digital Government, Principles and Best Practices, ed. Pavlichev, Alexei, and Garson, David, A., Idea Group Inc., 2004, 149-168.

Lawson, Roy, InformationWeek, 2006, More U.S. Workers Have IT Jobs Than Ever Before, Eric Chabrow, InformationWeek, Apr 24, 2006

Levy, Frank and Murnane, Richard, The New Division of Labor: How Computers are Creating the Next Job Market, Princeton University Press, 2004.

Liston, Robert A., Your Career in Civil Service, Messner Publishers, 1967.

Margetts, Helen, Information Technology in Government: Britain and America, Routledge Press, 1999.

McClure, C.R., Sprehe, T. and Eschenfelder, K. Performance Measures for Federal Agencies: Final Report. Retrieved December 13, 2001 from http://www.access.gpo.gov/su_docs/index.html

Mullen, Patrick R., Digital Government and Individual Privacy, in Digital Government, Principles and Best Practices, ed. Pavlichev, Alexei, and Garson, David, A., Idea Group Inc., 2004, 134-148.

National Research Council (NRC), Funding a Revolution: Government Support for Computing Research, National Academy Press, 1999.

O'Looney, J.A., Wiring Governments, Challenges and Possibilities for Public Managers, Quorum Books, 2002.
Patterson, David A., Association for Computing Machinery, 2006, http://www.acm.org/pubs/cacm/

Relyea, Harold C. and Hogue, Henry B., A Brief History of the Emergence of Digital Government in the United States, in Digital Government, Principles and Best Practices, ed. Pavlichev, Alexei, and Garson, David, A., Idea Group Inc., 2004, 16-33.

Richardson, Ronald E., Digital Government: Balancing Risk and Reward through Public/Private Partnerships, in Digital Government, Principles and Best Practices, ed. Pavlichev, Alexei, and Garson, David, A., Idea Group Inc., 2004, 200-217.

Society for Information Management, 2006, http://www.simnet.org/

Stowers, Genie, Issues in E-Commerce and E-Government Service Delivery, in Digital Government, Principles and Best Practices, ed. Pavlichev, Alexei, and Garson, David, A., Idea Group Inc., 2004, 169-185.

Sun Microsystems, http://www.sunmicrosystems.com.

U.S. Bureau of Labor Statistics, 2006, 2007, http://www.bls.gov.

VARBusiness, March 2006.

Zieger, Robert H., American Workers, American Unions, Second Edition, Johns Hopkins University Press, 1994.

Chapter Four
What IT Jobs Are Available
U.S. Federal – State – City

Information Technology Job Titles
Salaries & Pension Rates in U.S. Federal Government

Federal Government Hiring for U.S. Government
Federal Agencies

The Federal Government hires for 15 Executive Agencies & 101 Other Federal Agencies (Chart III). The range of Information Technology jobs required by these agencies is wide. The number of information technology jobs required is in the thousands. (USOPM, Executive Agencies, 2006.)

Competitive Hiring & Civil Service
in U.S. Federal Government Based on Qualifications

The U.S. Federal Government hires staff competitively, based on the best qualifications, hiring the best qualified candidate who applies for the job. "Competitive" means hiring the best candidate with the best qualifications for the job.

No Written Civil Service Exam Required for IT Jobs

There is No Written (Multiple Choice or Essay) Civil Service Exam required for Information Technology jobs. The job reviewer will review the candidate's work experience and education and qualifications for the particular job, based on a review of the candidate's information, submitted on the Form 612 (Appendix G) Job Application or Resume, and the Form C. The "Competitive" appointment is made, and the candidate hired, on the basis of Experience and Education.

Knowledge – Skills – Abilities (KSAs) Requirements

Each Job Announcement designates the requirements for the job. It lists the Knowledge, Skills, and Abilities that are required. These are the minimum requirements. Since the job reviewer will select the "best" qualified candidate, a job applicant should list as much applicable education and work experience as possible, to achieve a higher rank than another candidate.

To learn how the IT Job Title in the Job Announcement you are responding to has been classified, consult the "Job Family Position Classification Standard for Administrative Work in the Information Technology Group GS-2200" (USOPM, GS-2200, 2001, 2003). This document will tell you what the qualifications are for each information technology job and its salary grade on the career ladder.

Consult the "Introduction to the Position Classifications Standard" (USOPM, Position Classifications, 1995,) and "The Classifier's Handbook (USOPM, Classifier's Handbook, 1991) to understand further the instructions to the classifiers and reviewers for determining job title salary grading and reviewing candidate qualifications.

To learn how to provide additional pages to your Resume, with your Knowledge, Skills & Abilities see **Chapter V: Completing the Application & Hiring Process, and Appendix H: Knowledge, Skills, Abilities (KSAs) Formatting & Factors Response.**

Federal Government Job Group, Job Title & Salary Grade Pay System

When a position is needed, the Classifier assigns the position a Job Group, Job Title, and Salary Pay Grade, based on the job standards and qualifications required.

The Grade Pay will correspond to the U.S. Federal Government General Schedule of Annual Rates by Grade and Step. The U.S. Federal Government General Services Salary Table published below shows the GS Salary Grades 1-15, with their corresponding Salaries, and the Steps 1-10 for each Grade. Steps 1-10 are achieved by promotions based on experience and performance.

General Services Salary Table – Salary Grades 1-15
[See Appendix A: General Services Salary Table]

Information Technology Job Titles
Salaries & Pension Rates in U.S. Federal Government

Information Technology Job Group

The Information Technology Job Group GS-2200 was created to cover the occupational series:
Information Technology Management GS-2210

The Information Technology Management GS-2210 series provides job title classifications and occupational guidance for administrative positions that manage, supervise, lead, administer, develop, deliver, and support information technology (IT) systems and services. This series covers only those positions for which the paramount requirement is knowledge of IT principles, concepts, and methods; e.g., data storage, software applications, networking. Information technology refers to systems and services used in the automated acquisition, storage, manipulation, management, movement, control, display, switching, interchange, transmission, assurance, or reception ofinformation.

Information technology includes computers, network components, peripheral equipment, software, firmware, services, and related resources.

"Information technology refers to systems and services used in the automated acquisition, storage, manipulation, management, movement, control, display, switching, interchange, transmission, assurance, or reception of information. Information technology includes computers, network components, peripheral equipment, software, firmware, services, and related resources. Perhaps no other occupation has experienced the dramatic changes that have affected the information technology (IT) occupation in recent years. The growing use of information technology throughout our economy has resulted in an unprecedented explosion in the demand for skilled IT workers. This phenomenon affects virtually every aspect of the IT human resources management process from recruitment to retirement. The position classification function is no exception. Continuous, significant developments in the technology and its application dramatically influence the occupation, with a particular emphasis on information security. As more and more information, products, and services become widely available to customers by way of shared resources, the need to assure the confidentiality, integrity, and availability of systems, networks, and data has become increasingly important. Any effort to predict the future course and direction of the occupation would be no more than an educated guess. One indisputable fact is that the occupation will continue to evolve in a very rapid fashion. New functions and specializations will emerge and replace or be added to those currently in use (USOPM, GS-2200 Job Family, 2001, 2003.)"

For the **Information Technology Management Job Family Standards,** see the document "Job Family Position Classification Standard for Administrative Work in the Information Technology Group GS-2200" publishing the standard knowledge, skill and abilities qualifications for each job title, level and grade in the Information Technology Job Group (USOPM, GS-2200 Job Family, 2001, 2003.)

Information Technology Main Job Titles

The Job Group is called Information Technology Management. The Job Title series has two main job titles, with Supervisory and Team Leader levels, and 10 Competency Specialties. The Information Technology Job Group replaces an earlier job group known as **Computer Specialist GS-0334 and Telecommunications GS-0391.** Computer

The basic titles for the Information Technology occupation are:

Information Technology Manager

Work that involves directly managing information technology projects to provide a unique service or product. The title also applies to supervisory project manager positions evaluated under the General Schedule Supervisory Guide.

Information Technology Specialist or IT Specialist

Work that involves developing, delivering, and supporting IT systems and services is Information Technology Specialist or IT Specialist. Use the parenthetical specialty titles defined below with the basic title to further identify the duties and responsibilities performed and the special knowledge and skills needed. The Job Title Classification may have any combination of two parenthetical specialty titles in official position titles; e.g., Information Technology Specialist (Applications Software/Systems Analysis), where the two specialties are of significant importance to the position.

Information Technology Supervisory and Leader Job Positions

Further, IT Job Titles may be classified as **"Supervisory"** or **"Team Leader"** positions.

*Information Technology Management Series Grades GS-5-GS-15 (*GS-11-GS-15)*

The Information Technology Management Job Title Series offers salaries from GS-5 – GS-15.   However, a Survey of the IT Job Announcements on the http://www. USAJOBS.gov website over a 1-month period by Info Tech Employment indicates that most IT jobs in the IT Jobs Series listed offer a salary between GS-11 and GS-15 (*Info Tech Employment, IT Federal Jobs Survey, 2007). Each Job Announcement states the Job Salary Grade for the Title. Salary grades are negotiable at the time of hiring. Higher education and greater job experience will be considered to apply a higher Salary Grade.

Supervisory Positions may be assigned a Grade-Level Increase. Leader Positions may be assigned one or more Grade-Level Increases based on a points assessment of the work required. Supervisory Positions may earn a 1-Grade Level Increase per year. Team Leader positions may earn a 1-3 Grade Level Increases per year.

Experience and Performance in U.S. Federal Government employment lead to Salary Grade & Step Promotions. Step Promotions may be earned over the course of a career. No more than one Step Promotion may be earned in a single year for most job titles. See the GS Salary Schedule (Appendix A) for the Step increase rate amounts.

The IT Job Titles 5-Year Salary Projections Chart (Chart IV) calculates salary projections and estimated pensions based on some assumptions for the Step increase rate amounts over the course of a career.

Information Technology Ten (10) Specialties – Job Descriptions

An **IT Project Manager** job or **Information Technology Specialist (IT Specialist)** job may be defined with these ten (10) specialties. A job announcement and classification may call on up to two (2) of these Core Competency specialties in the job description. A general description of the relationships among the specialties is presented below:

• **Policy and Planning (PLCPLN)** – develop, implement, and ensure compliance with
  plans, policies, standards, infrastructures, and architectures that establish the

framework for the management of all IT programs.
- **Security (INFOSEC)** – plan, develop, implement, and maintain programs, polices, and procedures to protect the integrity and confidentiality of systems, networks, and data.
- **Systems Analysis (SYSANALYSIS)** – consult with customers to refine functional requirements and translate functional requirements into technical specifications.
- **Applications Software (APPSW)** – translate technical specifications into programming specifications; develop, customize, or acquire applications software programs; and test, debug, and maintain software programs.
- **Operating Systems (OS)** – install, configure, and maintain the operating systems environment including systems servers and operating systems software on which applications programs run.
- **Network Services (NETWORK)** – test, install, configure, and maintain networks including hardware (servers, hubs, bridges, switches, and routers) and software that permit the sharing and transmission of information.
- **Data Management (DATAMGT)** – develop and administer databases used to store and retrieve data and develop standards for the handling of data.
- **Internet (INET)** – provide services that permit the publication and transmission of information about agency programs to internal and external audiences using the Internet.
- **Systems Administration (SYSADMIN)** – install, configure, troubleshoot, and maintain hardware and software to ensure the availability and functionality of systems.
- **Customer Support (CUSTSPT)** – provide technical support to customers who need advice, assistance, and training in applying hardware and software systems.

(See Appendix B: Competencies Required for Federal IT Job Specialties)

Other Job Groups with Computer-Related, Technology-Related Job Titles Requiring Information Technology Knowledge

Other Job Groups in U.S. Federal Government have computer-related, technology-related job titles. When seeking a career in U.S. Federal Government, your information technology knowledge, skills, and abilities might apply and qualify you for a job in one of the following job titles. The following list of job titles provides examples of situations where the work may involve the application of related knowledge and skills, but not to the extent that it may warrant classification to IT job family. These job titles exist in other job groups.

These other job groups will look favorably on your computer-related, technology-related skills and experience. It is important to look for job announcements on http://www. USAJOBS.gov, in these Other Job Groups as well at the IT Job Group. Simply search on the job group and you will find job announcements and job descriptions for the available jobs in the group. The General Services Salary Grade possibilities for each of the groups or titles is listed in Parentheses, (i.e. GS-3-GS-9 means that job titles in this group may have a salary from GS-3 to GS-9).

GS-0335, Computer Clerk & Assistant (GS-3-GS-9)
Work involves IT support or services functions. Work requires a practical knowledge of IT systems, workflow, and controls rather than the broad and in depth knowledge of IT principles, concepts, and methods characteristic of positions covered by this standard

GS-0332, Computer Operation (GS-3-GS-9)
Work involves operating or supervising the operation of computer systems, including

the operation of peripheral equipment. Work requires knowledge of functions and features of computer systems and skill in reading, interpreting, and correctly responding to information transmitted through computer systems.

GS-0391, Telecommunications (GS-5-GS-11)
Work involves acquisition, technical acceptance, installation, testing, modification, or r eplacement of telecommunications equipment, services, and systems. Work requires paramount knowledge of:
• the operational and performance characteristics of telecommunications equipment;
• the relationships among component parts of telecommunications systems; and
• telecommunications equipment interoperability and compatibility characteristics; as well as an understanding of basic electronics theories and operating principles. Work in this series also typically requires knowledge of IT concepts that is secondary to the paramount knowledge requirements described above.

GS-0854, Computer Engineering (GS-5-GS-15)
Work involves professional knowledge of fundamentals and principles of computer engineering; computer hardware, systems, software, and computer systems architecture and integration; and mathematics as the paramount requirement.

GS-1550, Computer Science (GS 5-GS-15)
Work involves professional knowledge of theoretical foundations of computer science; specialized knowledge of design characteristics, limitations, and potential applications of information systems; and knowledge of relevant mathematical and statistical sciences.

GS-0300, Clerical, and Office Services Group, such as:
GS-0303, Miscellaneous Clerk and Assistant
GS-0318, Secretary (GS-2-GS-13)
Work involves skill in the use of personal computers and knowledge of specialized and/or general office software applications, e.g., desktop publishing, to provide administrative support.

GS-0200, Subject Area Computer Work, i.e. Human Resources Management Group (GS-1-GS-15)
Work involves knowledge of e.g., human resources management, even when performing IT assignments.

GS-2010, Inventory Management (GS-9-GS-11)

GS-1300P, Professional Work in the Physical Sciences Group, (GS-5-GS-15)
Work involves professional knowledge of mathematics, engineering, physics, or related fields as the paramount requirement even when performing IT assignments.

GS-0500, Accounting and Budget Group, (GS-2-GS-9)
Work involves designing new automated financial accounting systems or developing modifications to existing systems. Work requires knowledge of application of accounting theories, concepts, principles, and standards as the paramount requirement.

GS-0343, Management and Program Analysis, (GS-5-GS-9)
Work involves substantive knowledge of agency programs and activities; agency mission, policies, and objectives; management principles and processes; and analytical and evaluative methods as they relate to the evaluation of government programs and operations.

GS-0080, Security Administration, (GS-5-GS-15)

Work involves knowledge of security concepts, methods, practices, and procedures as the paramount requirement in developing, evaluating, maintaining, and/or operating systems, policies, devices, procedures, and methods used for safeguarding information, property, personnel, operations, and materials.

GS-1811, Criminal Investigating, (GS-5-GS-13)

Work involves knowledge of investigative techniques, rules of evidence, Federal laws and statutes, and criminal laws as the paramount requirement in planning and conducting investigations of computer and Internet related crimes.

GS-1410, Librarian, (GS-9-GS-14)

Work involves professional knowledge of the theories, principles, and techniques of library science as the paramount requirement in the collection, organization, preservation, and retrieval of recorded knowledge.

GS-1412, Technical Information Services, (GS-9-GS-14)

Work involves knowledge of one or more scientific, engineering, technical, or other fields and practical knowledge of techniques for organizing, accessing, or disseminating information as the paramount requirements in developing, coordinating, processing, and transmitting specialized information.

GS-1084, Visual Information, (GS-7-GS-12)

Work involves communicating information through visual means that requires knowledge of the principles of visual design and the ability to present subject matter i nformation in a visual form that will convey the intended message to, or have the desired effect on, the intended audience.

Appropriate Subject-Matter Series (GS-1-GS-15)

Work involves preparing and updating subject-matter information on an organization's Web site that requires knowledge of subject-matter programs and processes and knowledge of basic Web site development techniques rather than knowledge of IT principles, concepts, and methods as the paramount requirement.

GS-1910, Quality Assurance, (GS-5-GS-15)

Work involves knowledge of quality assurance methods, principles and practices as the paramount requirement in assuring the quality of products acquired and used by the Federal Government, including software used in manufacturing, maintenance, and operational applications.

GS-2600, Electronic Equipment Installation and Maintenance, (GS-5-GS-15 or Wage Grade)

Work involves operating computerized analytical test and diagnostic equipment to install, test, troubleshoot, maintain, and repair electronic equipment that requires knowledge of the operational capabilities and limitations of electronic equipment and systems and skill in the use of computerized testing and diagnostic equipment.

Information Technology Positions in Senior Executive Service (SES)

Members of the Senior Executive Service serve in the key positions just below the top Presidential appointees. SES members are the major link between these appointees and the rest of the Federal work force. They operate and oversee nearly every government activity in approximately 75 Federal agencies (USAOPM, 2006).

There are continuous opportunities for qualified Information Technology professionals to take key positions in the Senior Executive Service. Many governmental functions and departments rely keenly on information technology systems. Therefore, managing key information technology systems becomes a key responsibility in many Senior Executive Service positions. Jobs in information technology are also announced on http://www.USAJOBS.gov.

The SES pay range has a minimum rate of basic pay equal to 120 percent of the rate for GS-15, step 1, and the maximum rate of basic pay is equal to the rate for level III of the Executive Schedule. For any agency certified as having a performance appraisal system, the maximum rate of basic pay will be the rate for level II of the Executive Schedule (USAOPM, 2006).

U.S. Federal Government
Information Technology Exchange Program (ITEP)
for Federal & Private Sector IT Employees

The ITEP is a new and exciting professional development opportunity. If you are already employed in IT in the private sector, or if you are currently employed in IT in a federal agency, you may be eligible to participate. This program allows exceptional performers from the Federal and private IT sectors to participate in temporary assignments of three (3) months to 1 year, in the other sector. ITEP promotes the interchange of IT workers to develop, supplement, and modernize IT skills to expand the long term competencies of the Federal IT workforce. While Federal agencies have a strong interest in the areas of Enterprise Architecture, Solutions Architecture, IT Project Management, and IT Security, ITEP exchange opportunities can exist in all IT disciplines. Please visit, http://www.opm.gov for more details about the program.

The following Federal agencies are participating in this program. To contact the ITEP representative for jobs for IT professionals from the Private Sector for this program with these listed Agencies, visit http://www.usajobs.opm.gov/itep.asp

DEPARTMENT OF COMMERCE
DEPARTMENT OF DEFENSE
DEPARTMENT OF HEALTH AND HUMAN SERVICES
DEPARTMENT OF HOMELAND SECURITY (DHS)
DEPARTMENT OF JUSTICE (DOJ)
DEPARTMENT OF THE TREASURY
ENVIRONMENTAL PROTECTION AGENCY
FEDERAL BUREAU OF INVESTIGATION
OFFICE OF PERSONNEL MANAGEMENT (OPM)

To view ITEP opportunities in the private sector for existing Federal employees, visit http://www.actgov.org/ITEP.

Recruitment of IT Interns through
The Federal Career Intern Program

The Federal Career Intern Program is designed to help agencies recruit and attract exceptional individuals into a variety of occupations. It is intended for positions at grade levels GS-5, 7, and 9. In general, individuals are appointed to a 2-year internship. Upon successful completion of the internships, the interns may be eligible for permanent placement within an agency. Individuals interested in Career Intern opportunities must contact specific agencies directly (http://www.opm.gov/careerintern/.)

Factors in Determining Job Title Classification & Pay Grade

Federal IT Jobs are given job title and pay grades based on several factors:

☐ **Knowledge Factors in Determining Job Grade & Salary**
☐ **Competency Factors in Determining Job Grade & Salary**
☐ **Supervisory Factors**
☐ **Judgment Factors**
☐ **Nature of Assignment Factors**
☐ **Scope of Contacts – Purpose of Contacts**

Each IT Job Announcement lists Job Requirements. When you are preparing your Resume for a specific Job Announcement, refer to **Appendix C: Definitions of Factors Determining Job Title Classification & Pay Grade** to understand how you may write your Resume to reflect how your experience fulfills these Factors and Requirements of the job. **(See Appendix C: Definitions of Factors Determining Job Title Classification & Pay Grade).**

U.S. Federal Government
IT Job Series & Computer-Technology Related Job Titles -
Salaries, 5-Year Salary Projections & Estimated Pension

The Information Technology Management Series offers salaries from Salary Grades GS-5 – GS-15 (*GS-11-GS-15). However, a Survey of the IT Job Announcements on the http://www.USAJOBS.gov   website over a 1-month period by Info Tech Employment indicates that most IT jobs in the IT Jobs Series listed offer a salary between GS-11 and GS-15 (*Info Tech Employment, IT Federal Jobs Survey, 2007). Each Job Announcement will state the Job Salary Grade for the Title. Salary grades are negotiable at the time of hiring. Higher education and greater job experience will be considered to apply a higher Salary Grade. The Salary Grades possible for each Job Title are displayed on Chart IV.

Supervisory Positions may be assigned a Grade-Level Increase. Leader Positions may be assigned one or more Grade-Level Increases based on a points assessment of the work required. Supervisory Positions may earn a 1-Grade Level Increase per year. Team Leader positions may earn a 1-3 Grade Level Increases per year.

Other Computer-Related, Technology-Related Job Titles, offer salaries from GS-2-GS14. The Salary Grades possible for each Job Title are displayed on Chart IV.

Experience and Performance in U.S. Federal Government employment lead to Salary Grade & Step Promotions. Step Promotions may be earned over the course of a career. No more than one Step Promotion may be earned in a single year for most job titles. See the GS Salary Schedule (Appendix A) for the Step increase rate amounts.

The 5-Year Salary Projections and Estimated Pensions Chart (Chart IV) calculates the projected salaries, 5-year estimated salaries, and estimated pensions for the IT Job Titles and Other Job Group, Computer-Related, Technology-Related Job Titles. The calculations in the Chart are based on current actual salary base, assumptions for Step increase rate amounts over the course of a career, average Federal raises based on a 5-year past history, and current pension formula. Notes to Chart IV explain the calculations in greater detail.

Senior Executive Service Jobs in Information Technology (SES) are not represented separately in Chart V. The SES pay range has a minimum rate of basic pay equal to 120 percent of the rate for GS-15, step 1, and the maximum rate of basic pay is equal to the rate for level III of the Executive Schedule. For any agency certified as having a performance appraisal system, the maximum rate of basic pay will be the rate for level II of the Executive Schedule (USAOPM, 2006).

**[See Chart IV: U.S. Federal
IT Job Titles - Salaries, 5-Year Salary Projections & Estimated Pension]**

Sample Information Technology Job Announcements
U.S. Federal Government

Job Announcements for IT Jobs, Computer-Related jobs, Managements & Planning jobs, and Senior Executive Service (SES) positions that may require technology skills, will be found at http://www.USAJOBS.gov, the official U.S. Federal Job Web Portal. **See Appendix D: Sample Information Technology Job Announcements - U.S. Federal Government.**

The Job Package - U.S. Federal Government

Pay
A Federal job in information technology provides equal to or better pay than in the private sector, over the long term. There are no disruptions in employment, caused by private merger, downsizing or reorganization. Base pay factors could include performance-based pay, competency-based pay, geographic locality pay, structural and market adjustments, longevity pay, skills-based pay and other factors (USAOPM, Primer, 2006.) The Pay Benefit Package includes 13 Paid Holidays, 13 Paid Sick Days, between 13-26 Paid Annual Leave Days, and a Health Benefit Package that is equivalent to 33% salary. This is like adding an additional 1/3 on to your paycheck.

Permanence
A Career Service Federal employee will achieve job permanence after a probationary period, usually of one year, in the job title, and a successful performance evaluation. The Civil Service Merit System provides for a one-year Probationary Period, during which the employee's performance is evaluated to determine if it is satisfactory and permits Permanent Appointment. There are strict procedures and guidelines for severance from Federal employment service. An employee is entitled to Union Representation in any action toward severance. (USAOPM, Glossary, 2006).

Annual Raises
Annual Raises in Federal Career Service are typically 2.1%, 10.4% 5-Year cumulative, and 10.75% compounded over 5 years.
Longevity Increases

The Longevity-Competency and Performance-Based System makes pay increases on a regular basis based on a performance system .

Pension Plan
The Federal Employment Retirement System (FERS) is based on a 3-part benefit structure, allowing for:
□ *Social Security Benefits*
□ *Pension Benefits –Basic Benefit Plan*
Average 3-Years Highest Salary X Creditable Service X 1%
□ *Thrift Savings Program & Deferred Compensation Plan*
Your agency will set up a Thrift Savings Plan account for you and will automatically contribute an amount equal to 1% of your basic pay each pay period. These Agency Automatic (1%) Contributions are not taken out of your salary, and your agency makes these contributions whether or not you contribute your own money to the TSP.

Vacation Days – Annual Leave
Annual Leave is used for vacations, rest and relaxation, and personal business or emergencies. New full-time employees earn 4 hours of annual leave each 2 week pay period (13 Days per year). When you have 3 years of service this increases to 6 hours every 2 weeks (19.5 Days per year) , and at 15 years it increases to 8 hours every 2 weeks (26 Days per year).

Paid Holidays
□ **New Year's Day**
□ **Birthday of Martin Luther King, Jr.**
□ **Washington's Birthday**
□ **Memorial Day**
□ **Independence Day**
□ **Labor Day**
□ **Columbus Day**
□ **Veterans Day**
□ **Thanksgiving Day**
□ **Christmas Day**

Sick Leave
Federal Employees accrue 4 hours sick leave every two weeks, or 13 days of Sick Leave per year. You can accrue this leave without limit.
□ **Different Ways to Use Sick Leave**
Sick Leave for Family Care or Bereavement
Sick Leave for Adoption
12 Weeks of Paid or Leave without Pay Sick Leave for Family Care
Interaction with 13 days of Sick Leave for Family Care/Bereavement Purposes
The Family and Medical Leave Act (FMLA)
Interaction of Sick Leave for Family Care With the Family and Medical Leave Act
Leave Transfer And Leave Bank Programs
Interaction of Sick Leave for Family Care With the Leave Sharing Program
Leave for Childbirth;   Leave for Adoption
Sick Leave for Family Care or Bereavement

Student Loan Repayment Program
The Federal student loan repayment program permits agencies to repay Federally insured student loans as a recruitment or retention incentive for candidates.

Health & Benefits Package
☐ **Federal Employees Health Benefits Program (Over 350 Plans)**
   Individual Health Benefits
   Family health benefits
   Medical Health Plan
   Major Medical & Hospitalization
☐ **Prescription Plan**
☐ **Dental Plan & Vision Insurance Program**

Career Ladder - Advancement
☐ **Advancement in Job Title Grades (Steps I-IV)**
Federal Employees may achieve normal advancement through successful Performance
Evaluation, and advance within Job Title Series, from Steps 1-9 on the GS Pay Schedule, at a rate
of 1-2 Step Increases per year.
☐ **Advancement through Promotion (Grades I-IV)**
Federal Employees may advance through Promotions by achieving exceptional Performance
Evaluations, and advance within Job Title Series, from Steps 1-9 on the GS Pay Schedule, at a
rate of 1-3 Step Increases per year.
☐ **Advancement through Changing Positions within a Department, Agency, or Between
Agencies.** Federal Employees may achieve career advancement by changing positions within a
Department or Agency, or between Federal Agencies.

Multiple Employment Opportunities
☐ **Transfers within an Agency or Department**
☐ **Transfers between Agencies**

Training and Career Development
☐ **Intergovernmental Personnel Act Mobility Program**
The Intergovernmental Personnel Act Mobility Program provides for the temporary assignment
of personnel between the Federal Government and state and local governments, colleges and
universities, Indian tribal governments, federally funded research and development centers,
and other eligible organizations
☐ **Detail and Transfer of Federal Employees to International Organizations**
☐ **The Executives in Residence Program:** Executives in Residence (EIR)
☐ **Leadership & Knowledge Management Programs**
☐ **Individual Learning accounts (ILA)**
☐ **Individual Development Plans (IDP)**
☐ **Candidate Development Programs for Senior Executive Service -**Senior Executive
   Service (SES) Candidate Development Programs (CDP's)
☐ **Career Transition Resources-** Federal employees gain access to over 1 million jobs through
   Career One Stop in addition to other career transition resources .

Union Representation
Federal employees are entitled to full Union Representation in contracts, negotiations,
disputes and settlements, or unfair labor practice complaints .

Union Benefits
☐ **Major Medical Supplemental Health Benefits**
☐ **Educational Assistance**
☐ **Career Development Assistance**
☐ **Supplemental Life Insurance Policies**
☐ **Legal Representation at Hearings & Other Legal Support**

Long Term Care Insurance & Flexible Savings Account
The Federal Long Term Care Insurance Program (FLTCIP) helps cover long term care costs. Premium conversion uses Federal tax rules to let employees deduct their share of health insurance premiums from their taxable income, thereby reducing their taxes. John Hancock and MetLife provide this insurance, under a company called Long Term Care Partners, LLC to administer the Program.

The Federal Flexible Spending Account Program
The Federal Flexible Spending Account (FSA) Program lets the employee set aside pre-tax money to pay for health and dependent care expenses. The result can be a discount of 20% to more than 40% on services routinely paid for out-of-pocket.
☐ **Health Care Flexible Spending Account (HCFSA)**
The maximum annual amount that can be allotted for the HCFSA is $5,000. Covers eligible health care expenses not reimbursed by your FEHB Plan, or any other medical, dental, or vision care plan you or your dependents may have. The minimum annual amount is $250.
☐ **Dependent Care Flexible Spending Account (DCFSA)**
Covers eligible dependent care expenses incurred so you, or your spouse, if married, can work, look for work, or attend school full-time.

Federal Life Insurance Program
The Federal Employees' Group Life Insurance Program is the largest group life nsurance program in the world, covering over 4 million Federal employees and retirees, as well as many of their family members. FEGLI provides group term life insurance. The cost of Basic insurance is shared between you and the Government. You pay 2/3 of the total cost and the Government pays 1/3. Your age does not affect the cost of Basic insurance.

Survivor Benefits
If you die while you are a Federal employee, payments will be made in a particular order set by law from:
☐ **Life Insurance (FEGLI)**
☐ **Unpaid Salary**
☐ **Thrift Savings Plan funds**
☐ **Retirement Lump Sum**

Information Technology Job Titles
Salaries & Pension Rates in U.S. State and Municipal Government

U.S. State & Municipal Government Hiring
for State & City Agencies & Departments

Information Technology jobs exist in all 50 U.S. States and most major U.S. City government agencies and departments. A "Survey of IT Jobs in U.S. States & Major U.S. Cities" conducted by Info Tech Employment shows that most U.S. States and Major Cities offer between 10-35 Civil Service Information Technology Job Titles.

U.S. States and major U.S. Cities hire staff in Information Technology for most of their government departments and agencies. Agencies and Departments that are found in most U.S. States and Cities include:

Board of Elections
Buildings, Department of
City Clerk
State & City Employees' Retirement System
Civil Service Commission
Consumer Affairs, Department of
Correction, Department of
Cultural Affairs, Department of
Economic Development Corporation
Education, Department of
Emergency Management, Office of
Environmental Protection, Department of
Finance, Department of
Fire Department

Housing Authority
Human Resources Administration – Social Services
Information Technology and Telecommunications,
Investigation, Department of
Management and Budget, Office of
Mayor's Office
Parks and Recreation, Department of
Payroll Administration, Office of
Personnel, Department of
Police Department
Probation, Department of
Records, Department of
Sanitation, Department of
Transportation, Department of

Records, Department of
Sanitation, Department of
Transportation, Department of

IT Job Titles - Salaries - 5-Year Salary Projections
Estimated Pension in U.S. State & Municipal Government

The Salaries for IT Job Titles in State and City government are higher than for many trade, labor and administrative titles. The Average Raise per Year for IT Job Titles, according to the Info Tech Employment Survey, is 2.25%, with a cumulative 5-Year Raise of 11.25%, and a Compounded Raise of 11.75%. In addition, many States and Major Cities have Service in Job and Service in Title Longevity Increases, at 5 years, and at 10 years. These Longevity Increases, once earned, continue to be compounded as part of the Salary, and paid over the career of the employee. The Average Retirement Pension Percentage among the 50 U.S. States and Major U.S. Cities, found in the Survey, was found to be 1.5% (Info Tech Employment, 2007.)

Using the figures gathered in the Info Tech Employment Survey, a starting salary of $55,000 in an Information Technology job, a 2.25% raise per year yields an 11.75% compounded raise over 5 years (or $61,475.). The 20-Year Retirement Pension for a career employee at a starting salary of $55,000 (without Longevity added in) is an estimated $27,369 per year. The 25-Year Retirement Pension for a career employee at $55,000 (without Longevity) is estimated at $45,876 per year. The 30-year Retirement Pension for a career employee at $55,000 (without Longevity added in) is estimated at $61,530 per year (Info Tech Employment, Employment Survey, 2007); The Career Pension is in addition to Social Security Benefits. The Estimated Pension amount is in today's dollars.

The Information Technology Job Titles – Salaries – Salary Projections and Estimated Pensions are listed in the Charts below for representative U.S. States and Major Cities. These estimates are made on the basis of published current Salaries, published by each of the U.S. States and Cities (U.S. Government, Freedom of Information Act, 2006).

(See Chart V: U.S. States & Major Cities

IT Job Titles
 Salaries, 5-Year Salary Projections & Estimated Pension]

Sample Information Technology Job Descriptions
U.S. States & City Government

If you are seeking an IT position, you may read Job Descriptions to understand the job qualifications and levels of experience required. These Job Descriptions are found on the State and City, Personnel Department and Employment websites. Job Descriptions may also be obtained by sending an e-mail to the Contact person identified at the Personnel Website. We have provided Sample Information Technology Job Descriptions for some of the main job titles in Information Technology, published by U.S. States and major cities. **(See Appendix E: Sample Information Technology Job Descriptions & Qualifications - U.S. State & Municipal Government - Representative U.S. States & Major Cities)**

The Job Package – Benefits
U.S. State & City Government

Pay
A U.S. State or Municipal government job in information technology provides equal or better pay than in the private sector, over the long term. There are no disruptions in employment, caused by private merger, downsizing or reorganization. Base pay factors could include performance-based pay, competency-based pay, schedule differential pay, longevity pay, and other factors. The Pay Benefit Package includes 11 Paid Holidays, 13 Paid Sick Days, between 13-26 Paid Annual Leave Days, and a Health Benefit Package that is equivalent to 33% salary. This is like adding an additional 1/3 on to your paycheck.

Permanence
A U.S. State or Municipal employee will achieve job permanence after a probationary period in the job title, usually of one year, and a successful performance evaluation. The Civil Service Merit System provides for a one-year Probationary Period, during which the employee's performance is evaluated to determine if it is satisfactory and permits Permanent Appointment. There are strict procedures and guidelines for severance from employment. An employee is entitled to Union Representation and Legal Representation during any severance action that might, in rare cases, be taken.

Annual Raises
Annual Raises in U.S. State and Municipal government typically average between 2.25%-3%, per year, 11.25%-15% 5-Year cumulative, and 11.75%-15.75% compounded over 5 years (Info Tech Employment, Survey, 2007.)

Longevity Increases
U.S. States and Municipal government have a variety of In Service and/or In Title Longevity Increases, ranging from No Increase, to as much as $3,000 In Service Longevity after 10 years In Service, and $3,000 after 5 Years In Title. These Longevity Increases are rolled into Base Pay and Compounded over time, in most cases (Info Tech Employment, Survey, 2007.)

Pension Plan
The Employee Retirement Systems for most U.S. States and Cities make provisions for:

☐ *Social Security Benefits*
U.S. State and Municipal career employees pay full social security taxes and receive full social security benefits.

☐ *Pension Benefits – Basic Benefit Plan*
Employees pay either zero or a small contribution to the Pension Plan, ranging from 0% - 6% of pay, for a determined number of years, based on the specific Union or Non-Union hiring contract the employee is hired under. The Retirement Formula for the Pension is, on average: Average 3-Years Highest Salary X Creditable Service X 1.5%-2.25% (depending on specific U.S. State or City. Some States and Cities have undefined Pension Plans based on employee contributions.) (Info Tech Employment, Survey, 2007.)

☐ *Pre-Tax Deferred Compensation Savings Program*
Most U.S. State and Municipal government agencies offer a voluntary employee-funded retirement savings program, with choice of providers and investment options. You may defer a percentage of your base pay up to a specified amount, in before-tax dollars. Thus, you are paying less on your Income Taxes during the year you defer i ncome. Savings is taxed at the time of distribution.

☐ *After-Tax 401K or 401K Roth Retirement Savings Program*
A voluntary 401K or 401K Roth Retirement Savings Program is also available for most U.S. State and City government employees. You may save to a 401K or 401 Roth with a choice of providers and investment options. Taxes are paid at the time of saving. However, no taxes are paid at the time of withdrawal.

Vacation Days – Annual Leave

Annual Leave is used for vacations, rest and relaxation, and personal business or emergencies. While U.S. State and Municipal Labor-Management contracts vary from State-to-State and City-to-City, most new full-time employees earn 4 hours of annual leave each 2 week pay period (13 Days per year). When you have 3 years of service this often increases to 6 hours every 2 weeks (19.5 Days per year) , and at 15 years it often increases to 8 hours every 2 weeks (26 Days per year).

Paid Holidays

☐ **New Year's Day**
☐ **Birthday of Martin Luther King, Jr.**
☐ **Washington's Birthday (or President's Day)**
☐ **Memorial Day**
☐ **Independence Day**
☐ **Labor Day**
☐ **Columbus Day**
☐ **Election Day**
☐ **Veterans Day**
☐ **Thanksgiving Day**
☐ **Christmas Day**

Sick Leave

Most U.S. State and Municipal employees accrue 4 hours sick leave every two weeks, or 13 days of Sick Leave per year. You can accrue this leave without limit.

☐ **Different Ways to Use Sick Leave**

 ☐ Sick Leave for Family Care or Bereavement
 ☐ Sick Leave for Adoption
 ☐ The Family and Medical Leave Act (FMLA)
 ☐ Interaction of Sick Leave for Family Care With the Family and Medical Leave Act
 ☐ Leave Transfer And Leave Bank Programs

☐ Interaction of Sick Leave for Family Care With the Leave Sharing Program
☐ Leave for Childbirth
☐ Leave for Adoption
☐ Sick Leave for Family Care or Bereavement

Health & Benefits Package Health Care

Comprehensive Health Care coverage is available to U.S. State and City government employees and eligible dependents. Cost for coverage varies for each State or City, from No Cost to a specified bi-weekly fee, or maximum out of pocket expense per contract, per benefit year. Choices of Health Care Coverage Plans are offered. Health Care Coverage includes Doctor-Provider Coverage and Hospital Coverage. Employees may also choose to pay for uncovered Health Care Expenses out of a Medical Spending Account, that establishes their own pre-tax account to pay for medical or dental expenses for the employee and their dependents.

☐ **Individual Health Benefits**
☐ **Family health benefits**
☐ **Medical Health Plan**
☐ **Major Medical & Hospitalization**

Career Ladder -Advancement

☐ **Advancement in Job Title Levels (not Automatic in most cases)**
U.S. State and Municipal employees in certain titles, may advance to the next level of the title, based on performance or duties performed.

☐ **Advancement through Promotional Exams or Provisional Promotion**
U.S. State and Municipal employees may achieve Promotion either through successful completion of a Promotional Civil Service Exam and appointment by an Agency, or by Provisional Promotion to a higher job titles or level by an Agency or Department.

☐ **Advancement through Changing Positions within a Department, Agency, or Between Agencies**U.S. State and Municipal employees may achieve career advancement by changing positions within a Department or Agency, or between Federal Agencies, either by Transfer to a Higher Job Title or by taking a Civil Service Exam and achieving successful appointment, or applying for an achieving Provisional Appointment in the same of higher title with higher pay.

Multiple Employment Opportunities

☐ **Transfers within an Agency or Department**
U.S. State and Municipal employees may apply for any job opening within an Agency or Department and seek to obtain the position through competitive qualification.

☐ **Transfers between Agencies**
U.S. State and Municipal employees may apply for any job opening within an Agency or Department and seek to obtain the position through competitive qualification. This provides employees with an optimum opportunity to advance by bringing acquired skills and experience to a new job.

Training and Career Development

The Training and Career Development programs vary from State-to-State and City-to-City. They often include these types of training and career development:

☐ **Equal Opportunity Employment Opportunity Training**
☐ **On-Site Training in Emerging Technologies, Office Automation, & Information Technology**
☐ **Computer-Based Training from Learning Libraries**
☐ **Instructor-Led Courses**
☐ **Off Site Training in Emerging Technologies & IT**
☐ **Vendor Product Specific Training**

Union Representation

U.S. State and Municipal employees are entitled to full Union Representation in contracts, negotiations, disputes and settlements, or unfair labor practice complaints.

Union Benefits

Union Benefits vary from State-to-State and City-to-City. They often include these types of benefits:

- ☐ **Eyeglasses – VDT Glasses**
- ☐ **Major Medical Supplemental Health Benefits**
- ☐ **Educational Assistance**
- ☐ **Civil Service Exam Preparation Assistance**
- ☐ **Supplemental Life Insurance Policies**
- ☐ **Legal Representation at Hearings & Other Legal Support**
- ☐ **Prescription Plans and/or Dental Plans (varies by Union)**

Other Benefits

U.S. State and Municipal employees receive these other types of Benefits, which may vary from State-to-State and City-to-City.

- ☐ **Medical Spending Conversion Health Benefits Buy-Out Waiver Program**
- ☐ **Medical Spending Plan Premium Pre-Tax Conversion**
- ☐ **Health Care Flexible Spending Accounts**
- ☐ **Dependent Care Flexible Spending Account Program**
- ☐ **College Pre-Tax Savings Program**
- ☐ **Long Term Care Insurance**
- ☐ **Long-Term Disability Insurance**
- ☐ **Life Insurance**
- ☐ **Survivor Benefits**

REFERENCES

Info Tech Employment, "Employment Survey," 2007, http://www.infotechemployment.com.

Info Tech Employment, "IT Federal Jobs Survey," 2007, http://www.infotechemployment.com.

Info Tech Employment, "Survey of IT Job Titles in U.S. States & Major U.S. Cities," 2007, http://www.infotechemployment.com.

U.S. Federal Government, Office of Personnel Management, Career Transition Resources, 2006, http://www.careeronestop.org.

U.S. Government, Department of Justice, U.S. Freedom of Information Act, 2006.

U.S. Federal Government, Office of Personnel Management, Career Transition Resources, 2006, http://www.careeronestop.org.
U.S. Federal Government, Office of Personnel Management, Detail and Transfer of Federal Employees to International Organizations, 2006, http://www.opm.gov/employ/internat/.

U.S. Federal Government, Office of Personnel Management, 15 Executive Agencies & 101 Other Federal Agencies, 2006, http://www.loc.gov/rr/news/fedgov.html.

U.S. Federal Government, Office of Personnel Management, Individual Development Plans (IDP), 2006, http://www.opm.gov/hcaaf_resource_center/assets/Lead_tool3.pdf.;

U.S. Federal Government, Office of Personnel Management, Intergovernmental Personnel Act Mobility Program, 2006, http://www.opm.gov/programs/ipa/.

U.S. Federal Government, Office of Personnel Management, "Introduction to the Position Classifications Standards" and "The Classifier's Handbook" for Information Technology Job Groups, USOPM, GS-2200, 2001, 2003; http://www.opm.gov/FEDCLASS/gs2200a.pdf .

U.S. Federal Government, Office of Personnel Management, Introduction to the Position Classifications Standard,1995, http://www.opm.gov/fedclass/gsintro.pdf.

U.S. Federal Government, Office of Personnel Management, Job Family Position Classification Standard for Administrative Work in the Information Technology Group GS-2200, GS-2200, 2001, 2003; http://www.opm.gov/FEDCLASS/gs2200a.pdf .

U.S. Federal Government, Office of Personnel Management, Leadership & Knowledge Management Programs, 2006, http://apps.opm.gov/HumanCapital/standards/lkmq5b.html

U.S. Federal Government, Office of Personnel Management, The Classifier's Handbook, 1991, http://www.opm.gov/fedclass/clashnbk.pdf)."

U.S. Federal Government, Office of Personnel Management, The Executives in Residence Program, 2006, http://www.leadership.opm.gov/content.cfm?CAT=EIRP.

Chapter Five

Completing the Application and Hiring Process
U.S. Federal – State - City

Federal Employment Process

Learning about Information Technology Job Announcements with U.S. Federal Government Agencies

There are several ways to find all the job announcements for current available Federal jobs in Information Technology

1. **Search the Official Federal Government Website Portal –** http://www.USAJOBS.gov
2. **Locate Jobs Posted at Local Offices of Federal Agencies by contacting regional Federal Executive Boards for Agency Local Office & Personnel Department Listings**
3. **Locate Jobs Posted with Direct Hiring Authority and by Excepted Agencies (See Appendix F) by directly contacting these Agency Personnel Departments & searching** http://www.USAJOBS.gov
4. **Locate Entry Level Administrative Jobs (Administrative Careers with America -ACWA), Outstanding Scholar Program, and Student Employment - Search** http://www.opm.gov/qualifications/SEC-V/sec-v.asp; http://www.opm.gov/employ/luevano-archive.asp#Outstanding; http://www.studentjobs.gov;
5. **Search Supplemental Job Announcements - Search Career One Stop Centers –** http://www.careeronestop.org; **and America's Job Bank** http://www.ajb.org/

1. Official Federal Government Jobs Website Portal
http://www.USAJOBS.gov

Your Career in the U.S. Government Starts at the Official Federal Government Job Website Portal! USAJOBS is provided at no cost and offers information on 20,545 U.S. government job opportunities worldwide. USAJOBS.gov is the official job site of the United Stated Federal Government. You may search job announcements by Job Category, Job Location, and Job Salary Grade. You may also request E-Mail notifications about jobs in your job categories, locations and salary grades. For representative, sample job Announcements from USAJOBS.gov, see Appendix D.

2. Locate Jobs Posted at Local Offices of Federal Agencies by contacting regional Federal Executive Boards for Agency Local Office & Personnel Department Listings

Federal Executive Boards, located in each U.S. Region maintain a list of all Federal Agency Regional & Local Offices. Contact your regional Federal Executive Board for Agency local offices in your region. Contact or visit these Local Office Personnel Departments for Job Announcements http://www.feb.gov.

3. Locate Jobs Posted with Direct Hiring Authority and by Excepted Agencies (See Appendix F) by directly contacting these Agency Personnel Departments & searching http://www.USAJOBS.gov

While the traditional method to enter Federal service is by appointment through the competitive examining process, (Competitive Appointment Job Announcements are announced on USAJOBS.gov), Agencies may also appoint candidates directly to jobs. When an agency has a severe shortage of candidates or has a critical hiring need, direct hire provides a quick way to hire individuals into the Competitive Civil Service (GS-15 and below or equivalent) in permanent or nonpermanent positions. Direct hire allows the agency to attract a larger pool of candidates by advertising job openings. Jobseekers may go to USAJOBS.gov to see many Direct Hire positions. Jobseekers may also go to individual Agency websites to identify direct hire job openings, that may or may not be posted on USAJOBS.gov.

Information Technology Management (Information Security),
GS-2210, GS-9 and above, jobs at all locations, are Direct Hire jobs.

Excepted Service Positions, Senior Executive Positions, and Appointments Authorized by Statute, the "excepted service", consists of all positions in Excepted Service Agencies (See Appendix G). This includes the Executive Branch, the President, the Library of Congress, the Federal Bureau of Investigation and other agencies.

To locate Jobs posted with Direct Hire Excepted Agencies, search the list of Excepted Agencies provided in Appendix G and search the Agency's individual website employment page. You may also contact the Personnel Departments of Excepted Agencies for Posted Job Announcements. Appendix G provides website and personnel department contact information for Excepted Agencies.

4. Locate Entry Level Administrative Jobs (Administrative Careers with America (ACWA), Outstanding Scholar Program, and Student Employment Jobs-Search   http://www.opm.gov/qualifications/SEC-V/sec-v.asp;http://www.opm.gov/employ/luevano-archive.asp#Outstanding;   http://www.studentjobs.gov;

For Entry-Level Administrative Jobs (GS 5-GS-7) (with or without information technology skills), the Federal Government offers the *Administrative Careers with America Program (ACWA)*. Over 150 Federal Job occupations are eligible for ACWA appointments, whereby candidates will complete scannable questionnaires detailing their qualifications and experience. The U.S. Office of Personnel Management grades the questionnaires and provides Federal Agencies with a list of the best qualified candidates. For some positions, a written exam may be given by the hiring Agency. For a list of titles where a written and performance test may be given, see http://www.opm.gov/qualifications/.

Through the *Outstanding Scholar Program*, Agencies may appoint those college graduates from accredited schools who obtained a grade point average of 3.5 or higher on a 4.0 scale for all undergraduate courses completed toward a baccalaureate degree. They may also appoint those who stand in the upper 10% of a baccalaureate graduating class, or of a major university subdivision such as a College of Arts and Sciences. These appointments may be made without going through an examination procedure for jobs at grades GS-5 and GS-7 in covered occupations. To learn more about appointment through the Outstanding Scholar Program, see http://www.opm.gov/employ/luevano-archive.asp#Outstanding.

Student Job opportunities are available for students who are working towards a diploma, certificate, or degree. The *Student Temporary Employment Program (STEP)* and the *Student Career Experience Program (SCEP)* provide training and a means for students to achieve a career conditional appointment. To learn more about these appointment opportunities, see http://www.studentjobs.gov. The *Presidential Management Internship Program* (http://www.opm.gov/fedregis/1995/60rl1017.pdf) offers professional, entry-level positions to graduate students, leading to a permanent career position.

Plus, at http://www.studentjobs.gov you will find information for students on:
Apprenticeships
Cooperative Programs
Fellowships
Grants
Internships
Scholarships

5. Search Supplemental Job Announcements - Search Career One Stop Centers – http://www.careeronestop.org**; and America's Job Bank –** http://www.ajb.org/
CareerOneStop is an integrated suite of national web sites that help businesses, job seekers, students, and workforce professionals find employment and career resources. *CareerOneStop*, sponsored by the U.S. Department of Labor, includes three core products:
America's Career InfoNet (http://www.CareerInfoNet.org) provides national, state and local career information and labor market data using unique career tools, career reports, videos, a career resource library and other innovative web-based tools.
America's Job Bank (http://www.ajb.org) is the nation's largest online labor exchange. Businesses post job listings, create customized job orders, and search resumes. Job seekers post resumes and search for jobs that fit their career goals. A companion web site, *Department of Defense Job Search* (http://dod.jobsearch.org), is a career resource for businesses and military personnel transitioning to civilian careers to match work opportunities.
America's Service Locator (http://www.ServiceLocator.org) maps customers to a range of local services including workforce centers, unemployment benefits, job training, education opportunities, and other workforce services.

Completing a Federal Employment Application to Obtain a Federal Job

Responding to the Job Announcement comes after locating the position(s) you want to apply for. Responding to a Federal Job Announcement involves:

1. **Submitting a Federal Style Resume (by using the Resume Creator at USAJOBS.gov or other method), AND/OR**
2. **Completing a Standard Form OF-612 (Appendix G)**
3. **Customizing the Response to the Job Announcement**
4. **Completing a Standard OPM Form 1203, Form C, Supplemental Qualifications Statement (SQS),**
5. **Preparing a Knowledge, Skills, Abilities (KSA) Statement (Appendix H)**

It is Required that you Mail, Fax, or Electronically Submit your Standard Form OF-612, Form C, and KSAs. You may also submit a Federal Style Resume by preparing one with the Resume Creator at USAJOBS.gov and submitting it electronically at http:// www.USAJOBS.gov, in addition to Mailing, Faxing or Electronically Submitting the OF-612, Form C, and KSAs

1. Submitting a Federal Style Resume, using the Resume Creator at http://www.USAJOBS.gov

It is recommended that you use the Resume Creator at http://www.USAJOBS.gov. It provides the format the Federal Government expects to see in a resume, and will help you structure your resume. It is important to structure your Federal Resume and your KSAs to 1) respond to the specific Job Announcement, and 2) to clearly identify where your experience and education fill the specific requirements and demonstrate the specific experience and skills being asked for. Your Resume may be examined by someone who is not the hiring manager. Therefore, your Resume must read clearly and present the best possible case for why you are the right fit for the job announcement and what is being asked for. More on structuring and customizing your Resume will be found in the section on Customizing the Response.

2. Completing a Standard Form OF-612 (See Appendix G)

The Standard OF-612 may be downloaded and printed from http://www.opm.gov/forms/ pdf_fill/of612.pdf. The downloadable form may be filled in electronically online. You may Print the Form or Save the Form. Section C, Additional Work Experience pages, will need to be copied or duplicated, so you may fill your work experience that will take more space than the section on the form for Additional Work Experience provides. You need to Mail, Faxing or Electronically Submitting the OF-612, Form C, and KSAs. You will find a copy of OF-612 in Appendix G.

3. Customizing the Response to the Job Announcement

Your Response, in the Federal Resume, OF-612, and the KSAs Statement should mirror the words of the specific Job Announcement. Where the Job Announcement asks for the candidate to perform named task and duty, your response will indicate how and where you performed named task and duty. For example "Performed [Name Task & Duty] in this position, in this assignment, in this context, with these competencies and knowledge, skills, and abilities, with this degree of supervision or supervisory control, with this degree of difficulty, calling on this type of special knowledge or contacts with others (See Factors determining Salary Grade, Appendix C.)

In Responding to each Named Task or Duty required of the job, indicate how & where you previously performed or demonstrated the:

[Named Knowledge, Competencies or Specialties]
[Named degree of Supervisory control or Minimal Supervision Authority]
[Named Degree of Difficulty]
[Named Degree of Judgment called for]
[Named Special Knowledge (i.e. of Equipment, Software, Procedures, Legislation)]
[Named Nature of Assignment]
[Named Scope of Contacts]

Your Response should directly respond to the Requirements specified in the Job Announcement. Essentially, it is responding to 1) **Factors** and 2) **Factor Levels** used to determine the job classification and create the job announcement (Appendix C.)

In addition, your response should indicate, where you began on the job, what you had to learn, who you had to work with, what level of competency you achieved, what results you achieved, and the significance of the project, task or duty for the project, mission or employer. These "extra mile" responses will indicate to the reviewer that you are detail oriented, attuned to your working team environment, keen to your part in the organization and its purpose or mission, a life-long learner, and capable of handling complex thinking.

4. Completing a Standard OPM Form 1203, Form C, Supplemental Qualifications Statement (SQS)

The Job Announcement will indicate whether you need to fill out this form.

You may fill it out and submit it either electronically at http://www.USAJOBS.gov, or by downloading it, filling out the form, printing it, and mailing or Faxing the Form C.

If you choose to complete the Form C, Supplemental Qualifications Statement (SQS) online, go to http://www.USAJOBS.gov. Click on *Online Application*. Click on *Complete Online Supplemental Qualifications Statement*. Enter the Control Number of the Job Announcement to start filling out the form.

If you choose to download, fill out, print and send the Form C, it may be downloaded from http://www.opm.gov/forms/pdf_fill/OPM1203fx.pdf. It is a Scannable Occupational Questionnaire, where you answer occupational questions, and the answers are used by reviewers to assess your qualifications and rank them. The downloadable form may be filled in electronically online. You may Print the Form or Save the Form and Mail or Fax it before the Closing Date of the Job Announcement.

5. Preparing a Knowledge, Skills, Abilities (KSA) Statement

A Knowledge, Skills, Abilities (KSA) Statement is your opportunity to review and structure your Response to the Job Announcement to demonstrate that you qualify for the 1) **GS Salary Grade or Grades** indicated in the Job Announcement (if the job Grade is between GS-11-GS13, for example), and that you qualify for the 2) **Job Announcement Job Title Requirements and Factor Levels. (Appendix H).**

While a KSA Statement may tell a Reviewer about your Job History, it is designed to clarify to the Reviewer how your qualifications meet the job requirements in a particular Salary Grading Structure and Job Title Structure.

To learn how your Job Announcement has been classified and created, refer to the manual for "Introduction to the Position Classifications Standards" and "The Classifier's Handbook" for Information Technology Job Groups (USOPM, GS-2200, 2001, 2003; http://www.opm.gov/ FEDCLASS/gs2200a.pdf). This document will tell you how the job classification has been determined, and what is expected to meet the requirements. When the Classifier classified the position, they wrote the Job Announcement with certain expectations in mind. They expect someone to fill the position with the qualifications specified in the Job Announcement for the specified **Salary Grade** and for the **Job Title Requirements and Factor Levels.** These requirements include:

Knowledge
Competencies
Supervisory Background
Degree of Difficulty
Degree of Judgment
Special Knowledge (i.e. of Equipment, Software, Procedures, Legislation)]
Nature of Assignment
Scope of Contacts

Therefore, to write your KSA Statement, you need to indicate the Knowledge, Skills Abilities that you have demonstrated in previous experience that now qualify you for the **Salary Grade**, and for the **Job Title Requirements and Factor Levels** specified in the Job Announcement.

To demonstrate how a KSA Statement is written, we have prepared a KSA Statement (Appendix H) that responds to the Job Announcement for Information Technology Specialist Job Announcement shown in Appendix D. Note how the KSA Statement answers, point for point, the qualifications required, named in the Job Announcement, by matching the KSA Statements (Appendix H) with the Job Announcements (Appendix D).

After Completing the Application you will receive a Notice of Rating or Notice of Results within 2-4 weeks by mail or e-Mail.

The Interview

Preparing for the Interview
Preparing for the Interview involves 1) Learning about the Agency and its Mission, and 2) Preparing a Verbal Portrait of Yourself.

Learning about the Agency

Read the Agency's website. What is the Agency's Mission. What are the Agency's primary Information Technology applications, related to its Mission. Call or ask for the Agency's Mission Statement, and the individual Department's Mission Statement. Familiarize yourself with the individual Department where the job will be performed.

Preparing a Verbal Portrait of Yourself

To prepare a Verbal Portrait of Yourself, indicate in a few verbal sentences, who you are, what your major experience and focus has been, main skills, strengths, why you are interested in this Job Announcement, and why you are a good fit. Your emphasis should be on what you bring to this position, rather than on your previous employers. Preparing a Verbal Portrait, will help you structure strengths, work ethics, skills, and abilities. It will prepare you to bring a clear focus to the Interview.

The Interview

A good Interview is a discussion or dialog. You are expected to ask questions, to clarify what the Job and Job Context is about. Questions to ask may focus in these areas:

The Agency or Department
1. What are the Agency's Major Missions
2. What are the Agency's Major Functions
3. What are the Agency's Major Business Applications
4. What are the Agency's Major Information Technology Applications
5. What are the Agency's Major & Auxiliary Computer Platforms
6.   What is the scope of the Agency's IT/IS work

The Job Required
1. What will I be doing
2. Who will I be reporting to
3. Who will I be working with
4. What knowledge, skills, abilities will I be using the most
5. Questions-Discussion about the Specific Job

The Job Employment Status
1. What is the Employment Status of this Position (i.e. Competitive, Direct Hire, Non-Competitive, Senior Executive Service, Wage Grade, other)
2. Salary Discussion
3. What is the next step in the Interview process
4. What is the Interviewer's Name, Telephone, e-Mail

The U.S. State & City Employment Process

Learning about and Applying for a Provisional Information Technology Job in State or Municipal Government

1. State & City Government Websites - Job Application Websites
There are several ways to find all the job announcements for current available State and City jobs in Information Technology

2. Search the Official U.S. State & Municipal Government Website Portals –http://www.50States.com; or Search State or City on http://www.

google.com

Each U.S. State and Municipality has an official website portal. Your Career in U.S. State or City Government Starts at the Official State and Municipal Job Website Portals! An easy way to locate the official State or City website is to search for State of [Name State] or City of [Name City] on http://www.google.com. Or, you may use the website http://www.50states.com to click on the State or City, and go to its official website. Once you have gone to the official website, search for employment or job or personnel department links. These links will take you to job postings.

3. Locate Jobs Posted at the U.S. State or Municipal Government Personnel Department Website Portals or Personnel Offices

At the Official Website Portal for each U.S. State and Municipality, you will find links to individual State or City Agencies and Departments. Click on these individual Agencies and Departments; **search for** *employment or job or personnel department links.* **These links will take you to job postings.**

4. Locate Jobs Posted by Visiting Local Offices of individual Agencies in U.S. State & Municipal Government and reviewing jobs posted on the Job Bulletin Boards

One of the best ways to locate U.S. State and Municipal Government jobs is to visit the local office of the State Employment Services, State Personnel Department, City Personnel Department or Human Resources Department, or State or City Agency or Department Personnel Department where you want to work. Often, the most recent and most needed jobs are immediately posted by these departments on their Job Bulletin Boards. It is advised you contact the department by telephone before visiting, to find out the address, if they have a job bulletin board, and if you as a private citizen (rather than government employee) will have the required access to visit the location, office and job bulletin board.

5. Read about Advertised U.S. State or Municipal Government Provisional Jobs announced in local newspaper help wanted or business sections

Information Technology jobs, Managerial jobs and other professional jobs are often advertised in local newspaper help wanted or business sections. These are usually positions that are required immediately. They will customarily be filled on a Provisional basis. The employee will be hired and given a Provisional Appointment. The employee will work until the position is no longer required. The employee will be given the opportunity to take a Civil Service Exam for the position when the exam is given. Often, a Provisional Appointment will result in a full-time, permanent Career Competitive Appointment.

6. Search Supplemental Job Announcements -
Search Career One Stop Centers – http://www.careeronestop.org;
and America's Job Bank – http://www.ajb.org/

CareerOneStop is an integrated suite of national web sites that help businesses, job seekers, students, and workforce professionals find employment and career resources. *CareerOneStop*, sponsored by the U.S. Department of Labor, includes three core products:

America's Career InfoNet (http://www.CareerInfoNet.org) provides national, state and local career information and labor market data using unique career tools, career reports, videos, a career resource library and other innovative web-based tools.

America's Job Bank (http://www.ajb.org) is the nation's largest online labor exchange. Businesses post job listings, create customized job orders, and search resumes. Job seekers post resumes and search for jobs that fit their career goals. A companion web site, *Department of Defense Job Search* (http://dod.jobsearch.org), is a career resource for businesses and military personnel transitioning to civilian careers to match work opportunities.

America's Service Locator (http://www.ServiceLocator.org) maps customers to a range of local services including workforce centers, unemployment benefits, job training, education opportunities, and other workforce services.

Applying for a Posted or Advertised Provisional Position

When you locate a Posted or Advertised Provisional Position you want to apply for, the Announcement will state the application requirements. Typically, the application requires submitting a **Resume.** The same guidelines apply for preparing a Resume for U.S. State or Municipal government employment, as for Federal Employment. Your Resume and Skills Statement should mirror the words of the specific Job Announcement. Where the Job Announcement asks for the candidate to perform named task and duty, your response will indicate how and where you performed named task and duty. For example "Performed [Name Task & Duty] in this position, in this assignment, in this context, with these competencies and knowledge, skills, and abilities, with this degree of supervision or supervisory control, with this degree of difficulty, calling on this type of special knowledge or contacts with others.

While the term KSA or Knowledge, Skills, Abilities Statement is not used in U.S. State and Municipal government, a similar **Skills Statement**, in direct response to the Job Announcement, can be a valuable statement to send with the Resume. The Reviewer can easily discern why you meet the requirements of the job position.

Completing a U.S. State or City Employment Application to Obtain a Competitive Civil Service Information Technology Job Title

Most employment in U.S. State and City government comes by way of Civil Service Open Competitive (or Promotional) Exam and Appointment. A jobseeker makes an application to take a Civil Service Exam for a specific Job Title (or to fill out the Experience & Education Paper that will serve as an Exam). After applications are reviewed and scored for the Job Title, and candidates Ranked, a Certified Civil Service List is created for the Job Title. Agencies and Departments then use the list to Call, Interview, and Hire candidates. Candidates are called for Interview from the Certified List by list rank number. They are interviewed from a Civil Service Pool, during which 3 candidates are interviewed at a time, and an Agency must hire one of the three (or may hire more where there are more positions), before going on to interview the next three candidates. A candidate may accept or decline a position offered. If a jobseeker declines the job, they may be restored to the Certified List for the Job Title, and will be called for another Civil Service Pool and round of interviews. Certified Lists of Candidates may be in effect for one to three years, or until all the candidates have been hired and the list is exhausted. Certified Lists may contain a few or many certified qualified candidates. Open Competitive Exam Filings for a Job Title may be open for candidates to apply, from once a year to once every few years.

Obtaining a Civil Service Exam Application

To obtain a *Civil Service Exam Application* and *Schedule of Open Exam Filings*, go to the U.S. State or Municipal government website portal. Click on the *Personnel Department* or *Employment or Jobs link*. *Search Schedule of Exams or Schedule of Open Exam Filings*. *You may also call the telephone number for the Personnel Department and ask for a Schedule of Open Exam Filings and When [Named Job Title] Exam will have an open filing.*

Filing the Application during an Open Filing Period

After you determine when the Application should be filed, and will be accepted, you are ready to fill out the Application or Application for Exam.

The Civil Service Exam

The Civil Service Exam (or Experience and Education Paper) is a way of assessing your qualifications, as related to the Job Requirements for the Job Title. An *Experience & Education Application Form* is often a Substitute for Civil Service Exam for IT Job Titles in many cases. There are no multiple choice or essay exams for many IT titles in most States and Cities.

Filling out the *Application Form (and/or Experience and Education Paper)* for the Job Title is critical in receiving a high enough score to be certified to a Civil Service List. You are demonstrating your qualifications to perform the duties, tasks and responsibilities of the Job Title, as specified in the published Job Title Description. There are several key points in filling out the Application:

☐ **List all your Education**, indicating dates and number of months and years attended, and diplomas, certifications, or credits received. List Academic, Vendor and Employer Education and Training.

☐ **List all your Experience**, indicating dates and number of months and years for each position, assignment, specialty, project. These must meet the Experience and/or Education Requirements specified for the Job Title.

☐ **Respond to the Job Title Requirements.** Your Application and Experience and Education Paper should mirror the words of the specific Job Announcement. Where the Job Title Requirements ask for the candidate to demonstrate that they performed named task and duty, your response will indicate how and where you performed named task and duty. For example "Performed [Name Task & Duty] in this position, in this assignment, in this context, with these competencies and knowledge, skills, and abilities, with this degree of supervision or supervisory control, with this degree of difficulty, calling on this type of special knowledge or contacts with others."

☐ **Ask for Veteran's Preference points, if this applies.**

Ranking by Score

A Certified Civil Service List of Qualified Candidates for the Job Title will be created from 6 months to 1 year from the time you make your application. Your application will be graded and given points based on the degree to which you meet the qualifications. You will be ranked along with other candidates who applied. After a Certified Civil Services List for Job Title is created, you will be notified of your List Number. You will be called to a Job Hiring Pool based on your list number. While the process may seem slow, career employment is a valuable and honorable achievement.

Certified Civil Service Lists Created for the Job Titles

As State and City agency personnel departments need staff in the job title, they use the Certified Civil Service Job Title List and request a Civil Service Pool be formed of candidates to hire from.

Job Hiring Pools

Candidates are called for Interview from the Certified List by list rank number. They are interviewed from a Civil Service Pool, during which 3 candidates are interviewed at a time, and an Agency must hire one of the three (or may hire more where there are more positions), before going on to interview the next three candidates. A candidate may accept or decline a position offered. If a jobseeker declines the job, they may be restored to the Certified List for the Job Title, and will be called for another Civil Service Pool and round of interviews. Certified Lists of Candidates may be in effect for one to three years, or until all the candidates have been hired and the list is exhausted. Certified Lists may contain a few or many certified qualified candidates. Open Competitive Exam Filings for a Job Title may be open for candidates to apply, from once a year to once every few years.

Types of Employment Status

Your job and hiring status may be classified as:
☐ **Competitive Permanent**
☐ **Competitive Provisional**
☐ **Non-Competitive**
☐ **Labor**
☐ **Exempt**

A **permanent** employee is someone who has been appointed from a civil service list in a **competitive** class job title. The employee has taken and passed a competitive civil service exam for the job title. After being hired, the employee must complete a probationary period (typically one year). If performance during this probationary period is satisfactory, the employee will be appointed permanent status.

A **provisional** employee is someone who has been hired prior to the establishment of a civil service list for his/her job title in a **competitive, non-competitive exempt or labor** class job title, or because there is no civil service job title list. A provisional employee may be terminated any time, because services are no longer required, because a civil service list for the job title has been established and the provisional employee's name does not appear on the list or is too low on the list to be reached, or because of poor performance. Most provisional employees will take and pass the civil service exams to secure their position career path.

An employee in a **non-competitive** class job title may be hired because the position has been classified as non-competitive due to its unique nature, and is appointed on the basis of educational background and or experience, and is not required to take a civil service examination. The non-competitive position may be eliminated and the employee may no longer be required.

An employee in an **exempt** class works at the executive level, in an administrative position reporting to a commissioner level or executive level officer. An exempt class position. The exempt class position may be eliminated and the employee may no longer be required.

An employee in a **labor** job class works in one of the trade titles, not otherwise classified as competitive or non-competitive.

Employees **pay status** may be per annum (full-time whose salary is determined on an annual basis, eligible for longevity in title and longevity in service pay), or per diem (full time or part time whose salary is determined and paid by the hour only for the hours worked.) (The City of New York, 2006; AFSCME, CWA Local 1180, 2006).

REFERENCES

APPENDIX F: Locate Jobs at Direct Hire Authorities & Excepted Agencies through Excepted Agency Personnel Departments

Americas Job Bank, http://www.ajb.org

Career One Stop Centers, http://www.careeronestop.org

U.S. Federal Government, Office of Personnel Management, 15 Executive Agencies & 101 Other Federal Agencies, 2006, http://www.loc.gov/rr/news/fedgov.html .

U.S. Federal Government, Office of Personnel Management, Administrative Careers with America -ACWA), http://www.opm.gov/qualifications/SEC-V/sec-v.asp

 U.S. Federal Government, Office of Personnel Management, Leadership & Knowledge Management Programs, 2006, http://apps.opm.gov/HumanCapital/standards/lkmq5b.html

U.S. Federal Government, Office of Personnel Management, Career Transition Resources, 2006, http://www.careeronestop.org .

U.S. Federal Government, Office of Personnel Management, Detail and Transfer of Federal Employees to International Organizations, 2006, http://www.opm.gov/employ/internat/ .

U.S. Federal Government, Office of Personnel Management, Direct Hiring Authority and by Excepted Agencies
http://apps.opm.gov

U.S. Federal Government, Office of Personnel Management, Form OF-612 may be downloaded and printed from http://www.opm.gov/forms/pdf_fill/of612.pdf.

. U.S. Federal Government, Office of Personnel Management, Supplemental Questionnaire, Form C Section C. Form C, it may be downloaded from http://www.opm.gov/forms/pdf_fill/OPM1203fx.pdf.

U.S. Federal Government, Office of Personnel Management, Leadership & Knowledge Management Programs, 2006, http://apps.opm.gov/HumanCapital/standards/lkmq5b.html

U.S. Federal Government, Office of Personnel Management, General Services Salary Schedule, 2006, http://www.opm.gov .

U.S. Federal Government, Office of Personnel Management, Individual Development Plans (IDP), 2006, http://www.opm.gov/hcaaf_resource_center/assets/Lead_tool3.pdf .

U.S. Federal Government, Office of Personnel Management, Intergovernmental Personnel Act Mobility Program, 2006, http://www.opm.gov/programs/ipa/

U.S. Federal Government, Office of Personnel Management, Introduction to the Position Classifications Standard,1995, http://www.opm.gov/fedclass/gsintro.pdf

U.S. Federal Government, Office of Personnel Management, Job Family Position Classification Standard for Administrative Work in the Information Technology Group GS-2200, GS-2200, 2001, 2003; http://www.opm.gov/FEDCLASS/gs2200a.pdf .

U.S. Federal Government, Office of Personnel Management, Leadership & Knowledge Management Programs, 2006, http://apps.opm.gov/HumanCapital/standards/lkmq5b.html
U.S. Federal Government, Office of Personnel Management, Outstanding Scholar Program, http://www.opm.gov/employ/luevano-archive.asp#Outstanding

U.S. Federal Government, Office of Personnel Management, Student Employment; http://www.studentjobs.gov

U.S. Federal Government, Office of Personnel Management, Leadership & Knowledge Management Programs, 2006, http://apps.opm.gov/HumanCapital/standards/lkmq5b.html

U.S. Federal Government, Office of Personnel Management, The Classifier's Handbook, 1991, http://www.opm.gov/fedclass/clashnbk.pdf.

U.S. Federal Government, Office of Personnel Management, The Executives in Residence Program, 2006, http://www.leadership.opm.gov/content.cfm?CAT=EIRP.

U.S. Federal Government, USAJOBS.gov, Official Jobs Web Portal, http://www.USAjobs.gov

Chapter Six
Today's Tech Jobs in America

C++ Computer Programmer Jobs and C++ Programmer Consultants

Employers are placing increasing emphasis on new, object-oriented programming languages and tools, such as C++ and Java. Additionally, employers are seeking persons familiar with fourth- and fifth-generation languages that involve graphic user interface (GUI) and systems programming. Having a strong skill set with C++, Java, JavaScript, and VisualBasic along with Report Writing Tools will put a jobseeker in a strong position.

C++ programmer jobs primarily involve writing, compiling, testing, troubleshooting, and maintaining computer programs and/or application software written in the C++ programming language. C++ programmer employment generally requires skills and experience in other object-oriented programming languages. The C++ programmer job market remains very stable, despite the formidable presence of the Java programming language. Like their colleagues in other software programmer jobs, IT professionals in C++ programmer jobs may also prepare documentation and reports on computer programs for use by other programmers, C++ programmer consultants, users, and computer support specialists. C++ programmer employment may start with C++ programmer jobs and advance to software development or programming consultancy.

C++ programmer consultants work with C++ programmers and other programming personnel to determine user requirements, manage program design activities, oversee actual writing of program code, supervise the deployment of computer programs and systems, and monitor program maintenance functions. To be hired, C++ programmer consultants will be expected to hold experience in IT project management, maintain the latest and highest level of skills in object-oriented programming, and have an extensive knowledge of software development life cycles. Due to the highly specialized skills required, C++ programmer consultants are highly sought after.

Software Programmer Jobs & Software Programmer Consultants

Software programmer jobs, as a group, focus on design, development, testing, and evaluation of software programs and systems. Software programmer jobs in applications development involve responsibility over tasks such as designing, developing, and customizing computer applications software based on an analysis of users' needs. IT professionals who work in software programmer jobs may also expect to prepare documentation and reports on the operation, status, and maintenance of software for use by software programming staff, software programming consultants, software users, and technical support personnel. IT companies will also frequently hire software programmer consultants in order to develop, manage, implement, and provide training for software projects. Software programmer consultants are generally hired outside the company on a per-project or contractual basis.

Software programmer jobs requires people who know their C++, Java, JavaScript, VisualBasic, Cobol or Fortran programming language and who can think logically and pay close attention to detail. The job calls for patience, persistence, and the ability to work on exacting analytical work, especially under pressure. Ingenuity, creativity, and imagination also are particularly important for the software programmer job when programmers design solutions and test their work for potential failures. The ability to work with abstract concepts and to do technical analysis is especially important for systems programmers, because of the work with the software that controls the computer's operation. Because programmers are expected to work in teams and interact directly with users, employers want programmers who are able to communicate with non-technical personnel.

Java Programmer Jobs, JavaScript Programmer Jobs, Visual Basic Programmer Jobs

Java and JavaScript created quite a buzz in the computer industry when client-server technology mounted, creating the need for Java, JavaScript and Visual Basic Programmers able to do GUI interfaces and direct to web scripting.

Java (not to be confused with JavaScript) is the programming language developed by Sun Microsystems that enables programmers to build an application for one platform and run it on another. For example, building applications for small handheld devices or a mission-critical enterprise-wide application becomes possible with Sun's Java. The Java programming language is a robust and versatile programming language, enabling developers to:

- Write software on one platform and run it on another.
- Create programs to run within a web browser.
- Develop server-side applications for online forums, stores, polls, processing HTML forms, and more.
- Write applications for cell phones, two-way pagers, and other consumer devices.

JavaScript is not Java
JavaScript was developed by Brendan Eich at Netscape. Because of its linkage to web browsers, it instantly became popular. It is well suited to client programming.

Skill Sets for Java Programmer Jobs, JavaScript Programmer Jobs Successful software programmer jobs, Java programmer employment or JavaScript employment hinges on solid skills in Sun Microsystem's Java application development product, with knowledge of the JavaScript programming language to script direct to web. Java Programmer jobs and JavaScript programmer jobs also require related Web development scripting languages, such as HTML, CGI, Perl, CSS, ASP, and PHP. In addition, Java and JavaScript programmer jobs may require some level of proficiency in Macromedia Flash, DREAMWEAVER, Adobe Photoshop, and FrontPage. Working with a Java staff requires familiarity with Windows, UNIX, and LINUX platforms. Excellent communication skills will come in handy when you work with fellow Java and JavaScript staff members and deal with end-users. You stand a better chance at finding lucrative Java employment if you have experience developing Web or Java/J2EE-based applications with JSP, SERVLETS,

Java, and EJB. Another highly desirable qualification is achievement of Sun Microsystems JAVA Programmer Certification or Sun Microsystems JAVA Developer Certification.

Responsibilities of Java Programmer Jobs & JavaScript Programmer Jobs

Java programmer jobs and JavaScript employment cover a broad range of responsibilities, ranging from writing, maintaining, and debugging Web sites to directly providing customer technical support. Java programmer jobs and JavaScript programmer jobs involve:

- ☐ system testing Java modules and components,
- ☐ documentation of Java modules and components,
- ☐ creating code files,
- ☐ troubleshooting code files,
- ☐ updating code files,
- ☐ and direct to web scripting.

You may also be asked to coordinate with Visual Basic programmer consultants and other members of the Java staff to modify and adapt modules and code files to specific applications. Together with Visual Basic programmer consultants, you will analyze current programming needs and develop solutions that maximize existing resources.

Like Visual Basic programmer jobs, Java programmer jobs and JavaScript programmer jobs serve many functions in the information technology career spectrum.

The Java job market as well as the JavaScript job market and JavaScript employment could mean working in such specialized areas as enterprise, e-commerce, portals, content management, databases, data warehousing, and custom applications development. Java and JavaScript programming jobs apply to both in-house software development and outsourced functions. As part of the staff, you will develop, implement and maintain robust Web and client-server applications. In addition, Java staff members holding software programmer jobs are expected to deliver solutions that add new functionality to existing systems. Your expertise as a member of the Java staff may be applied to the preparation of user and technical support manuals. From time to time, you will be participating in professional development and training programs related to Java employment or JavaScript employment.

Outlook and venues for Java Programmer Jobs and JavaScript Programmer Jobs

Landing a rewarding information technology job or software programmer job means having the necessary skill sets and ability to apply them in a specific situation. A large number of Java and JavaScript Programmer jobs will be delivered on a temporary or contract basis with work as independent consultants, as companies demand expertise with new programming languages or specialized areas of application. Rather than hiring programmers as permanent employees and then laying them off after a job is completed, employers can contract with temporary help agencies, consulting firms, or directly with programmers themselves. A marketing firm, for example, may require the services of several programmers only to write and debug the software necessary to get a new customer resource management system running. This practice also enables companies to bring in people with a specific set of skills-usually in one of the latest technologies-as it applies to their business needs.

IT professionals with experience in the Java programming language will have no trouble finding a good position in information technology. The Java job market and JavaScript employment market will continue to be solid as these languages are among the leading software programmer job languages to do client-server and web interface programming.

Sun Solaris, Unix, Linux, Network Tech Jobs

Client-server technologies, coupled with LAN and WAN networks are the success story of the 21st Century. Many software programmer jobs and network programmer jobs will exist in many business, scientific and technical settings for IT professionals learning Unix-based operating systems such as Sun Solaris, IBM AIX and Linux. The creation of high-speed servers with the UNIX operating system now allows programmers to do things they couldn't do previously. The UNIX operating system was designed to let a number of programmers access the computer at the same time and share its resources. In addition, it provides an environment so powerful that many telecommunications switches and transmission systems are controlled by administration and maintenance systems based on UNIX. The features that made UNIX a hit from the start are:

☐ Multitasking capability
☐ Multiuser capability
☐ Portability
☐ UNIX programs
☐ Library of application software

While initially designed for medium-sized minicomputers, the UNIX-based operating systems have been rolled out to mainframes and personal computers. Sun Solaris, IBM AIX5L, and Linux are Unix-based operating systems.

They allow users to:

☐ easily share printers and files across any network
☐ break down barriers between platforms to make resource sharing easy
☐ provide Windows file and print services
☐ integrate web and hosting services
☐ painlessly manage network access
☐ develop enterprise applications
☐ manage storage
☐ accelerate and extend the network
☐ secure the network
☐ enable desktop environments

Software programmer jobs and network programmer jobs will exist in many business, scientific and technical settings for IT professionals learning Unix-based operating systems such as Sun Solaris, IBM AIX and Linux. Jobs for system administrator UNIX and UNIX teaching jobs are offered by leading companies. IT professionals gaining experience in Sun Solaris, IBM AIX, and Linux will have no difficulty finding a good Sun Solaris job, software programmer job or network programmer job.

IT professionals with experience in the Java programming language will likewise have no trouble finding a good software programmer job. The Java programming language is a robust and versatile programming language, making the perfect marriage to client-server technology, enabling developers to:

☐ Write software on one platform and run it on another.
☐ Create programs to run within a web browser.
☐ Develop server-side applications for online forums, stores, polls, processing HTML forms, and more.
☐ Write applications for cell phones, two-way pagers, and other consumer devices.

The challenges and opportunities for the 21st Century are robust. To be part of it you need to find the companies that can use you, your talents, your experience, and your potential in the right way. Info Tech Employment has put together a catalog of leading companies with IT contracts looking to provide services and staff to their clients. We invite you to take advantage of this research. Embrace how big the opportunity really is.

Wireless Network Engineers are in hot demand. The field in wireless is so new that companies who need to implement the technology have high demands for wireless network engineers. IT Staffing Firms, IT Outsourcers, and IT Service Providers have network programmer jobs and will pay top dollar for contract, contract to permanent, or permanent wireless network engineers.

Oracle, SQL, Foxpro, PowerBuilder, Sybase, Database Programming Jobs, Database Administration, Database Management Jobs

With the Internet and electronic business generating large volumes of data, there is a growing need to be able to store, manage, and extract data effectively. Database administrator jobs are on the rise. Database management jobs work with database management systems software and determine ways to organize and store data. Database administrators identify user requirements, set up computer databases, and test and coordinate modifications to the systems.

An organization's database administrator ensures the performance of the system, understands the platform on which the database runs, and adds new users to the system. Because they also may design and implement system security, database administrators often plan and coordinate security measures. With the volume of sensitive data generated every second growing rapidly, data integrity, backup systems, and database security have become increasingly important database jobs and aspects of the job of database administrators. Other database management jobs require use of database tools like SQL and Crystal Reports to pull extracts and reports from databases.

Database developers are employed in almost every industry. Database jobs exist as part of every information technology operation. The development of new 4th and 5th generation database languages has created the need for developers to be on the front-end of application development in structuring the database, and to be on the inside track in creating and maintaining the databases of an organization. Additional database jobs will be given to department database managers, and to database specialists who understand database structure and report querying functions in order to pull reports and provide input on departmental needs.

One of the latest forms of database management has come in the form of data warehouse jobs. Data warehouses house information that may be used by an entire organization for different applications. This person who holds this database administrator job is responsible for working with an organization to let department heads know how they can use the data and then implementing their report requirements.

Database Programmer Jobs

Database Developers/Administrators and Programmer Consultants are responsible for planning, implementation, configuration, and administration of relational database management systems. There are Sybase Programmers, PowerBuilder Programmers, Oracle Programmers, SQL Programmers and FoxPro Programmers. Other database administrator employment is available in structure and support for DB2 and CICS for IBM mainframes.

Database Programmer Jobs Profile

Database Developers/Administrators and Database Programmer Consultants are responsible for the development and maintenance of database programs and use of SQL Servers. This database job requires the database developer/administrator to suggest solutions to improve performance and to think out of the box.

Database Developers/Administrators and Database Programmer Consultants plan and coordinate all testing efforts on a project, generate complex test plans, test cases, and test scripts. This database job requires the database developer/administrator to identify any bugs and follow necessary steps to provide seamless operation of the database with any GUI interfaces and programs.

Pre-requisites for Database Programmer Jobs

A Database Administrator or Database Manager is usually required to have formal training in PHP, Oracle, MySQL, and Sybase, FoxPro, or PowerBuilder, or one of the mainframe database products such as DB2. It is important to have knowledge of different database platforms. Minimum Educational Qualifications and requirements usually include experience and education in computer science, and knowledge of how a database is structured and interfaces with programs.

Oracle Programmer Jobs Oracle Programmer Jobs

Oracle Programmer consultants, often called developers, provide solutions to empower organizations for quick and effective building of refined client server and web-based systems that can range from a simple workgroup to big corporate systems.

Oracle Programmer Job Profile

Typically, Oracle programmer consultants are accountable for management of the design, programming and the production units. Oracle Programmer Consultants are required to provide backup to Programming Leaders or Managers, interpret the business requirements for different type of clients, and do quality checks. This database job requires the database developer/administrator or Oracle Programmer job to design, implement and test the database structure besides creating support documents, defined by the Project Managers.

Pre-requisites for Oracle Programmer Jobs

A Masters degree in Computer Applications (MCA), Bachelors/ Masters in Information Technology or hands-on experience is usually the pre-requisite to get into an Oracle Programmer Job. This database job or Oracle Programmer job requires the database developer/administrator to be well versed with the latest technologies, standards and policies in Oracle Programming and designing. Other abilities include good analytical and assessment skills, effective client management skills and strong communication skills.

Fortunately, for the person who wants an Oracle Programmer Job, there is vendor-sponsored certification to learn the product and product line. The vendor http://www. oracle.com can provide you with a list of certification vendors and sites.

Oracle Certified Professional Certifications

Oracle Certified Professional (OCP) - Application Developer. This certification is for those who develop Oracle applications.

Oracle Certified Professional (OCP) - Database Operator (DBO). This path is primarily for database operators who have completed Oracle's Education training for database operators and have hands-on experience with Oracle databases before taking Oracle8 Certified Database Operator exam.

Oracle Certified Solution Developer - JDeveloper. This track is for those who use Oracle JDeveloper. This is part of the multi-vendor Certification for Enterprise Development.

FoxPro Programmer Jobs

FoxPro Programmers work with databases, which include database maintenance; data removal and data transfer related work. This database job requires the Foxpro programmer understand the customer's requirements and translate them into meaningful products.

FoxPro Programmer Jobs Profile

The responsibilities of FoxPro Programmers generally include creation and enhancement of FoxPro applications.

Pre-requisites for FoxPro Programmer Jobs

A Bachelors/ Masters degree in Computer Applications or hands-on experience is usually the pre-requisite to get a FoxPro Programmer Job. This database job requires the Foxpro programmer to have other skills including good analytical, documentation and communication skills. A good understanding of the machine-to-machine product line is required with a complete grasp of network technologies.

SQL Programmer Jobs

SQL Programmer Consultants are responsible for the development and maintenance of

all Corporate SQL Servers
SQL Programmer Jobs Profile
SQL Programmer Consultant is responsible for database structuring

Pre-requisites for SQL Programmer Jobs

A graduate degree in Computer Science or formal training in Oracle, MySQL or Sybase, Database Management and Coding is usually required to be an SQL Programmer Consultant. This database job requires good knowledge of programming, use of database design tools, with knowledge of C, C++. SQL Programmer Consultant requires a strong understanding of SQL and other multiple platforms.

Why Application Development/ Database Management Jobs?

Application development/Database management is one of the "in" IT career choices for obvious reasons. Besides the tremendous demand for professional application programmers and database specialists, a database job position, once learned, will put you at the center of an organization's needs. You will be highly regarded because you have central knowledge about the information technology and how critical business applications are structured. This special knowledge, hard won with hard work and vital training, will ensure your place within an organization.

If you have database management training or experience and are ready for a new database job position, you may actively seek the information technology service providers, staffing firms, and IT outsourcers who are looking for your experience and know-how.

Software Programmer Jobs; Software Engineer Jobs
Software Programmer Jobs

Software programmer jobs, as a group, focus on design, development, testing, and evaluation of software programs and systems. Software programmer jobs in applications development involve responsibility over tasks such as designing, developing, and customizing computer applications software based on an analysis of users' needs. IT professionals who work in software programmer jobs may also expect to prepare documentation and reports on the operation, status, and maintenance of software for use by software programming staff, software programmer consultants, software users, and technical support personnel. IT companies will also frequently hire software programmer consultants in order to develop, manage, implement, and provide training for software projects. Software programmer consultants are generally hired outside the company on a per-project or contractual basis.

The software programmer job requires people who know their C++, Java, JavaScript, VisualBasic, Cobol or Fortran programming language and who can think logically and pay close attention to detail. The job calls for patience, persistence, and the ability to work on exacting analytical work, especially under pressure. Ingenuity, creativity, and imagination also are particularly important for the software programmer job when programmers design solutions and test their work for potential failures. The ability to work with abstract concepts and to do technical analysis is especially important for systems programmers, because of the work with the software that controls the computer's operation. Because programmers are expected to work in teams and interact directly with users, employers want programmers who are able to communicate with non-technical personnel.

C++ programmer jobs primarily involve writing, compiling, testing, troubleshooting, and maintaining computer programs and/or application software written in the C++ programming language. C++ programmer employment generally requires skills and experience in other object-oriented programming languages. The C++ programmer job market remains very stable, despite the formidable presence of the Java programming language. Like their colleagues in other software programmer jobs, IT professionals in C++ programmer jobs may also prepare documentation and reports on computer programs for use by other programmers, C++ programmer consultants, users, and computer support specialists. C++ programmer employment may start with C++ programmer jobs and advance to software development or programming consultancy.

Employers are placing increasing emphasis on new, object-oriented programming languages and tools, such as C++ and Java. Additionally, employers are seeking to fill software programmer jobs with persons familiar with fourth- and fifth-generation languages that involve graphic user interface (GUI) and systems programming. To fill a software programmer job, having a strong skill set with C++, Java, JavaScript, and VisualBasic along with Report Writing Tools will put a jobseeker in a strong position.

Skill Sets for Java Programmer Jobs, JavaScript Programmer Jobs
Successful Java programmer employment or JavaScript employment hinges on solid skills in Sun Microsystem's Java application development product, with knowledge of the JavaScript programming language to script direct to web. Java Programmer jobs and JavaScript programmer jobs also require related Web development scripting languages, such as HTML, CGI, Perl, CSS, ASP, and PHP. In addition, Java and JavaScript programmer jobs may require some level of proficiency in Macromedia Flash, DREAMWEAVER, Adobe Photoshop, and FrontPage. Working with a Java staff requires familiarity with Windows, UNIX, and LINUX platforms. Excellent communication skills will come in handy when you work with fellow Java and JavaScript staff members and deal with end-users. You stand a better chance at finding lucrative Java employment if you have experience developing Web or Java/J2EE-based applications with JSP, SERVLETS, Java, and EJB. Another highly desirable qualification is achievement of Sun Microsystems JAVA Programmer Certification or Sun Microsystems JAVA Developer Certification.

Fortran Programmer Jobs
Fortran Programmers write computer programs, implement databases, work under supervision to support the activities of Software programmers and perform other functions like debugging computer programs.

Fortran Programmer Jobs Profile
The responsibilities of a Fortran Programmer include implementation of the algorithms in the code, working under supervision to support the activities of Software programmers, writing the computer programs and software functions.

Pre-requisites for Fortran Programmer Jobs

Educational qualification required to get into this line is a BS Engineering/Technical or equivalent. A good knowledge of C, C++ and FORTRAN programming languages are a must to make it as a Fortran Programmer. To fill a Fortran software programmer job one should be familiar with database systems such as DB2, Oracle, Sybase, and MySQL.

Software Engineer Jobs

While client-server technologies are moving rapidly toward client-server programming languages such as C++ and Java and JavaScript, there are still millions of programs written in COBOL to be maintained for mainframe processors.

COBOL Programmers will continue to be required.

Software Engineer Jobs

IT service providers, IT staffing companies, and IT outsourcers hire to fill Software Engineer Jobs to provide a variety of needs for their corporate and government clients.

Computer software engineers may work for companies to configure, implement, and install complete computer systems. They may be members of the marketing or sales staff, serving as the primary technical resource for sales workers and customers. They also may be involved in product sales and in providing their customers with continuing technical support. All these possibilities for computer software engineer employment are available.

Computer software engineers often work as part of a team that designs new hardware, software, and systems, or that designs an IT strategy for a project or organization. A core team of software engineers, consisting of engineering, marketing, manufacturing, and design people may work together to address a project challenge and work until the product is released or implementation is rolled out.

By contacting an IT service provider, and networking with their representatives you may find your niche in handling their client's need.

Software engineers, working in applications or systems development, analyze user needs. They may design, construct, test, and maintain computer applications software or systems. Software engineers can be involved in the design and development of many types of software, including software for operating systems and network distribution, and compilers, which convert programs for execution on a computer. In programming, or coding, software engineers instruct a computer, line by line, how to perform a function. They may also solve technical problems that arise. Software engineers must possess strong programming know-how, and have an ability to address a particular project or challenge.

Computer applications software engineers analyze user needs. They may design, construct, and maintain general computer applications software or specialized utility programs. They may use C, C++, and Java, with Fortran and COBOL depending on need or platform or programming specialization. Some software engineers develop both packaged systems and systems software or create customized applications.

Computer systems software engineers may coordinate the construction and maintenance of a company's computer systems and plan their future growth. Working with a company, they may coordinate a department's business applications in order fulfillment, inventory, billing, and payroll. They may outline and direct strategy for corporate intranet or internet presence and database interfaces with front-end operations.

Computer Programming Jobs in the "hidden" job marketplace

Where are these software programmer jobs, C++ programmer jobs, and network programmer jobs? They are in the "hidden" marketplace - hidden from popular job board view, yet in the mainstream of American business. Many of these computer programming jobs and other computer jobs can be found through IT service providers with contracts to supply IT staff to government agencies and private corporations. IT staffing companies are authorized to recruit IT staff for a wide range of computer programming jobs. Outsourcing companies are authorized to hire software programmer consultants, C++ programmer consultants, and network programmer consultants for data centers, infrastructures and various IT-related projects in government and private enterprises.

Network Systems and Data Communications Analyst Jobs, Network Management Software Jobs, Network Engineer and Network Programming Consultants

Network is the word for the 21st Century. Network Analyst Jobs, Network Systems and Data Communications Analyst Jobs and Network Engineer Jobs are plentiful. Network security has created a special demand for Network Security Specialists and the Network Security Job. The management of large networks has created the special demand for Network Management Software Specialists or Network Management Software Programmers who will analyze the structure of the network, loads on servers, and resource allocation. If you are a Wireless Network Programmer you will be in high immediate demand because this area of IT is the newest and there are few trained people to implement wireless networks.

Network programmer jobs are concerned with maintaining the software settings that ensure the operation and security of the computer networks. IT professionals using Microsoft NT, Sun Solaris Network Operating Systems, IBM Operating and Network Management Systems configure and troubleshoot network settings. They work with the software program settings that regulate file access and sharing across the network. Network programmer consultants will be hired to make quick assessments and quick implementations of new critical networks. They may supervise the implementation and new vendor networking products or organization rollouts.

To get set for your first or next network programmer job, you need to bring your familiarity with a network management system along with your head for teamwork and troubleshooting. Few network setups are without their quirks and changing demands. That is why an IT service provider, IT staffing firm, or IT outsourcer will hire you. Customization for their client will require up-to-date knowledge of products and layers in the infrastructure and the ability to add on new products and make new settings.

Network security has created a special demand for Network Security Specialists. Network programming jobs with a security specialization require use of the latest security products, Firewalls, Virtual Private Networks, and Proxy Servers. An IT service provider or outsourcer may hire you to establish a security program for an organization involving physical security, data security, and user access security.

The management of large networks has created a special type of Network Programming Job: the Network Management Software Specialist or Network Management Software Programmers will analyze the structure of the network, loads on servers, and resource allocation. There are niches and opportunities with IT service providers and IT outsourcers for Network Management Software Programmers and Engineers who will provide the assessment of IT infrastructure and resources for an organization. These people are the architects of the organizations IT house making sure the stresses on the network are not too great and throughput and capacity demands are met and will be met in an organization's future. These network programming jobs require training in vendor products such as Veritas.

Network Systems and Data Communications
Analysts, and Network Engineer Jobs

The "networking", or connecting of all computers together, internally-in an individual office, department, or establishment-or externally through a WAN, VPN or the Internet, has created the core Network Programming Job -- the Network Systems and Data Communications Analyst Job and the Network Engineer Job. Since networks come in many sizes and shapes, Network Systems and Data Communications Analysts are required to design, test, and evaluate systems such as local area networks (LANs), wide area networks (WANs), the Internet, intranets, and other data communications systems. Systems can range from a connection between two offices in the same building to globally distributed networks, voice mail, and e-mail systems of a multinational organization. Network systems and data communications analysts perform network modeling, analysis, and planning; they also may research related products and make necessary hardware and software recommendations. The Telecommunications Analyst or Telecommunications Engineer job requires focus on the interaction between computer and communications equipment. You design voice and data communication systems, supervise the installation of those systems, and provide maintenance and other services to clients after the system is installed.

Increasingly Network Engineers will work with Application Programmers to facilitate the transformation of data over internal and external networks. The data may vary according to the business function of the application. It may be vital real-time information, financial transactions, or data pulled from a multi-user data warehouse. The network engineer may be called on to customize the connections, security layers, and other settings to provide vital use of the information on the network.

The IT professional with experience in network may easily parlay that experience into their next position. IT service providers and outsourcers seek to capitalize on experience in network to bring it to their new clients and projects.

Telecommunications Jobs
Telecommunications Jobs and Telecommunications Analyst's Jobs

For the 21st Century, telecommunications, wireless, cellular, and voice over IP industries will radically transform communications. These growth industries guarantee that more telecommunications jobs and telecommunications analysts jobs will be created. The corporate and consumer demands for better and cheaper, faster, more elaborate means of information technology and personal communications will continue to prime the industry. The telecommunications industry will develop newer and more sophisticated products and services to make the global village smaller. These products will require sales, customer support, installers and repairers, telecommunications analysts, computer software engineers, tech support troubleshooters, call center managers and staff and workers to fill in the special niches for this growing industry.

Telecommunications jobs will multiply and diversify. Rapid technological change, falling prices of consumer telecommunications equipment, and favorable regulatory climates will be the primary drivers of the industry's unprecedented growth. While significant debt among telecommunications firms may limit employment within telecommunications firms, the use of increasingly sophisticated computer technology will increase the opportunities for IT service providers to deliver the services of computer professionals, including computer software engineers, computer support specialists, and computer systems analysts.

There are new telecommunications jobs in Sales. The sophistication of telecommunications services and products now calls for sophisticated Sales Personnel in telecommunications. This telecommunications employment is open territory for the IT professional willing to learn the product and the technology behind it and work with the client to customize scalable solutions and customize applications.

Telecommunications jobs are now available for Computer Engineers to work in the fiber optics and wireless technology potions of the industry. Rapidly increasing wireless demand, and the construction of a new generation of wireless systems, now advance the need for wireless network developers.

Telecommunications employment now covers a new territory. Telecommunications jobs call for cross-functional responsibilities as a result of increasing convergence of information and communications technologies.

In order to design state-of-the-art infrastructures, to customize applications, and to streamline networks and voice and information communications, companies will contract services and staff in order to quickly implement projects, boost staff know-how or obtain the best telecommunications hands-on work available. Telecommunications jobs will be filled by IT service and solutions providers with the staff to advise and support. IT service providers, staffing firms and outsourcers will be hiring.

Qualifications & Responsibilities for Telecommunications Jobs and Telecommunications Analyst's Jobs

Telecommunications jobs are concerned primarily with the design, construction, implementation, troubleshooting, and maintenance of wire line and wireless communication networks and voice over IP telephone systems. Because of the diversified nature of telecommunications jobs, the educational background, skill sets, and experience required may vary. New occupational specialties have emerged based on the industry's innovations and new technologies.

Telecommunications jobs in Sales require an ability to grasp the nature of the product and the industry, to understand the fundamentals of telecommunications, and to work with the client to know where the product and service will fit into their strategy. Employers are looking for someone who can actually sell the software and systems. Dual experience in technology and sales will land a job in telecommunications software and service.

Telecommunications Customer Service personnel help customers understand the new and varied types of services offered by telecommunications providers. Some customer service representatives also are expected to sell services and may work on a commission basis.

Most corporations and government agencies have telecommunications departments. These departments offer telecommunications employment. Billions of dollars are spent every year by companies on their telecommunications systems, and especially on telecommunications services. The telecommunications jobs track installs, repairs and moves for the organization. Telecommunications analysts perform work to maintain an organization's voice data infrastructure. They monitor security, fraud usage, network privacy, and costs. These jobs require solid experience in the principles of business analysis, purchasing and accounting. Telecommunications administrative support workers include financial, information, and records clerks; secretaries and administrative assistants; and first-line supervisors/managers of office and administrative support workers. These workers keep service records, compile and send bills to customers, and prepare statistical and other company reports, among other duties. IT Outsourcers provide telecommunications services for their clients and hire for telecommunications jobs for their departments as well.

For telecommunications firms, and for companies with large telecommunications systems and networks, telecommunications jobs exist for Line Installers and Tech Support Staff to install, repair, and maintain telephone equipment, cables and access lines, and telecommunications systems. This work includes setting up, rearranging, and removing the complex switching and dialing equipment used in central offices. When customers move or request new types of service, such as a high-speed Internet connection, a fax, or an additional line, installers relocate telephones or make changes in existing equipment. They assemble equipment and install wiring. Many of these are scientific and technical personnel such as engineers and computer specialists. They may also solve network-related problems and program equipment to provide special features. To obtain and hold one of these telecommunications jobs, on-the-job experience, or training from a technical school, 2 or 4-year college programs in electronics or communications, trade schools, or training provided by telecommunications companies and/or equipment and software manufacturers is usually required. Telecommunications equipment installers and repairers may advance to jobs maintaining more sophisticated equipment or to network engineering technician positions. Tech support staff in telecommunications jobs develop, install, and diagnose telecommunications equipment, as well as provide maintenance and other services to clients after the equipment is installed. Additionally, tech support professionals in telecommunications jobs may program, analyze, and resolve problems related to telecommunications software. Professionals in higher-level telecommunications jobs may supervise a team of telecommunications network engineers, software designers, network systems designers, test engineers, field engineers, and electrical/electronic technicians.

Telecommunications analyst's jobs focus on systems development, maintenance, and technical support for various telecommunication hardware and software systems, particularly mainframe, microcomputer, and minicomputer hardware and software and a variety of operating systems. Workers in telecommunications analyst's jobs are expected to document installation of telecommunication systems and propose system design changes when necessary. Telecommunications analyst's jobs involve the coordination of telecommunication system evaluation, equipment and service purchasing, and systems deployment. Additionally, professionals in telecommunications analyst's jobs may advise managers and service users on equipment acquisitions and system deployments. Information systems analysts and telecommunications analyst's jobs, share many similar responsibilities with computer tech jobs. These telecommunications jobs often require training and experience on-the-job, or to begin, a liberal arts degree or a Bachelor's degree in computer science, information systems, or related discipline.

Telecommunications network services require network engineers and network test engineers. Engineers plan cable and microwave routes, central office and PBX equipment installations, and the expansion of existing structures, and solve other engineering problems. Some engineers also engage in research and development of new equipment. Many specialize in telecommunications design or voice, video, or data communications systems, and integrate communications equipment with computer networks. They work closely with clients, who may not understand sophisticated communications systems, and design systems that meet their customers' needs. Computer software engineers and network systems and data communications analysts design, develop, test, and debug software products. These include computer-assisted engineering programs for schematic cabling projects; modeling programs for cellular and satellite systems; and programs for telephone options, such as voice mail, e-mail, and call waiting.

Telecommunications specialists coordinate the installation of these systems and may provide follow up maintenance and training. These network engineers, systems designers and other holders of telecommunications jobs often enter the field with software programmer experience or with a technical degree, in electrical/electronics and communications engineering. These telecommunications jobs require the ability to learn, the ability to troubleshoot, and the ability to move with developments in the industry. Knowledge of the principles of both digital and analog communications technologies and exposure to various telecommunications architectures and protocols are necessary for technical telecommunications jobs. Telecommunications analyst's jobs require a combination of hardware and software skills, including knowledge of mainframe, minicomputer, and microcomputer hardware and software, local and wide area networks, and a variety of operating systems.

Telecommunications employment exists for telecommunications marketing managers and telecommunications lawyers. They advise and support on the telecommunications industry and developments in marketing and law. These people often start with liberal arts degrees or an undergraduate degree in business, marketing, or management. There are opportunities for developing expertise in the burgeoning fields of telecommunications marketing and telecommunications law and bringing that expertise to clients companies.

Analysts of IT employment trends for telecommunications jobs emphasize the importance of upgrading skills and knowledge to keep pace with technological innovation and maintain labor market mobility. Professional development through vendor-related seminars and workshops, certifications, and technical courses help keep you on the cutting edge for your telecommunications job. Strong communication, team working, problem solving, and analytical skills are important across all telecommunications job categories.

While there is no universally accepted way to prepare for a job as a computer professional, most employers place a premium on some formal college education. Computer software engineers usually have learned on the job on the way up or hold a degree in computer science or in software engineering. For systems analyst, computer scientist, or database administrator positions, many employers seek applicants who have training from a 2 or 4 year college or trade school or hold a Bachelor's degree in computer science, information science, or management information systems.

Due to the rapid introduction of new technologies and services, the telecommunications industry is among the most rapidly changing in the economy. This means workers must keep their job skills up to date. From managers to communications equipment operators, increased knowledge of both computer hardware and software is of paramount importance.

Several major companies and the telecommunications unions have created a Web site that provides free training for employees, enabling them to keep their knowledge current and helping them to advance.

Telecommunications industry employers now look for workers with knowledge of and skills in computer programming and software design; voice telephone technology, known as telephony; laser and fiber optic technology; wireless technology; data compression; cellular; and voice over IP. Individuals with sales ability enhanced by interpersonal skills and knowledge of telecommunications terminology also are sought. IT service providers, staffing firms and outsourcers are hiring.

Web Developer Jobs
Web Developers Employment, Web Developers Consultants and Web Developers Staff

The growth of the Internet and the expansion of the World Wide Web (the graphical portion of the Internet) have generated a variety of occupations related to the design, development, and maintenance of Web sites and their servers. Because the Intranet and Internet presence will be so important to an organization, many companies and government agencies draw on the experience of IT specialists and hire from outside the company to develop the Intranet or Internet applications.

Drawing on the experience gained by working with other clients, IT service providers who specialize in web development will bring together the players and components needed to provide the right application.

IT service providers who specialize in web developers employment provide an opportunity for these team players to produce an output that can be seen and used by the client's entire organization or by millions of Internet users. These assignments may vary from creating a website that is an organization's impression or face to the world, to creating complicated Internet business applications that deliver information, receive information, or perform complex business or financial

A case in point comes to mind with the development of website portals for several U.S. States. While digital government has increasingly come into play in government, IT is not the primary business of government. As States have decided on the function and importance of their web portal in their relation to the public, they have determined how essential it is to develop the knowledge base to develop and maintain their web portals. Kansas and Missouri went to outsourcers to develop and maintain their web portals. New York, California, Colorado and many other States kept the web developer jobs in the State IT departments.

IT service providers and outsourcers are providing extensive web developer employment.

People who work as Web developers, web developer consultants or as part of a Web developers staff are concerned with developing solutions that enhance the online computing experience. They may design an Intranet for an organization's wide area network to serve information and business applications. Or they may design Internet applications for an organization. From creating a user-friendly Web interface to maintaining an extensive online shopping catalog, Web developers, web consultants and other Web developer jobs carry out a host of duties that support the proper functioning of an entire Web site.

Because developing a website with full functionality may require different parts or components, there will be different players holding web developer jobs in the web development process.

Web designer architects may be part of a business team that determines the architecture of the site, the business function, the back-end databases that will be required, and how the disparate pieces of the web application fit together. The web development team leader will determine what is required and who the other players will be and how the parts will come together. Java computer programmers may design the computer application that will operate over the Intranet or Internet. Database administrators or data warehouse administrators may create and maintain the databases that will hold the information to be transacted.

Internet developers or Web developers, also called Web designers, are responsible for website design and creation. They may employ the services of computer graphics designers using Macromedia Dreamweaver and Flash, or computer programmers using ColdFusion to add database functionality. Among all the people who hold a computer tech job, the web developer and web developers consultant sees the business parts of an application come together to communicate and interact with the intended audience. Data and visual communication come together in the web developers job.

Webmasters are responsible for the technical aspects of a Web site. They deal with performance issues such as speed of access, operability, errors and error messages, links and changing content.

Graphic artists and computer animators fill graphic design jobs and computer animation jobs as an essential component of the web development endeavor. (For more on Graphic Design Jobs and Computer Animation Jobs see the next article.)

Required Skills for Web Developers Jobs

Web development promises unlimited opportunities to those who possess knowledge and experience in several programming languages and Web protocols. To be able to meet the multiple demands of Web developers employment, one must demonstrate expertise in a combination of the following: HTML, CSS, CGI, Perl, XML, ASP, PHP, Java, JavaScript, ASP, VB, SQL, and Cold Fusion. Web developer job holders and web developer staff members may be asked to modify the graphical user interface of a Web site, so proficiency in Adobe PhotoShop, Macromedia Flash, DREAMWEAVER, and MS Front Page would come in handy. Web developers consultants occupy a lofty position in the computer jobs hierarchy, therefore their job demands more specialized knowledge.

Web developer consultants should have adequate exposure in some of the following client-server technologies: Web Logic, WEBSPHERE, SUNONE, Enterprise Java Beans, WEBMETHODS, TIBCO, Tuxedo, Netscape Enterprise Server, and Web Services. In addition, Web developers consultants must possess excellent communication and teamwork skills in order to work effectively with other information technology professionals.

Job Responsibilities of Web Developers Consultants

Web developer consultants are involved in every step of Web project development, starting from conceptualization of the Web site up to its maintenance. Together with a Web developers staff, Web developers consultants formulate strategies for improving the Web site's interface and performance. Like other computer tech jobs, Web developers jobs require writing, debugging, and maintaining code, as well as modifying existing code files for use in specific applications. Web developers employment covers a broad spectrum of applications which include enterprise, e-commerce, portals, content management, databases, and multimedia.

The all-encompassing nature of Web developers jobs brings the Web developer and web developer consultant in constant contact with professionals in other computer tech jobs, such as Visual Basic programmer consultants or members of a Java staff. A typical day for Web developer consultants could start with a meeting with the project manager and Web developers staff to discuss changes that need to be incorporated into a Web site. Afterwards, Web developers consultants might sit down and perform some coding, testing, troubleshooting, and documentation for the site. In some instances, web developer consultants might interact directly with end-users to provide technical support or gather feedback about the site's user-friendliness and performance. Throughout the day and for most of the project life cycle, Web developer consultants will be putting on different hats-sometimes manager, other times team member-in order to accomplish the task at hand.

As with other careers in information technology, web developer jobs require contact with trends in the industry, the Internet and developments that require upgrading skills. More than other tech jobs, data knowledge and visual knowledge or graphic design come into play. Visual literacy and training in visual arts will be considered highly in combination with computer skills.

IT Procurement Jobs- IT Training Jobs - Project Management IT Security Jobs

Information technology has become so integral to American business and government life that it has created new occupations to provide auxiliary support to the IT infrastructure and endeavor.

IT Procurement Jobs have grown up to manage the creation of RFPs (Requests for Proposals), Bid Analysis, Purchase and Maintenance Contracts, Personnel Contracting and the management of contracts. These jobs require special knowledge of the IT industry and the procurement field. People may enter an IT procurement job from another department and learn-as-you-go. Or they may be hired as a computer programmer or systems engineer to facilitate the procurement function for the hardware and software requirements. Computer Project managers often manage IT procurement contracts for staff and services. There is usually continuous communication between staff holding IT procurement jobs and technical staff delineating hardware and software contracts and outlining staffing needs.

IT Training Jobs exist both within an organization and with the numerous information technology training suppliers. Companies and government agencies contract for information technology training on new software and hardware. They may also contract for on-site or off-site information technology training for their employees. People may enter an information technology training job with a liberal arts or other degree or with hands-on business or training experience. IT trainers who work for a software or hardware vendor will be expected to know their product. IT trainers who train on software use will expand their tech jobs horizons by knowing may software products used in the workplace. Information technology training will be an integral part of any organization's employee development program. Both specialized information technology training and generic information technology training will ensure a modern organization where employees are conversant with software and the ability to handle information.

IT Project Management jobs, utilizing project management software such as Microsoft Project, Crystal Reports, Network Associates Magic, and Visio, are required in many departments. They are especially integral to the IT and Telecommunications departments of an organization. Project managers and systems analysts using project management software create project plans outlining system development life cycles and timelines. They gather statistics of call centers, tech support centers and organization groups to analyze IT operations. They use drawing and visualization software to map IT center server configurations. IT project management jobs usually do not require a degree in computer science. They require project management software skills, an ability to understand the parts of an organization and IT operation, and good communication skills.

IT Security jobs may fall under the web development group of an organization, under the telecommunications department, or in tech support. Information technology security jobs may reside in a separate security department responsible for facility and data security. IT service providers and outsourcers often hire IT staff to do security planning for their clients. Outsourcers may perform the access control function for their clients. Access control managers and access control specialists carry out access control functions for computer users, workgroups, and applications. Security specialist jobs exist for network engineers to establish secure network connections, decide on proxy servers to control content, and to determine firewall requirements. Systems analysts jobs are required to determine security requirements for safe electronic file transmissions, electronic file payment systems, HIPPA data release requirements and e-commerce systems.

While some tech jobs are clearly "technical" in nature, requiring math experience, there are so many non-technical tech jobs that no one should consider themselves out of the running for info tech employment. Skills are transferable from one industry to another and from one business process to another. Information technology employment will grow extensively over the next decade. IT service providers, staffing firms and outsourcers are hiring to fill new occupations created by this growth.

Computer Graphics Jobs, Computer Animation Jobs
Computer Graphics Jobs: Career Profile of Graphic Design

When Disney's "Beauty and the Beast" earned a Best Picture nomination in the Academy Awards, computer graphic artists working in the motion picture industry finally received the recognition they deserved. Almost a decade and a half later, artists and other creative professionals working in computer graphics jobs and computer animation jobs are still creating vivid images that seamlessly fuse life and art, not just in the movies but also in nearly every field of information technology employment. The convergence of data and visual communication over corporate Intranets and Internet will bring graphic artists into the mainstream of American business and government.

The explosive growth of the Internet and multimedia has left many companies scrambling to find qualified people to fill computer graphics jobs and computer animation jobs. There is the "coolness" factor of working in creative computer jobs. However, this factor alone for the graphic artist has never paid the bills consistently. Now the need for sophisticated computer graphics, to accompany sophisticated business applications, has raised the career profile of graphic design. Macromedia designer jobs now command as much respect and remuneration do other computer tech jobs.

An increasing number of graphic designers are developing material for Internet Web pages, computer interfaces, and multimedia projects. Graphic designers plan, analyze, and create visual solutions to communications problems. They use a variety of print, electronic, and film media and technologies to execute a design that meet clients' communication needs. They consider cognitive, cultural, physical, and social factors in planning and executing designs appropriate for a given context. In addition graphic designers use computer software to develop the overall layout and production design of magazines, newspapers, journals, corporate reports, and other publications. They also produce promotional displays and marketing brochures for products and services, design distinctive logos for products and businesses, and develop signs and signage systems-called environmental graphics-for business and government. Graphic designers also produce the credits that appear before and after television programs and movies.

Qualifications for Computer Graphics Jobs

Computer graphics jobs are about creating artwork that communicates a message visually. Producing eye-catching, compelling, organized images that convey information effectively requires a mind that is creative, logical, and analytical-all at the same time. These skills are acquired and harnessed through study and practice, which is why most professionals who work in computer graphics jobs hold bachelor's degrees in art or design.

Computer graphic artists usually supplement their formal art education with courses in computer graphics, computer animation, and Web and electronic publishing design. Getting computer graphics jobs is also possible for people with no formal degree in art or design, as long as they have demonstrable artistic and computer graphics skills and adequate experience.

Computer animation jobs and Macromedia designer jobs involve their own type of coding, unique to the graphic design and animation software. Like programming jobs, individuals who wish to work in these fields must know how to write, test, troubleshoot, and maintain scripts and codes to test their work. As with other computer jobs, computer graphics jobs involve a lot of collaboration with other people involved in the project, as well as constant communication with the client. Computer graphic artists must have good communication, team working, and interpersonal skills to be able to handle the responsibilities of computer graphics jobs.

Computer animation jobs

Information technology employment trends indicate that computer animation jobs are growing at almost the same pace as computer tech jobs. The increase in computer animation jobs is partly a result of expanding applications of computer animation. Computer animation jobs can be found in motion pictures, television, advertising, video games, CD-ROMs, and the Web-practically in any field where the medium is as important as the message.

Computer animation jobs require more specialized skills and training than do general computer animation jobs. Skills and experience in computer graphics, vector illustration, 3D animation, 3D modeling, computer rendering, and electronic and Web publishing are indispensable to workers in computer animation jobs. IT professionals in computer animation jobs should also be proficient in the use of Macromedia Flash, Dreamweaver, Director, Maya, 3D Studio Max, PowerAnimator, Softimage, Lightwave, and other computer animation programs.

Macromedia Designer Jobs

Macromedia Designer Jobs are computer graphics jobs held by people who specialize in the use of the Macromedia suite of graphics applications. Macromedia designer jobs generally involve developing and creating animation for the Web, advertising, games, and CD-ROMs. Macromedia Flash is currently the most widely used application for developing Web-integrated animation, and this has created a niche for Macromedia designers. Although Macromedia Designer Jobs emphasize the use of Macromedia products such as Flash, Dreamweaver, Director, Studio MX, FreeHand, and FlashPaper, knowledge of other computer animation and graphics programs is also necessary in this field.

Contract and Permanent Computer Graphics Jobs

The opportunity to work contract, contract to permanent, or permanent exists for computer graphics artists and computer animators. While some computer graphic artists choose to work as part of a company's creative department, others choose to work on a freelance and or contract basis. There are opportunities for computer graphic artists to be hired by IT service providers, staffing firms and outsourcers.

Outsourcers offer their services to companies and government agencies to design and maintain websites. They bring their expertise as IT providers to the table. These outsourcers hire and employ computer graphics artists and computer animators as part of their team to perform the work for their clients. Computer graphics artists and computer animators should seek work with outsourcers; staffing firms and IT service providers who have the clients. The opportunity to work permanent for an outsourcer, and contract for many clients for Telecommuting, or working at home, becomes available for computer graphics artists and computer animators. If you are a computer graphic artist or computer animator, finding contract or contract-to-permanent employment is easy once you have the right contacts. Employers will often ask that you start on a project and work at full pay on a trial basis. If they like your work, they will bring you on board full time. By expanding your contacts and building your network of companies, you will have choices to pursue the type of work you specialize in.

Charts

CHART I: IT Skills Sets-IT Jobs

Application Development, Programmer & Database Jobs

Programming Languages & Tools
- AS/400 RPG
- C,C,C++, Visual C++
- CGI
- Cobol
- CICS
- Extensile Markup Language (XML)
- Groove (peer-to-peer development environment)
- Java, Java Beans, Enterprise Java, JavaScript
- Lotus Notes/Domino
- Microsoft Exchange
- Perl
- PowerBuilder
- Universal Modeling Language (UML)
- Visual Basic (VB)
- Wireless Applications Protocol (WAP)

Operating Systems
- AS/400/OS
- Linux
- MVS
- Novell NetWaree
- PalmOS
- Unix (including Sun Solaris, IBM AIX, Hewlett-Packard)
- Windows 95/98/2000/XP
- Windows CE
- Windows NT

Database Languages
- IBM DB2
- Informix
- Microsoft Access
- Microsoft SQL Server
- Oracle 8i
- Sybase

Reporting Tools
- Crystal Reports
- Impromptu
- Oracle Reports
- SAS Enterprise Reporter

Online Analytical Processing Tools
- IBM Intelligent Decision Server
- Microsoft SQL Server OLAP Services
- SAP Business Information Warehouse
- SAS Software

Enterprise-Wide Application Suites
- J.D. Edwards
- Lawson
- Oracle Enterprise Apps
- PeopleSoft
- SAP

Application Development, Programmer & Database Jobs

Data Warehouse & Data Mining Tools
- Cognos Scenario
- Cognos Visualizer
- IBM Intelligent Miner
- Oracle Darwin
- SAS Enterprise Miner
- GUI Interfaces

Systems Analysis Tools
- CASE Management Software
- Microsoft Project
- Visio

Systems Analysis Work
- Feasibility Studies
- Hardware & Software Configuration
- Requests for Proposals
- Vendor Evaluation & Bid Analysis
- Design System Programming Specifications

Application Development, Database Work
- Customer Relationship Management System
- Data Warehouse & Data Mining
- Digital Libraries
- E-Commerce Web
- Electronic Data Interchange Systems
- Financial Data Processing Systems
- GIS Systems
- Paperless Office Systems
- Personnel Management Systems
- Real-time Reservation Systems
- SCM Systems
- Supply Chain Management System
- Web to Backend Integration
- Wireless Real-Time Dispatch & Proof-of-Delivery Systems

PC Support & Help DeskCall Center Jobs

PC Support Work
- HW/SW Installation
- PC Operating System & Application Software Troubleshooting
- Directory Mapping
- HW/SW Inventory
- HW/SW Licensing

Networking & Infrastructure Jobs

Hardware
- Bridges
- Brouters
- Cables (Fiber optic, coaxial, twisted-pair)
- Hubs
- Modems

Networking & Infrastructure Jobs

- Networked storage devices
- Routers
- Switches

LAN & WAN Technologies & Protocols
- AppleTalk/AppleShare
- Domain Name System (DNS)
- Ethernet
- File Transfer Protocol (FTP)
- IBM's System Network Architecture (SNA)
- Novell's Internetwork Packet Exchange
- OSI Reference Model
- Peer-to-peer networking
- Simple Network Management Protocol (SNMP)
- Storage area networks
- Sun's Network Fine System (NFS)
- TCP/IP
- Token Ring
- Virtual Private Network (VPN)
- Wireless Application Protocol (WAP)
- X-500 Directory Services, Directory Access Protocol (DAP), Lightweight Directory Access Protocol (LDAP)

Network Management Tools
- IBM, HP, SUN Middleware
- Veritas Network Management Software

Security
- Antivirus Software
- Data encryption/cryptography
- Digital certificates
- Firewalls (Checkpoint, Nokia, Symantec)
- Internet Protocol Security (Ipsec)
- Sniffer programs

Telecommunications Technologies
- Asynchronous Transfer Mode (ATM)
- Digital Subscriber Line (DSL)
- Frame Relay
- Hybrid Fiber Coaxial (HFC) networks
- Integrated Services Digital Network (ISDN)
- Inereactive Voice Response (IVR)
- Private Branch Exchange (PBX)
- Voice Over IP

Operations Jobs

Operations Hardware
- DEC
- HP
- IBM
- SUN
- Unisys

Operations Jobs

Operating Systems
- IBM MVS
- IBM OS
- Linux
- Microsoft 95/98/2000/XP
- Microsoft NT
- Unix (HP, IBM, SUN)

Storage Management Systems
- Computer Associates Unicenter
- EMC
- IBM
- Microsoft
- Storage Area Networks (SANs)

Disaster Recovery Planning Tools
- Comdisco ComPAS
- Strohl Business Impact Analysis (BIA)
- Strohl Living Disaster Recovery (LDRPS)
- SunGard Comprehensive Business Recovery
- SunGard ePlanner
- Tivoli Disaster Recovery Manager

Change Management & Capacity Planning Tools
- Network Associates Sniffer/RMON
- Peregrine
- SAS/STAT Statistical Analysis Tools
- Sniffer System

System Management Tools
- Computer Associates Unicenter
- Hewlett Packard OpenView
- IBM
- Veritas

Web Developer, e-Business & Internet Jobs

Web Development & DatabaseTools
- Active Server Pages (ASP)
- ATG Dynamic Server Suite
- CGI
- ColdFusion
- Dynamic HTML (DHTML)
- HTML E-mail Design
- Java, JavaScript
- Perl
- Visual Basic
- Wireless Application Protocol (WAP)
- XML
- Lotus Notes/Domino
- Microsoft Exchange
- Microsoft SQL Server
- Oracle

Web Developer, e-Business & Internet Jobs

Operating Systems & Server Software
- Linux
- Microsoft Internet Information Server
- Sun Solaris, HP Unix
- Windows 95/98/2000/XP
- Windows NT

Website Design Tools & Standards
- IP Multicas
- Macromedia Dreamweaver
- Macromedia Fireworks
- Macromedia Flash
- Macromedia MX
- Microsoft FrontPage
- Real Networks Streaming Media
- Shockwave

E-Business Platforms
- Ariba b2b Commerce Platform
- ATG Dynamo E-business Platform
- Blue Martini Software Customer Intereaction Software
- InterWorld Commerce Suite
- Vignette E-business Application Platform

Content Management Tools
- Artesia Technologies TEAMS Software Suite
- Vignette Content Management Server

E-business Applications
- Chordiant Software Customer Relation Management
- i2 Supplier Relationship Management Suite
- Siebel Systems e-business Customer Relationship Management

Networking & Security Technologies & Protocols
- Cisco Routers & Switches
- Emerging Internet2 Standards
- Firewalls
- PCP Encryption
- Secure Socket Layer (SSL)
- TCP/IP

Web Development, E-Commerce Work
- Ecommerce Website
- Flash Animation
- Flash MX
- HTML E-mail Design
- Internet Marketing
- Online Forms & Database Integration
- Search Engine Optimization (SEO)
- Web Design & Development
- Usability & Interface Design
- Web Hosting
- Web Programming

Graphic Design & Art Jobs

Graphic Design Software
- Adobe Illustrator
- Adobe Photoshop
- Adobe/Other
- Macromedia MX
- Macintosh Software
- Quark xPress

Graphic Design & Art Work
- 3D Graphics
- Annual Reports
- Art & Art Direction
- Banner Ads
- Billboards & Signage
- Brochures & Catalogs
- Computer Animation
- Datasheets & Press Kits
- Digital Imaging
- Direct Mail
- Graphic Design
- Illustration
- Logos
- Package Design
- Page & Book Layout
- Photo Retouching
- Photography
- Print Ads
- Printing
- Product Design

IT Management & Planning Jobs

IT Management & Planning Work
- Computer Center Planning
- Contract Management
- Contractor Management
- Enterprise Planning
- IT Personnel/Staffing/Human Resources
- IT Procedures & Policies
- IT Procurement
- IT Training & Development
- Project Management
- Requests for Proposals & Bid Analysis
- Vendors Relations

IT Planning Tools
- Microsoft Project
- Visio

Administrative Support Tech Jobs

Administrative Support Tools
- Custom Applications
- Microsoft Office
- Microsoft Word
- Microsoft Excel
- Microsoft Access
- Microsoft PowerPoint
- Microsoft Publisher

Administrative Support Tech Jobs

Administrative Support Tools
- Bulk Mailing
- Customer Response
- Data Entry
- Fact Checking
- Mailing List Development
- Office Management
- Research
- Transcription
- Travel Planning
- Word Processing

IT Training & Development
- Business Skills
- Business Software
- Media Training
- Policies & Manuals
- Programming Languages
- Technical Training

IT Certifications
- Certified Information Systems Auditor (CISA)
- Certified Network Professional (CNP)
- Cisco Certified Internetwork Expert (CCIE)
- Cisco Certified Network Associate (CCNA)
- Cisco Certified Network Professional (CCNP)
- Microsoft Certified Systems Engineer + Internet (MCSE+I)
- Microsoft Certified Trainer (MCT)
- Oracle Certified Professional (OCP)
- PMI Project Management Professional (PMP)

Sample IT Job Titles
- Applications Developer/Programmer Mainframe
- Systems Manager Mainframe
- Applications Developer/Programmer Mid Range
- Systems Manager Mid Range
- Applications Developer PC-Systems Manager PC
- Business Process Analyst (BPA) &
- Business Process Re-Engineering Analyst
- C++ Programmer
- Computer Aided Design & Drafting Specialist (CADD)
- Computer Animation Designer
- Computer Graphics Designer
- Computer Programmer
- Computer Software Engineer/Computer Software Programmer
- Database Administrator/Programmer/Specialist
- Data Conversion Specialist
- Desktop Asset Manager/Specialist
- Desktop Support Specialist
- Electronic Commerce (EC) & Electronic

Sample IT Job Titles
- Data Interchange (EDI) Developer
- Director of IT/IT Manager
- Documentation Specialist
- E-Commerce Manager/Director of E-Business
- Electronic Output Manager
- Electronic Output Manager
- Enterprise Resource Planning (ERP) Consultant
- Geographic Information Systems (GIS) Systems Analyst/Manager
- Help Desk Analyst/Manager
- Imaging Services Analyst/Manager/Director
- Information Security Analyst/Manager/Director
- Interactive Voice Response (IVR) Application Developer
- Internet/Intranet Applications Developer/Programmer
- IT Administrative Support Specialist
- IT Management & Planning: CIO/CTO/Development Director/
- IT Policies & Procedures Director/Specialist/Analyst
- IT Procurement & Contracting Specialist/Manager
- IT Trainer
- Java Programmer
- JavaScript Programmer
- Local Area Network Services (LANs) Administrator/Technician
- Network Architect//Administrator
- Network Architect//Administrator
- Network Engineer
- Operations/Data Center Specialist/Director
- Oracle Database Programmer
- PeopeSoft Programmer
- Point-Of-Sale Systems (POS)
- Quality Assurance Specialist
- Sales: Technical Sales Representative
- SAP Specialist
- Security Administrator/Specialist/Technician
- Security Administrator/Specialist/Technician
- Software Engineer
- Software Programmer
- Sun Solaris Systems Engineer
- Systems Integration Director/Specialist
- Technical Trainer
- Tape Librarian
- Technical Writer
- Technology Procurement (Marketwatching) Specialist
- Telecommunications Engineer/Director/Specialist/Analyst
- Web Designer/Site Designer
- Web Developer/Programmer/Content Editor
- Webmaster
- Wide Area Network (WAN) Administrator/Specialist
- Workflow Management Services

CHART II: Sample IT Job Classifications

Sample IT Contract Job Classifications show how employers are looking for levels of experience. Work experience translates into levels of experience. The sample IT contract Job Classifications demonstrate how IT service providers often translate their client's need into placement of the right person for the job. When a client says "I need a team leader," that will translate into a level of experience and expertise, and a pay level the IT service provider and client will agree on. Learn how to make optimum use of existing IT Contract Job Classifications in assessing your qualifications and seeking your position. Here's a very useful guide to understanding the positioning scheme of most IT service providers and positioning yourself when you negotiate with an IT service company for your position in your skill and at your level

Project Managers

Entry Level (EL) Project Manager - Less than 2 years experience in overseeing small scaled, non-complex projects, comprised of a small number of deliverables and/or a small number of phases; typically coordinates and delegates the assignments for the consultant project staff numbering up to 5; focal point of contact for Issuing Entity regarding project status, meetings, reporting requirements, scope changes, and issues and concerns raised by consultant staff or Issuing Entity.

Project Manager I - Minimum of 2 years experience in overseeing small scaled, non-complex projects, comprised of a small number of deliverables and/or a small number of phases; typically coordinates and delegates the assignments for the consultant project staff numbering up to 10. Focal point of contact for Issuing Entity regarding project status, meetings, reporting requirements, scope changes/extensions, and issues and concerns raised by consultant staff or Issuing Entity.

Project Manager II - Minimum 4 years experience in overseeing medium scaled projects comprised of sub-projects and distinct deliverables; typically coordinates and delegates the assignments for the consultant project staff numbering over 10. Focal point of contact for Issuing Entity regarding project status, meetings, reporting requirements; scope changes/ extensions, and financial, administrative, and technical issues and concerns raised by consultant staff or Issuing Entity.

Project Manager III - Minimum 8 years experience in overseeing medium to large scaled projects comprised of sub-projects and distinct deliverables; typically coordinates and delegates the assignments for the consultant project staff numbering over 20. Focal point of contact for Issuing Entity regarding project status, meetings, reporting requirements, scope changes/extensions, and financial, administrative, and technical issues and concerns raised by consultant staff or Issuing Entity.

Programmer/Analysts

Entry Level (EL) Programmer/Analyst- Less than 2 years experience with writing application software, data analysis, data access, data structures, data manipulation, databases, design, programming, testing and implementation, technical and user documentation, software conversions; environments include but are not limited to mainframe, mid range, personal computers, laptops.

Programmer/Analyst I - Minimum of 2 years experience with writing application software, data analysis, data access, data structures, data manipulation, databases, design, programming, testing and implementation, technical and user documentation, software conversions; environments include but are not limited to mainframe, mid range, personal computers, laptops.

Programmer/Analyst II - Minimum of 4 years experience with writing application software, data analysis, data access, data structures, data manipulation, databases, programming, testing and implementation, technical and user documentation, software conversions; environments include but are not limited to mainframe, mid range, personal computers, laptop; available to assist and/or lead in the design of program specifications and the implementation of software solutions.

Programmer/Analyst III - Minimum of 8 years experience with writing application software, data analysis, data access, data structures, data manipulation, databases, programming, testing and implementation, technical and user documentation, software conversions; environments include but are not limited to mainframe, mid range, personal computers, laptop; available to assist and/or lead in the design of program specifications and the implementation of software solutions.

Specialists

Entry Level (EL) Specialist - Less than 2 years experience in a particular technical and/or business application which is beyond the requirements addressed in the Programmer/Analyst (Entry level) Job Classification/Title as defined in a Project Definition/Specifications.

Specialist I - Minimum of 2 years experience in a particular technical and/or business application which is beyond the requirements addressed in the Programmer/Analyst I Job Classification/Title as defined in a Project Definition/Specifications. Examples include but are not limited to:

Certified Network Engineer (CNE)
Lotus Notes Certified Application Developer
Microsoft Certified Systems Engineer (MCSE)

PC Computer Designer
Web Master

Specialist II - Minimum of 4 years experience in a particular technical and/or business application which is beyond the requirements addressed in the Programmer/Analyst II Job Classification/Title as defined in a Project Definition/Specifications. See Specialist I list for examples.

Specialist III - Minimum of 8 years experience in a particular technical and/or business application which is beyond the requirements addressed in the Programmer/Analyst III Job Classification/Title as defined in a Project Definition/Specifications. See Specialist I list for examples.

CHART II: Sample IT Contract Hourly Rate Schedule

Expertise Selected: Application Development Mainframe, Systems Management Mainframe, Application Development Mid Range, Systems Management Mid Range, Application Development PC, Systems Management PC, LAN, WAN, Network, Security, Internet

Multi-Vendor Contract Not-To-Exceed Rates Effective: Current Year
(Hourly Rates Inclusive of Expenses)

[ITE Note: Average Hourly Rate to Employee: 65-85% Actual Rate charged to Client.]

Company   Job Classification/Title   Click on Individual Job Titles for Descriptions

Company	Entry Project Manager	Proj Manager I	Proj Manager II	Proj Manager III	Entry Prog Analyst	Prog Analyst I	Prog Analyst II	Prog Analyst III	Entry Spclst	Spclst I	Spclst II	Spclst III
A Company MBE SBE	$240.72	$272.09	$299.97	$340.81	$212.18	$237.54	$258.30	$278.65	$179.63	$217.81	$254.97	$299.97
B Company WBE	$221.00	$246.00	$276.00	$320.00	$195.00	$219.00	$236.00	$256.00	$177.00	$201.00	$236.00	$276.00
C Company LLP	$294.52	$329.35	$385.64	$441.93	$141.76	$170.62	$297.83	$357.50	$190.33	$223.53	$297.83	$381.14
D Company SBE WBE	$225.00	$275.00	$300.00	$330.00	$200.00	$225.00	$275.00	$295.00	$180.00	$210.00	$275.00	$300.00
E Company	$181.94	$216.77	$273.06	$329.35	$109.12	$137.97	$166.11	$188.63	$110.39	$143.60	$216.77	$273.06
F Company	$153.79	$188.63	$244.92	$301.21	$154.15	$183.00	$239.29	$273.06	$149.80	$183.00	$216.77	$261.81
G Company SBE	$185.77	$218.60	$235.15	$263.90	$150.53	$177.72	$195.40	$218.60	$169.63	$200.92	$218.60	$247.33
H Company	$200.00	$265.00	$310.00	$380.00	$180.00	$240.00	$280.00	$320.00	$200.00	$250.00	$290.00	$340.00
I Company	$233.55	$267.71	$328.41	$344.97	$145.61	$173.89	$195.97	$212.52	$163.42	$195.97	$240.12	$317.38
J Company	$279.09	$312.42	$364.49	$416.56	$258.78	$286.38	$312.42	$338.45	$228.59	$260.35	$312.42	$364.49
K Company WBE	$148.16	$183.00	$211.15	$244.92	$109.12	$137.97	$166.11	$194.26	$132.91	$166.11	$194.26	$216.77
L Company	$129.01	$161.84	$236.10	$283.84	$124.04	$151.23	$214.89	$257.32	$146.46	$177.75	$236.10	$283.84
M Company SBE	$265.00	$295.00	$335.00	$385.00	$230.00	$255.00	$285.00	$310.00	$210.00	$240.00	$285.00	$335.00
N Company	$143.23	$166.23	$174.60	$185.05	$120.23	$143.23	$159.96	$208.05	$122.32	$163.10	$174.60	$214.33
O Company	$248.24	$283.08	$304.86	$326.63	$243.34	$272.19	$283.08	$293.97	$238.99	$272.19	$283.08	$293.97
P Company	$250.00	$300.00	$350.00	$400.00	$175.00	$200.00	$250.00	$300.00	$200.00	$225.00	$275.00	$325.00
Q Company	$210.08	$244.92	$267.44	$340.61	$142.89	$171.74	$233.66	$278.69	$155.43	$188.63	$239.29	$295.58
R Company	$170.25	$210.08	$260.41	$310.25	$155.65	$185.84	$215.37	$255.89	$142.56	$160.85	$210.37	$250.64
S Company	$288.74	$322.90	$350.49	$378.08	$156.64	$184.93	$240.12	$256.67	$135.82	$168.38	$212.52	$295.30
T Company SBE	$172.55	$203.00	$253.75	$279.13	$101.50	$126.88	$152.25	$177.63	$116.73	$147.18	$213.15	$294.35
U Company	$144.92	$177.75	$257.32	$363.41	$124.04	$151.23	$177.75	$257.32	$172.99	$204.28	$257.32	$363.41
V Company SBE	$158.76	$193.08	$230.63	$321.80	$89.57	$118.00	$139.45	$176.99	$106.74	$139.45	$214.54	$300.35
W Company MBE SBE WBE	$210.13	$281.88	$312.63	$358.75	$184.50	$210.13	$240.88	$292.13	$164.00	$179.38	$194.75	$210.13
X Company SBE	$226.97	$261.81	$273.06	$357.50	$232.95	$261.81	$273.06	$357.50	$228.60	$261.81	$273.06	$357.50
Y Company SBE	$197.97	$230.80	$257.32	$283.84	$150.56	$177.75	$204.28	$230.80	$172.90	$204.28	$230.80	$257.32
Z Company	$235.97	$270.81	$305.71	$364.25	$194.68	$223.53	$270.81	$300.08	$190.33	$223.53	$270.81	$364.25
AA Company	$290.25	$323.08	$363.41	$416.45	$256.65	$283.84	$310.37	$336.89	$232.56	$263.85	$310.37	$363.41

CHART II: Sample IT Contract Hourly Rate Schedule

Company   Job Classification/Title   Click on Individual Job Titles for Descriptions

Company	Entry Project Manager	Proj Manager I	Proj Manager II	Proj Manager III	Entry Prog Analyst	Prog Analyst I	Prog Analyst II	Prog Analyst III	Entry Spclst	Spclst I	Spclst II	Spclst III
AB Company MBE	$117.09	$151.08	$206.00	$260.91	$89.98	$118.13	$134.60	$184.03	$91.23	$123.62	$140.10	$184.03
AC Company	$174.88	$208.37	$262.47	$316.58	$148.17	$175.90	$219.19	$240.82	$165.63	$197.54	$240.82	$284.11
AD Company	$155.29	$201.88	$293.30	$279.53	$110.78	$136.66	$163.58	$196.71	$131.48	$160.47	$186.35	$222.59
AE Company	$125.65	$160.49	$216.77	$273.06	$92.23	$121.08	$132.34	$143.60	$110.39	$143.60	$160.49	$188.63
AF Company MBE WBE	$297.25	$333.13	$374.13	$430.50	$264.45	$292.13	$321.85	$348.50	$240.88	$271.63	$319.80	$374.13
AG Company	$142.53	$177.37	$199.89	$216.77	$103.49	$132.34	$143.60	$154.86	$110.39	$143.60	$160.49	$183.00
AH Company SBE	$107.17	$140.00	$180.00	$220.00	$92.81	$120.00	$160.00	$220.00	$108.71	$140.00	$180.00	$220.00
AI Company	$114.39	$149.23	$166.11	$194.26	$97.86	$126.71	$143.60	$154.86	$99.14	$132.34	$149.23	$188.63
AJ Company	$261.37	$318.88	$350.24	$407.74	$261.37	$271.83	$303.19	$324.10	$198.64	$245.69	$303.19	$355.47
AK Company	$277.21	$308.58	$347.10	$397.75	$245.13	$271.10	$296.44	$321.77	$221.62	$252.02	$296.44	$347.10
AL Company SBE	$164.00	$215.25	$276.75	$338.25	$123.00	$158.88	$215.25	$276.75	$138.38	$225.50	$297.25	$358.75
AM Company	$105.00	$119.00	$127.00	$141.00	$89.00	$99.00	$109.00	$119.00	$93.00	$104.00	$117.00	$129.00
AN Company MBE	$102.50	$137.34	$143.53	$168.65	$80.35	$109.21	$128.36	$146.67	$155.67	$188.88	$207.28	$225.67
AO Company SBE	$200.00	$210.00	$230.00	$250.00	$150.00	$160.00	$180.00	$200.00	$150.00	$160.00	$180.00	$200.00
AP Company	$103.90	$138.73	$158.56	$265.06	$97.85	$126.70	$161.90	$318.97	$95.15	$128.36	$170.52	$239.28
AQ Company SBE WBE	$103.22	$136.87	$159.51	$182.16	$109.00	$136.87	$148.19	$159.51	$104.80	$136.87	$170.84	$204.81
AR Company	$295.80	$331.50	$372.30	$428.40	$265.20	$290.70	$321.30	$346.80	$239.70	$270.30	$321.30	$372.30
AS Company SBE	$125.65	$160.49	$216.77	$261.81	$126.00	$154.86	$211.15	$250.55	$116.02	$149.23	$205.52	$239.29
AT Company	$205.96	$240.12	$267.71	$322.90	$184.23	$212.52	$267.71	$295.30	$207.56	$240.12	$267.71	$322.90
AU Company	$209.10	$261.37	$313.65	$365.92	$209.10	$235.24	$287.51	$339.79	$235.24	$261.37	$313.65	$365.92
AV Company MBE SBE	$174.96	$208.28	$260.35	$312.42	$128.61	$156.21	$177.04	$208.28	$145.28	$177.04	$218.69	$249.93
AW Company MBE	$118.00	$135.00	$159.00	$177.00	$112.50	$139.50	$153.00	$199.50	$117.00	$154.50	$163.50	$205.50
AX Company SBE	$112.14	$146.98	$163.86	$175.12	$100.11	$128.96	$146.98	$158.23	$101.33	$134.54	$154.12	$176.08
AY Company	$147.12	$181.96	$208.43	$260.14	$107.24	$136.09	$163.73	$193.26	$121.60	$146.44	$182.24	$239.23
AZ Company SBE	$148.16	$183.00	$228.03	$273.06	$154.15	$183.00	$228.03	$273.06	$149.80	$183.00	$228.03	$273.06
BA Company	$216.84	$251.67	$286.57	$327.10	$132.76	$161.61	$211.15	$226.91	$123.90	$157.11	$222.40	$273.06

CHART III: U.S. FEDERAL EXECUTIVE BRANCH   INDEPENDENT AGENCIES

Executive Office of the President (EOP)	Advisory Council on Historic Preservation (ACHP)
White House	American Battle Monuments Commission
Office of Management and Budget (OMB)	Central Intelligence Agency (CIA)
United States Trade Representative (USTR)	Commodity Futures Trading Commission (CFTC)
Executive Agencies	Consumer Product Safety Commission (CPSC)
Department of Agriculture (USDA)	Corporation for National Service
Agricultural Research Service	Environmental Protection Agency (EPA)
Animal & Plant Health Inspection Service	Equal Employment Opportunity Commission (EEOC)
Economic Research Service	Farm Credit Administration (FCA)
Farm Service Agency	Federal Communications Commission (FCC)
Forest Service	Federal Deposit Insurance Corporation (FDIC)
National Agricultural Library	Federal Election Commission (FEC)
Natural Resources Conservation Service	Federal Energy Regulatory Commission (FERC)
Rural Development	Federal Labor Relations Authority (FLRA)
Department of Commerce (DOC)	Federal Maritime Commission
Bureau of the Census	Federal Reserve System, Board of Governors of the Federal Reserve
Bureau of Economic Analysis (BEA)	
STAT-USA Database	Federal Retirement Thrift Investment Board (FRTIB)
FEDWorld	Federal Trade Commission (FTC)
International Trade Administration (ITA)	General Services Administration (GSA)
National Institute of Standards & Technology (NIST)	Federal Consumer Information Center (Pueblo, CO)
National Marine Fisheries Service (NMFS)	Institute of Museum and Library Services (IMLS)
National Oceanic & Atmospheric Administration (NOAA)	International Boundary and Water Commission
National Ocean Service	International Broadcasting Bureau (IBB)
National Technical Information Service (NTIS)	Merit Systems Protection Board (MSPB)
National Telecommunications & Information Administration	National Aeronautics and Space Administration (NASA)
National Weather Service	National Archives and Records Administration (NARA)
Patent and Trademark Office Database	National Capital Planning Commission (NCPC)
Department of Defense (DOD)	National Commission on Libraries and Information Science (NCLIS)
Department of Education	National Council on Disability
Educational Resources Information Center (ERIC)	National Credit Union Administration (NCUA)
Clearinghouses	National Endowment for the Arts (NEA)
National Library of Education (NLE)	National Endowment for the Humanities (NEH)
Other Federal Government Internet Educational Resources	National Indian Gaming Commission (NIGC)
Department of Energy	National Labor Relations Board (NLRB)
Environment, Safety and Health (ES&H)	National Mediation Board (NMB)
Federal Energy Regulatory Commission	National Railroad Passenger Corporation (AMTRAK)
Los Alamos National Laboratory	National Science Foundation (NSF) Board
Office of Science	National Transportation Safety Board (NTSB)
Southwestern Power Administration	Nuclear Regulatory Commission (NRC)

Department of Health and Human Services (HHS)	US Nuclear Waste Technical Review Board (NWTRB)
HHS Agencies	Occupational Safety and Health Administration (OSHA)
National Institutes of Health (NIH)	Office of Federal Housing Enterprise Oversight (OFHEO)
National Library of Medicine (NLM)	Office of Personnel Management (OPM)
Department Homeland Security (DHS)	Overseas Private Investment Corporation (OPIC)
Customs & Border Protection	Peace Corps
Coast Guard	Pension Benefit Guaranty Corporation
Federal Emergency Management Agency (FEMA)	Postal Rate Commission
Federal Law Enforcement Training Center	Railroad Retirement Board (RRB)
Secret Service	Securities and Exchange Commission (SEC)
US Citizenship and Immigration Services	Selective Service System (SSS)
U.S. Intelligence Community (Jobs)	Small Business Administration (SBA)
Department of Housing and Urban Development (HUD)	Social Security Administration (SSA)
Government National Mortgage Association (Ginnie Mae)	Tennessee Valley Authority (TVA)
Office of Healthy Homes and Lead Hazard Control	Thrift Savings Plan (TSP)
Office of Public and Indian Housing (PIH)	United States Agency for International Development (USAID)
Department of the Interior (DOI)	United States Arms Control and Disarmament Agency (ACDA)
Bureau of Indian Affairs	United States International Trade Commission (USITC)
Bureau of Land Management	Dataweb (Import/export data)
Bureau of Reclamation	United States Office of Government Ethics (OGE)
Fish and Wildlife Service	United States Postal Service (USPS)
Geological Survey	United States Trade and Development Agency
Minerals Management Service	Voice of America (VOA)

CHART IV: U.S. Federal
IT Job Titles & Computer-Technology Related Job Titles Salaries, 5-Year Salary Projections & Estimated Pensions

LEGEND:

*Salary minimum and maximum amounts are projected estimates, based on actual base published salaries, from base year in the U.S. Federal GS Schedule, plus the estimated raise percentage. The raise percentage used is based on a 5-year average of actual published raises for the U.S. Federal Government from over the most recent 5 years (USAOPM, GS Pay Schedule, 2006.).

** Cumulative 5-Year Raise Estimate, is based on 5-Year Average Raise Estimate, as determined from actual published raise figures from over the most recent 5 years. Compounded 5-Year Raise Estimate (not shown) is greater than Cumulative 5-Year Raise Estimate.

***Estimated Pension at 20-Years, 25-Years, and 30-Years is based on the Pension Formula for the U.S. Federal Government 3 part plan: 1) The Basic Benefit annual pension of Average of 3 Highest Years Salaries times Pension Percentage 1.1% times Number of Years. The Pension Benefit is based on a fixed formula. 2) Social Security Benefits are paid in addition to The Basic Plan Benefits. 3) The Thrift Savings Plan pays an Automatic Agency Contribution of 1% of base salary per year. Employees may make additional contributions to the Thrift Savings Plan; contributions will be matched by the Agency at a rate of $1.00 for $1.00 for the first 3% of base salary contributed, and $.50 for $1.00 for the second 2% of base salary contributed (USAOPM, FERS, 2006.)

****Retirement Benefit from Agency Thrift Savings Plan. The Retirement Benefit calculated here from The Thrift Savings Plan is calculated as 1% of base salary minimum or maximum per year, plus an estimated 4.5% estimated Interest accrued per year on the 1%. Employees may choose to save their Thrift Savings in any of a variety of investment savings vehicles; interest rates may vary. This calculation shown for demonstration purposes is made without any additional Employee Contributions (USAOPM, TSP, 2006.)

*****Senior Executive Service: The SES pay range has a minimum rate of basic pay equal to 120 percent of the rate for GS-15, step 1, and the maximum rate of basic pay is equal to the rate for level III of the Executive Schedule. For any agency certified as having a performance appraisal system, the maximum rate of basic pay will be the rate for level II of the Executive Schedule (USAOPM, SES, 2006.)

Disclaimer: The Salary & Pension performance data featured is based on past performance, which is no guarantee of future results. Current Salary & Pension may be higher or lower than the performance data quoted.

REFERENCEs:
U.S. Federal Government, Office of Personnel Management, Federal Employee Retirement System 2006, http://www.opm.gov/forms/pdfimage/RI90-1.pdf

U.S. Federal Government, Office of Personnel Administration, GS Pay Schedule, 2006, http://www.opm.gov/oca/06tables/pdf/gs.pdf; http://www.opm.gov/oca/06tables/indexGS.asp.

U.S. Federal Government, Office of Personnel Administration, Senior Executive Service, 2006, http://www.opm.gov/oca/06tables/pdf/es.pdf http://www.opm.gov/ses.

U.S. Federal Government, Office of Personnel Administration, Thrift Savings Plan, 2006, http://www.opm.gov/benefits/correction/faq/Thrift.htm

U.S. Federal Government Agencies Information Technology Group Jobs

Job	2008 GS-11 (Min)*	2008 GS-15 (Max)	2009 GS-11 (Min)	2009 GS-15 (Max)	2010 GS-11 (Min)	2010 GS-15 (Max)	2011 GS-11 (STEP 2) (Min)	2011 GS-15 (STEP 2) (Max)	2012 GS-11 (Min)	2012 GS-15 (Max)	5-Year Average % Raise	5-Year Cumulative Raise Estimate**	20-Year Annual Pension Benefit Estimate	20-Year Annual Pension Benefit Estimate (Max.)	25-Year Annual Pension Benefit Estimate (Min.)	25-Year Annual Pension Benefit Estimate (Max.)	30-Year Annual Pension Benefit Estimate (Min.)	30-Year Annual Pension Benefit Estimate (Max.)	Agency Automatic Contributions 1% Thrift Savings Plan 20 Year Savings Plus 4.5% Interest	Agency Automatic Contributions 1% Thrift Savings Plan 20 Year Savings Plus 4.5% Interest (Max)	Agency Automatic Contributions 1% Thrift Savings Plan 25 Year Savings Plus 4.5% Interest (Min)	Agency Automatic Contributions 1% Thrift Savings Plan 25 Year Savings Plus 4.5% Interest (Max)	Agency Automatic Contributions 1% Thrift Savings Plan 30 Year Savings Plus 4.5% Interest (Min)	Agency Automatic Contributions 1% Thrift Savings Plan 30 Year Savings Plus 4.5% Interest (Max)
Information Technology Project Manager*	47,351	93,809	47,943	94,982	48,542	96,169	50,689	100,421	51,323	101,676	2.00%	10.00%	15,534	30,773	22,026	43,635	29,884	59,201	12,471	24,707	16,652	32,990	21,369	42,334
Information Technology Project Manager (Supervisor)****	47,351	93,809	47,943	94,982	48,542	96,169	50,689	100,421	51,323	101,676	2.00%	10.00%	15,534	30,773	22,026	43,635	29,884	59,201	12,471	24,707	16,652	32,990	21,369	42,334
Information Technology Project Manager (Team Leader)****	47,351	93,809	47,943	94,982	50,082	99,219	50,708	100,459	51,342	101,715	2.00%	10.00%	14,988	29,692	21,351	42,297	29,076	57,600	12,546	24,855	16,751	33,185	21,495	42,584
Information Technology Specialist*	47,351	93,809	47,943	94,982	50,082	99,219	50,708	100,459	51,342	101,715	2.00%	10.00%	14,988	29,692	21,351	42,297	29,076	57,600	12,546	24,855	16,751	33,185	21,495	42,584
Information Technology Specialist (Supervisor)****	47,351	93,809	47,943	94,982	50,082	99,219	50,708	100,459	51,342	101,715	2.00%	10.00%	14,988	29,692	21,351	42,297	29,076	57,600	12,546	24,855	16,751	33,185	21,495	42,584
Information Technology Specialist (Team Leader)****	47,351	93,809	47,943	94,982	50,082	99,219	50,708	100,459	51,342	101,715	2.00%	10.00%	14,988	29,692	21,351	42,297	29,076	57,600	12,546	24,855	16,751	33,185	21,495	42,584

Other Job Groups with IT-Computer-Technical Services Work

Job	2008 GS-5 (Min)*	2008 GS-15 (Max)	2009 GS-5 (Min)	2009 GS-15 (Max)	2010 GS-5 (Min)	2010 GS-15 (Max)	2011 GS-5 (STEP 2) (Min)	2011 GS-15 (STEP 2) (Max)	2012 GS-5 (Min)	2012 GS-15 (Max)	5-Year Average % Raise	5-Year Cumulative Raise Estimate**	20-Year Annual Pension Benefit Estimate (Min.)***	20-Year Annual Pension Benefit Estimate (Max.)	25-Year Annual Pension Benefit Estimate (Min.)	25-Year Annual Pension Benefit Estimate (Max.)	30-Year Annual Pension Benefit Estimate (Min.)	30-Year Annual Pension Benefit Estimate (Max.)	Agency Automatic Contributions 1% Thrift Savings Plan 20 Year Savings Plus 4.5% Interest	Agency Automatic Contributions 1% Thrift Savings Plan 20 Year Savings Plus 4.5% Interest (Max)	Agency Automatic Contributions 1% Thrift Savings Plan 25 Year Savings Plus 4.5% Interest (Min)	Agency Automatic Contributions 1% Thrift Savings Plan 25 Year Savings Plus 4.5% Interest (Max)	Agency Automatic Contributions 1% Thrift Savings Plan 30 Year Savings Plus 4.5% Interest (Min)	Agency Automatic Contributions 1% Thrift Savings Plan 30 Year Savings Plus 4.5% Interest (Max)
Computer Engineering (GS-0854) (GS-5- GS-15)	26,213	95,204	26,737	97,108	27,272	99,050	28,317	104,081	28,884	106,163	2.00%	10.00%	8,769	33,756	12,246	47,468	16,651	64,472	7,239	27,402	9,653	36,793	12,378	47,362
Computer Science (GS-1550) (GS 5-GS-15)	26,213	95,204	26,737	97,108	27,272	99,050	28,317	104,081	28,884	106,163	2.00%	10.00%	8,646	33,008	12,077	46,435	16,427	63,104	7,182	27,053	9,562	36,242	12,251	46,587

U.S. Federal Government Agencies Information Technology Group Jobs	2008 GS-11 (Min)*	2008 GS-15 (Max)	2009 GS-11 (Min)	2009 GS-15 (Max)	2010 GS-11 (Min)	2010 GS-15 (Max)	2011 GS-11 (STEP 2) (Min)	2011 GS-15 (STEP 2) (Max)	2012 GS-11 (Min)	2012 GS-15 (Max)	5-Year Average % Raise	5-Year Cumulative Raise Estimate**	20-Year Annual Pension Benefit Estimate	20-Year Annual Pension Benefit Estimate (Max.)	25-Year Annual Pension Benefit Estimate (Min.)	25-Year Annual Pension Benefit Estimate (Max.)	30-Year Annual Pension Benefit Estimate (Min.)	30-Year Annual Pension Benefit Estimate (Max.)	Agency Automatic Contributions 1% Thrift Savings Plan 20 Year Savings Plus 4.5% Interest	Agency Automatic Contributions 1% Thrift Savings Plan 20 Year Savings Plus 4.5% Interest (Max)	Agency Automatic Contributions 1% Thrift Savings Plan 25 Year Savings Plus 4.5% Interest (Min)	Agency Automatic Contributions 1% Thrift Savings Plan 25 Year Savings Plus 4.5% Interest (Max)	Agency Automatic Contributions 1% Thrift Savings Plan 30 Year Savings Plus 4.5% Interest (Min)	Agency Automatic Contributions 1% Thrift Savings Plan 30 Year Savings Plus 4.5% Interest (Max)
Subject Area Computer Work, GS-0200 (GS-1-GS-15)	26,213	95,204	26,737	97,108	27,272	99,050	28,317	104,081	28,884	106,163	2.00%	10.00%	8,646	33,008	12,077	46,435	16,427	63,104	7,182	27,053	9,562	36,242	12,251	46,587
Physical Sciences Group (GS-1300P) (GS-5-GS-15)	26,213	95,204	26,737	97,108	27,272	99,050	28,317	104,081	28,884	106,163	2.00%	10.00%	8,646	33,008	12,077	46,435	16,427	63,104	7,182	27,053	9,562	36,242	12,251	46,587
Security Administration (GS-0080) (GS-5-GS-15)	26,213	95,204	26,737	97,108	27,272	99,050	28,317	104,081	28,884	106,163	2.00%	10.00%	8,646	33,008	12,077	46,435	16,427	63,104	7,182	27,053	9,562	36,242	12,251	46,587
Subject Matter Series (GS-5-GS-15)	26,213	95,204	26,737	97,108	27,272	99,050	28,317	104,081	28,884	106,163	2.00%	10.00%	8,646	33,008	12,077	46,435	16,427	63,104	7,182	27,053	9,562	36,242	12,251	46,587
Quality Assurance (GS-1910) (GS-5-GS-15)	26,213	95,204	26,737	97,108	27,272	99,050	28,317	104,081	28,884	106,163	2.00%	10.00%	8,646	33,008	12,077	46,435	16,427	63,104	7,182	27,053	9,562	36,242	12,251	46,587
Electronic Equipment Installation & Maint (GS-2600) (GS-5-GS-15	26,213	95,204	26,737	97,108	27,272	99,050	28,317	104,081	28,884	106,163	2.00%	10.00%	8,646	33,008	12,077	46,435	16,427	63,104	7,182	27,053	9,562	36,242	12,251	46,587
Telecommunications (GS-0391) (GS-5-GS-11)	26,213	95,204	26,737	97,108	27,272	99,050	28,317	104,081	28,884	106,163	2.00%	10.00%	8,646	33,008	12,077	46,435	16,427	63,104	7,182	27,053	9,562	36,242	12,251	46,587
Management & Program Analysis (GS-0343) (GS-5-GS-9)	26,213	39,717	26,737	40,512	27,272	41,322	28,317	45,198	28,884	46,102	2.00%	10.00%	8,646	16,082	12,077	23,077	16,427	32,156	7,182	12,682	9,562	17,298	12,251	22,594
Criminal Investigating (GS-1811) (GS-5-GS-13)	26,213	68,492	26,737	69,861	27,272	71,259	28,317	75,734	28,884	77,249	2.00%	10.00%	8,646	24,859	12,077	35,190	16,427	48,205	7,182	20,134	9,562	27,122	12,251	35,037

U.S. Federal Government Agencies Information Technology Group Jobs

Job Group	2008 GS-11 (Min)*	2008 GS-15 (Max)	2009 GS-11 (Min)	2009 GS-15 (Max)	2010 GS-11 (Min)	2010 GS-15 (Max)	2011 GS-11 (STEP 2) (Min)	2011 GS-15 (STEP 2) (Max)	2012 GS-11 (Min)	2012 GS-15 (Max)	5-Year Average % Raise	5-Year Cumulative Raise Estimate**	20-Year Annual Pension Benefit Estimate	20-Year Annual Pension Benefit Estimate (Max.)	25-Year Annual Pension Benefit Estimate (Min.)	25-Year Annual Pension Benefit Estimate (Max.)	30-Year Annual Pension Benefit Estimate (Min.)	30-Year Annual Pension Benefit Estimate (Max.)	Agency Automatic Contributions 1% Thrift Savings Plan 20 Year Savings Plus 4.5% Interest	Agency Automatic Contributions 1% Thrift Savings Plan 20 Year Savings Plus 4.5% Interest (Max)	Agency Automatic Contributions 1% Thrift Savings Plan 25 Year Savings Plus 4.5% Interest (Min)	Agency Automatic Contributions 1% Thrift Savings Plan 25 Year Savings Plus 4.5% Interest (Max)	Agency Automatic Contributions 1% Thrift Savings Plan 30 Year Savings Plus 4.5% Interest (Min)	Agency Automatic Contributions 1% Thrift Savings Plan 30 Year Savings Plus 4.5% Interest (Max)
Visual Information (GS-1084) (GS-7-GS-12)	32,470	57,597	33,119	58,749	33,782	59,923	34,957	64,172	35,656	65,455	2.00%	10.00%	10,555	21,536	14,711	30,603	19,917	42,128	8,802	17,313	11,698	23,402	14,956	30,325

Other Job Groups with IT-Computer-Technical Services Work~
(Column headers for this section: 2008 GS-9 (Min)* | 2008 GS-11 or 14 (Max) | 2009 GS-9 (Min) | 2009 GS-11 or 14 (Max) | 2010 GS-9 (Min) | 2010 GS-11 or 14 (Max) | 2011 GS-9 or 14 (STEP 2) (Min) | 2011 GS-11 or 14 (STEP 2) (Max) | 2012 GS-9 (Min) | 2012 GS-11 or14 (Max) | 5-Year Average % Raise | 5-Year Cumulative Raise Estimate** | 20-Year Annual Pension Benefit Estimate (Min.)*** | 20-Year Annual Pension Benefit Estimate (Max.) | 25-Year ... (Min.) | 25-Year ... (Max.) | 30-Year ... (Min.) | 30-Year ... (Max.) | ... TSP columns as above)

Job Group																								
Inventory Management (GS-2010) (GS-9-GS-11)	39,717	48,055	40,512	49,016	41,322	49,997	43,421	52,536	44,290	53,587	2.00%	10.00%	13,505	18,168	19,006	25,519	26,009	34,609	11,143	14,396	14,905	19,442	19,169	25,114
Librarian (GS-1410) (GS-9-GS-14)	38,175	77,793	38,175	77,793	38,175	77,793	39,448	80,386	39,448	80,386			9,739	20,738	12,524	26,636	15,823	33,247	8,780	18,442	11,199	23,584	13,724	28,889
Technical Information Services (GS-1412) (GS-9-GS-14)	38,175	77,793	38,175	77,793	38,175	77,793	39,448	80,386	39,448	80,386			9,739	20,738	12,524	26,636	15,823	33,247	8,780	18,442	11,199	23,584	13,724	28,889

Other Job Groups with IT-Computer-Technical Services Work~~
(Column headers for this section: 2008 GS-3 (Min)* | 2008 GS-7, 9, or 13 (Max) | 2009 GS-3 (Min) | 2009 GS-7, 9, or 13 (Max) | 2010 GS-3 (Min) | 2010 GS-7, 9, or 13 (Max) | 2011 GS-3 9, or 13 (STEP 2) (Min) | 2011 GS-7, 9 or 13 (STEP 2) (Max) | 2012 GS-3 (Min) | 2012 GS-7, 9, or 13 (Max) | 5-Year Average % Raise | 5-Year Cumulative Raise Estimate** | 20-Year Annual Pension Benefit Estimate (Min.)*** | 20-Year ... (Max.) | 25-Year ... (Min.) | 25-Year ... (Max.) | 30-Year ... (Min.) | 30-Year ... (Max.) | ... TSP columns as above)

Job Group																								
Computer Clerk & Assistant (GS-0335) (GS-3-GS-9)	20,565	39,135	20,822	39,625	21,082	40,120	22,015	41,894	22,290	42,418	2.00%	10.00%	7,009	14,447	9,928	20,424	13,630	27,440	5,560	11,217	7,444	15,095	9,593	19,427
Computer Operation GS-0332) (GS-3-GS-9)	20,565	39,135	20,822	39,625	21,082	40,120	22,015	41,894	22,290	42,418	2.00%	10.00%	7,009	14,447	9,928	20,424	13,630	27,440	5,560	11,217	7,444	15,095	9,593	19,427

U.S. Federal Government Agencies Information Technology Group Jobs	2008 GS-11 (Min)*	2008 GS-15 (Max)	2009 GS-11 (Min)	2009 GS-15 (Max)	2010 GS-11 (Min)	2010 GS-15 (Max)	2011 GS-11 (STEP 2) (Min)	2011 GS-15 (STEP 2) (Max)	2012 GS-11 (Min)	2012 GS-15 (Max)	5-Year Average % Raise	5-Year Cumulative Raise Estimate**	20-Year Annual Pension Benefit Estimate	20-Year Annual Pension Benefit Estimate (Max.)	25-Year Annual Pension Benefit Estimate (Min.)	25-Year Annual Pension Benefit Estimate (Max.)	30-Year Annual Pension Benefit Estimate (Min.)	30-Year Annual Pension Benefit Estimate (Max.)	Agency Automatic Contributions 1% Thrift Savings Plan 20 Year Savings Plus 4.5% Interest	Agency Automatic Contributions 1% Thrift Savings Plan 20 Year Savings Plus 4.5% Interest (Max)	Agency Automatic Contributions 1% Thrift Savings Plan 25 Year Savings Plus 4.5% Interest (Min)	Agency Automatic Contributions 1% Thrift Savings Plan 25 Year Savings Plus 4.5% Interest (Max)	Agency Automatic Contributions 1% Thrift Savings Plan 30 Year Savings Plus 4.5% Interest (Min)	Agency Automatic Contributions 1% Thrift Savings Plan 30 Year Savings Plus 4.5% Interest (Max)
Admin Work Accounting & Budget (GS-0500) (GS-2-GS-9)	18,848	39,135	19,083	39,625	19,322	40,120	20,063	41,894	20,314	42,418	2.00%	10.00%	6,320	14,447	8,913	20,424	12,209	27,440	5,043	11,217	6,735	15,095	8,660	19,427
Miscellaneous Clerk & Assistant (GS-0303) (GS-1-GS-7)	16,763	31,994	16,973	32,394	18,725	35,849	19,459	37,337	19,702	37,804	2.00%	10.00%	7,295	14,151	10,844	21,085	15,123	29,457	5,369	10,368	7,412	14,340	9,799	18,988
Secretary (GS-0318) (GS-2-GS-13)	18,848	67,488	19,083	68,332	19,322	69,186	20,063	72,245	20,314	73,148	2.00%	10.00%	6,320	23,744	8,913	33,607	12,209	45,196	5,043	18,672	6,735	25,052	8,660	32,187

Senior Executive Service (SES)*****	2008 GS-15 (Min)*	2008 GS-15 (Max)	2009 GS-15 (Min)	2009 GS-15 (Max)	2010 GS-15 (Min)	2010 GS-15 (Max)	2011 GS-15 (STEP 2) (Min)	2011 GS-15 (STEP 2) (Max)	2012 GS-15 (Min)	2012 GS-15 (Max)	5-Year Average % Raise	5-Year Cumulative Raise Estimate**	20-Year Annual Pension Benefit Estimate (Min.)***	20-Year Annual Pension Benefit Estimate (Max.)	25-Year Annual Pension Benefit Estimate (Min.)	25-Year Annual Pension Benefit Estimate (Max.)	30-Year Annual Pension Benefit Estimate (Min.)	30-Year Annual Pension Benefit Estimate (Max.)	Agency Automatic Contributions 1% Thrift Savings Plan 20 Year Savings Plus 4.5% Interest	Agency Automatic Contributions 1% Thrift Savings Plan 20 Year Savings Plus 4.5% Interest (Max)	Agency Automatic Contributions 1% Thrift Savings Plan 25 Year Savings Plus 4.5% Interest (Min)	Agency Automatic Contributions 1% Thrift Savings Plan 25 Year Savings Plus 4.5% Interest (Max)	Agency Automatic Contributions 1% Thrift Savings Plan 30 Year Savings Plus 4.5% Interest (Min)	Agency Automatic Contributions 1% Thrift Savings Plan 30 Year Savings Plus 4.5% Interest (Max)
Agencies with a Certified SES Performance Appraisal System	112,570	169,358	113,978	171,475	115,402	173,618	118,385	178,839	119,865	181,074	2.00%	10.00%	34,571	52,826	48,299	74,069	64,694	99,524	28,392	43,149	37,566	57,216	47,796	72,947
Agencies without a Certified SES Performance Appraisal System	112,570	155,824	113,978	157,772	115,402	159,744	118,385	164,791	119,865	166,850	2.00%	10.00%	34,571	48,875	48,299	68,617	64,694	92,301	28,392	39,845	37,566	52,876	47,796	67,463

CHART V: U.S. States & Major Cities
Information Technology Job Titles
Salaries, 5-Year Salary Projections & Estimated Pensions

* *Salary minimum and maximum amounts are projected estimates, based on actual base published salaries, from base year, plus the estimated raise percentage. The raise percentage used is based on a 5-year average of actual published raises for the State or City from over the most recent 5 years.
** Cumulative 5-Year Raise Estimate, is based on 5-Year Average Raise Estimate, as determined from actual published raise figures from over the most recent 5 years. Compounded 5-Year Raise Estimate (not shown) is greater than Cumulative 5-Year Raise Estimate.

***Estimated Pension at 20-Years, 25-Years, and 30-Years is based on the Pension Formula for the individual U.S. State or City. (Some U.S. States and Cities have an "undefined" Pension Benefit System based on a employee individual' contributions to a Pension Fund. Most U.S. States and Cities have "defined" pension plans.) The Pension Benefit is based on a fixed formula. The Pension Formula is commonly: Average of 3 Highest Year Salaries times Pension Percentage times Number of Years. Career Pension Benefits are paid in addition to Social Security Benefits.

Disclaimer: The Salary & Pension performance data featured is based on past performance, which is no guarantee of future results.
Current Salary & Pension may be higher or lower than the performance data quoted.

AZ-Phoenix

AZ-Phoenix	2008 (Min)	2008 (Max)	2009 (Min)	2009 (Max)	2010 (Min)	2010 (Max)	2011 (Min)	2011 (Max)	2012 (Min)	2012 (Max)	5-Year Average % Raise	5-Year Cumulative Raise Estimate**	20-Year Annual Pension Benefit Estimate (Min.)***	20-Year Annual Pension Benefit Estimate (Max.)	25-Year Annual Pension Benefit Estimate (Min.)	25-Year Annual Pension Benefit Estimate (Max.)	30-Year Annual Pension Benefit Estimate (Min.)	30-Year Annual Pension Benefit Estimate (Max.)
Information Technology Analyst/ Programmer I	51,241	76,514	52,420	78,274	53,625	80,074	54,859	81,916	56,121	83,800	2.30%	11.50%	33,947	50,690	48,649	72,643	68,381	102,107
Information Technology Analyst/ Programmer II	56,683	84,633	57,987	86,579	59,321	88,571	60,685	90,608	62,081	92,692	2.30%	11.50%	37,552	56,069	53,815	80,351	75,643	112,942
Information Technology Analyst/ Programmer III	62,647	93,428	64,088	95,577	65,562	97,775	67,070	100,024	68,613	102,324	2.30%	11.50%	41,503	61,895	59,478	88,701	83,603	124,679
Information Technology Project Manager	69,374	103,266	70,970	105,641	72,602	108,071	74,272	110,557	75,980	113,100	2.30%	11.50%	45,960	68,413	65,865	98,042	92,580	137,808
Information Technology Service Specialist	46,474	69,374	47,543	70,970	48,637	72,602	49,755	74,272	50,900	75,980	2.30%	11.50%	30,789	45,960	44,123	65,865	62,020	92,580
Information Technology Supervisor	48,782	72,813	49,904	74,488	51,052	76,201	52,226	77,954	53,427	79,747	2.30%	11.50%	32,318	48,238	46,314	69,130	65,099	97,169
Information Technology Systems Specialist	59,622	88,857	60,993	90,900	62,396	92,991	63,831	95,130	65,299	97,318	2.30%	11.50%	39,499	58,867	56,605	84,361	79,565	118,579

CA-Los Angeles

CA-Los Angeles	2008 (Min)	2008 (Max)	2009 (Min)	2009 (Max)	2010 (Min)	2010 (Max)	2011 (Min)	2011 (Max)	2012 (Min)	2012 (Max)	5-Year Average % Raise	5-Year Cumulative Raise Estimate**	20-Year Annual Pension Benefit Estimate (Min.)***	20-Year Annual Pension Benefit Estimate (Max.)	25-Year Annual Pension Benefit Estimate (Min.)	25-Year Annual Pension Benefit Estimate (Max.)	30-Year Annual Pension Benefit Estimate (Min.)	30-Year Annual Pension Benefit Estimate (Max.)
Applications Programmer	51,300	63,720	52,634	65,376	54,002	67,076	55,406	68,820	56,847	70,609	2.60%	13.00%	37,030	45,994	52,625	65,366	71,798	89,180
Database Architect	85,017	105,635	87,228	108,382	89,496	111,199	91,823	114,091	94,210	117,057	2.60%	13.00%	59,826	74,334	85,022	105,641	115,998	144,129
Programmer Analyst	58,049	97,898	59,558	100,443	61,107	103,055	62,695	105,734	64,325	108,483	2.60%	13.00%	40,848	68,889	58,052	97,904	79,202	133,572
Systems Programmer	75,764	109,635	77,734	112,486	79,755	115,410	81,829	118,411	83,956	121,490	2.60%	13.00%	53,314	77,149	75,769	109,642	103,373	149,587

State of Colorado	2008 (Min)	2008 (Max)	2009 (Min)	2009 (Max)	2010 (Min)	2010 (Max)	2011 (Min)	2011 (Max)	2012 (Min)	2012 (Max)	5-Year Average % Raise	5-Year Cumulative Raise Estimate**	20-Year Annual Pension Benefit Estimate (Min.)***	20-Year Annual Pension Benefit Estimate (Max.)	25-Year Annual Pension Benefit Estimate (Min.)	25-Year Annual Pension Benefit Estimate (Max.)	30-Year Annual Pension Benefit Estimate (Min.)	30-Year Annual Pension Benefit Estimate (Max.)
Computer Operator Intern	27,413	38,454	28,030	39,319	28,661	40,204	29,306	41,108	29,965	42,033	2.25%	11.25%	21,389	30,004	29,883	41,918	40,079	56,221
Computer Operator I	30,224	42,393	30,904	43,347	31,599	44,322	32,310	45,320	33,037	46,339	2.25%	11.25%	23,582	33,078	32,946	46,213	44,188	61,981
Computer Operator II	36,735	51,477	37,561	52,635	38,407	53,819	39,271	55,030	40,154	56,268	2.25%	11.25%	28,663	40,165	40,044	56,114	53,708	75,261
Computer Operations Supervisor I	49,218	69,003	50,326	70,556	51,458	72,144	52,616	73,767	53,800	75,427	2.25%	11.25%	38,403	53,840	53,652	75,220	71,959	100,886
Computer Operations Supervisor II	62,291	83,858	63,693	85,745	65,126	87,674	66,591	89,647	68,090	91,664	2.25%	11.25%	48,603	65,431	67,903	91,413	91,073	122,604
Computer Operations Manager	75,603	109,013	77,304	111,466	79,043	113,974	80,822	116,538	82,640	119,160	2.25%	11.25%	58,989	85,058	82,414	118,834	110,535	159,382
Computer Production Coordinator Intern	23,674	33,197	24,207	33,944	24,752	34,708	25,309	35,489	25,878	36,287	2.25%	11.25%	18,472	25,902	25,807	36,188	34,613	48,535
Computer Production Coordinator I	26,108	36,597	26,696	37,420	27,297	38,262	27,911	39,123	28,539	40,004	2.25%	11.25%	20,371	28,555	28,461	39,894	38,172	53,506
Data Entry Intern	23,674	33,197	24,207	33,944	24,752	34,708	25,309	35,489	25,878	36,287	2.25%	11.25%	18,472	25,902	25,807	36,188	34,613	48,535
Data Entry Operator I	25,406	35,631	25,977	36,433	26,562	37,252	27,160	38,091	27,771	38,948	2.25%	11.25%	19,823	27,801	27,695	38,841	37,144	52,094
Data Entry Operator II	28,806	40,386	29,454	41,295	30,117	42,224	30,794	43,174	31,487	44,145	2.25%	11.25%	22,476	31,511	31,401	44,024	42,115	59,046
Data Specialist	33,310	46,709	34,059	47,760	34,826	48,835	35,609	49,933	36,410	51,057	2.25%	11.25%	25,990	36,445	36,311	50,917	48,701	68,291
Data Supervisor	37,550	52,631	38,395	53,815	39,259	55,026	40,143	56,264	41,046	57,530	2.25%	11.25%	29,299	41,065	40,933	57,372	54,900	76,949
Information Technology Technician I	39,207	56,595	40,089	57,869	40,991	59,171	41,913	60,502	42,856	61,863	2.25%	11.25%	30,591	44,159	42,739	61,694	57,322	82,745
Information Technology Technician II	43,246	62,404	44,219	63,808	45,214	65,244	46,232	66,712	47,272	68,213	2.25%	11.25%	33,743	48,691	47,142	68,026	63,228	91,238
Information Technology Professional I	47,688	68,778	48,761	70,325	49,858	71,907	50,980	73,525	52,127	75,180	2.25%	11.25%	37,209	53,664	51,984	74,974	69,722	100,556
Information Technology Professional II	52,556	75,816	53,738	77,522	54,947	79,266	56,183	81,050	57,448	82,873	2.25%	11.25%	41,007	59,156	57,290	82,646	76,839	110,846
Information Technology Professional III	57,938	83,569	59,241	85,450	60,574	87,372	61,937	89,338	63,331	91,348	2.25%	11.25%	45,206	65,205	63,158	91,098	84,708	122,182

State of Colorado	2008 (Min)	2008 (Max)	2009 (Min)	2009 (Max)	2010 (Min)	2010 (Max)	2011 (Min)	2011 (Max)	2012 (Min)	2012 (Max)	5-Year Average % Raise	5-Year Cumulative Raise Estimate**	20-Year Annual Pension Benefit Estimate (Min.)***	20-Year Annual Pension Benefit Estimate (Max.)	25-Year Annual Pension Benefit Estimate (Min.)	25-Year Annual Pension Benefit Estimate (Max.)	30-Year Annual Pension Benefit Estimate (Min.)	30-Year Annual Pension Benefit Estimate (Max.)
Information Technology Professional IV	67,109	96,768	68,619	98,945	70,163	101,171	71,742	103,448	73,356	105,775	2.25%	11.25%	52,362	75,504	73,155	105,486	98,116	141,479
Information Technology Professional V	79,367	110,393	81,152	112,877	82,978	115,417	84,845	118,013	86,754	120,669	2.25%	11.25%	61,926	86,135	86,517	120,338	116,037	161,399
Information Technology Professional VI	83,319	110,393	85,193	112,877	87,110	115,417	89,070	118,013	91,074	120,669	2.25%	11.25%	65,010	86,135	90,825	120,338	121,815	161,399
Information Technology Professional VII	87,484	110,393	89,452	112,877	91,465	115,417	93,523	118,013	95,627	120,669	2.25%	11.25%	68,260	86,135	95,365	120,338	127,905	161,399
Applications Programmer Intern	37,375	53,898	38,216	55,111	39,076	56,351	39,955	57,619	40,854	58,915	2.25%	11.25%	29,162	42,054	40,742	58,754	54,644	78,801
Applications Programmer I	41,176	59,393	42,103	60,730	43,050	62,096	44,019	63,493	45,009	64,922	2.25%	11.25%	32,128	46,342	44,886	64,744	60,202	86,835
Applications Programmer II	45,417	65,491	46,439	66,964	47,484	68,471	48,552	70,011	49,644	71,587	2.25%	11.25%	35,437	51,099	49,509	71,391	66,401	95,750
Applications Programmer III	50,059	72,203	51,185	73,827	52,337	75,488	53,514	77,187	54,719	78,924	2.25%	11.25%	39,059	56,337	54,569	78,708	73,188	105,564
Applications Programming Manager	67,109	96,768	68,619	98,945	70,163	101,171	71,742	103,448	73,356	105,775	2.25%	11.25%	52,362	75,504	73,155	105,486	98,116	141,479

State of Florida	2008 (Min)	2008 (Max)	2009 (Min)	2009 (Max)	2010 (Min)	2010 (Max)	2011 (Min)	2011 (Max)	2012 (Min)	2012 (Max)	5-Year Average % Raise	5-Year Cumulative Raise Estimate**	20-Year Annual Pension Benefit Estimate (Min.)***	20-Year Annual Pension Benefit Estimate (Max.)	25-Year Annual Pension Benefit Estimate (Min.)	25-Year Annual Pension Benefit Estimate (Max.)	30-Year Annual Pension Benefit Estimate (Min.)	30-Year Annual Pension Benefit Estimate (Max.)
Computer & Information Sys Mgrs Exec 1	48,500	199,705	49,591	204,199	50,707	208,793	51,848	213,491	53,014	218,294	2.25%	11.25%	23,176	95,432	32,380	133,328	43,428	178,821
Computer & Information Sys Mgrs Exec 2	58,200	239,646	59,509	245,038	60,848	250,552	62,217	256,189	63,617	261,953	2.25%	11.25%	27,812	114,518	38,856	159,993	52,113	214,585
Computer & Information Sys Mgrs Level 2	27,107	111,619	27,717	114,130	28,341	116,698	28,979	119,324	29,631	122,009	2.25%	11.25%	12,954	53,339	18,098	74,519	24,273	99,946
Computer & Information Sys Mgrs Level 3	33,884	139,523	34,647	142,662	35,426	145,872	36,223	149,154	37,038	152,510	2.25%	11.25%	16,192	66,673	22,622	93,149	30,341	124,932
Computer & Information Sys Mgrs Level 4	42,354	174,400	43,307	178,324	44,282	182,336	45,278	186,439	46,297	190,634	2.25%	11.25%	20,240	83,340	28,277	116,434	37,925	156,162
Computer Programmers Level 1	22,235	57,223	22,735	58,511	23,247	59,827	23,770	61,173	24,305	62,550	2.25%	11.25%	10,625	27,345	14,845	38,203	19,910	51,239
Computer Programmers Level 2	26,419	67,989	27,013	69,518	27,621	71,083	28,242	72,682	28,878	74,317	2.25%	11.25%	12,625	32,489	17,638	45,391	23,656	60,879
Computer Programmers Level 3	31,388	80,777	32,094	82,595	32,816	84,453	33,555	86,353	34,310	88,296	2.25%	11.25%	14,999	38,601	20,955	53,929	28,106	72,330
Computer Programmers Level 4	34,212	88,045	34,982	90,026	35,769	92,052	36,574	94,123	37,397	96,241	2.25%	11.25%	16,349	42,074	22,841	58,781	30,634	78,838
Computer Support Specialists Level 1	22,235	57,223	22,735	58,511	23,247	59,827	23,770	61,173	24,305	62,550	2.25%	11.25%	10,625	27,345	14,845	38,203	19,910	51,239
Computer Support Specialists Level 2	26,419	67,989	27,013	69,518	27,621	71,083	28,242	72,682	28,878	74,317	2.25%	11.25%	12,625	32,489	17,638	45,391	23,656	60,879
Computer Support Specialists Level 4	34,212	88,045	34,982	90,026	35,769	92,052	36,574	94,123	37,397	96,241	2.25%	11.25%	16,349	42,074	22,841	58,781	30,634	78,838
Computer Systems Analysts Level 3	31,388	80,777	32,094	82,595	32,816	84,453	33,555	86,353	34,310	88,296	2.25%	11.25%	14,999	38,601	20,955	53,929	28,106	72,330

State of Florida	2008 (Min)	2008 (Max)	2009 (Min)	2009 (Max)	2010 (Min)	2010 (Max)	2011 (Min)	2011 (Max)	2012 (Min)	2012 (Max)	5-Year Average % Raise	5-Year Cumulative Raise Estimate**	20-Year Annual Pension Benefit Estimate (Min.)***	20-Year Annual Pension Benefit Estimate (Max.)	25-Year Annual Pension Benefit Estimate (Min.)	25-Year Annual Pension Benefit Estimate (Max.)	30-Year Annual Pension Benefit Estimate (Min.)	30-Year Annual Pension Benefit Estimate (Max.)
Computer Systems Analysts Level 4	34,212	88,045	34,982	90,026	35,769	92,052	36,574	94,123	37,397	96,241	2.25%	11.25%	16,349	42,074	22,841	58,781	30,634	78,838
Database Admin. Level 2	26,419	67,989	27,013	69,518	27,621	71,083	28,242	72,682	28,878	74,317	2.25%	11.25%	12,625	32,489	17,638	45,391	23,656	60,879
Database Admin. Level 4	34,212	88,045	34,982	90,026	35,769	92,052	36,574	94,123	37,397	96,241	2.25%	11.25%	16,349	42,074	22,841	58,781	30,634	78,838
Network & Computer Systems Admin Level 2	26,419	67,989	27,013	69,518	27,621	71,083	28,242	72,682	28,878	74,317	2.25%	11.25%	12,625	32,489	17,638	45,391	23,656	60,879
Network & Computer Systems Admin Level 4	34,212	88,045	34,982	90,026	35,769	92,052	36,574	94,123	37,397	96,241	2.25%	11.25%	16,349	42,074	22,841	58,781	30,634	78,838
Network System & Data Commun Analyst 1	22,235	57,223	22,735	58,511	23,247	59,827	23,770	61,173	24,305	62,550	2.25%	11.25%	10,625	27,345	14,845	38,203	19,910	51,239
Network System & Data Commun Analyst 2	26,419	67,989	27,013	69,518	27,621	71,083	28,242	72,682	28,878	74,317	2.25%	11.25%	12,625	32,489	17,638	45,391	23,656	60,879
Network System & Data Commun Analyst 3	31,388	80,777	32,094	82,595	32,816	84,453	33,555	86,353	34,310	88,296	2.25%	11.25%	14,999	38,601	20,955	53,929	28,106	72,330
Network System & Data Commun Analyst 4	34,212	88,045	34,982	90,026	35,769	92,052	36,574	94,123	37,397	96,241	2.25%	11.25%	16,349	42,074	22,841	58,781	30,634	78,838
Computer Specialists Level 1	22,235	57,223	22,735	58,511	23,247	59,827	23,770	61,173	24,305	62,550	2.25%	11.25%	10,625	27,345	14,845	38,203	19,910	51,239
Computer Specialists Level 2	26,419	67,989	27,013	69,518	27,621	71,083	28,242	72,682	28,878	74,317	2.25%	11.25%	12,625	32,489	17,638	45,391	23,656	60,879
Computer Specialists Level 3	31,388	80,777	32,094	82,595	32,816	84,453	33,555	86,353	34,310	88,296	2.25%	11.25%	14,999	38,601	20,955	53,929	28,106	72,330

State of Florida	2008 (Min)	2008 (Max)	2009 (Min)	2009 (Max)	2010 (Min)	2010 (Max)	2011 (Min)	2011 (Max)	2012 (Min)	2012 (Max)	5-Year Average % Raise	5-Year Cumulative Raise Estimate**	20-Year Annual Pension Benefit Estimate (Min.)***	20-Year Annual Pension Benefit Estimate (Max.)	25-Year Annual Pension Benefit Estimate (Min.)	25-Year Annual Pension Benefit Estimate (Max.)	30-Year Annual Pension Benefit Estimate (Min.)	30-Year Annual Pension Benefit Estimate (Max.)
Computer Specialists Level 4	34,212	88,045	34,982	90,026	35,769	92,052	36,574	94,123	37,397	96,241	2.25%	11.25%	16,349	42,074	22,841	58,781	30,634	78,838
Telecomm Equp Instal/Repr ExLline-eInstal 1	17,170	44,188	17,557	45,182	17,952	46,199	18,356	47,238	18,769	48,301	2.25%	11.25%	8,205	21,116	11,463	29,501	15,375	39,567
Telecomm Equp Instal/Repr Ex Lline Instal 3	26,419	67,989	27,013	69,518	27,621	71,083	28,242	72,682	28,878	74,317	2.25%	11.25%	12,625	32,489	17,638	45,391	23,656	60,879
Electric/Electron Repr/Comr Indust Equip 1	17,170	44,188	17,557	45,182	17,952	46,199	18,356	47,238	18,769	48,301	2.25%	11.25%	8,205	21,116	11,463	29,501	15,375	39,567
Electric/Electron Repr/Comr Indust Equip 2	22,235	57,223	22,735	58,511	23,247	59,827	23,770	61,173	24,305	62,550	2.25%	11.25%	10,625	27,345	14,845	38,203	19,910	51,239
Electric/Electron Repr/Comr Indust Equip 3	26,419	67,989	27,013	69,518	27,621	71,083	28,242	72,682	28,878	74,317	2.25%	11.25%	12,625	32,489	17,638	45,391	23,656	60,879
Electric & Electron Repairer-Powerhouse 1	17,170	44,188	17,557	45,182	17,952	46,199	18,356	47,238	18,769	48,301	2.25%	11.25%	8,205	21,116	11,463	29,501	15,375	39,567
Computer Operators Level 1	17,170	44,188	17,557	45,182	17,952	46,199	18,356	47,238	18,769	48,301	2.25%	11.25%	8,205	21,116	11,463	29,501	15,375	39,567
Data Entry Keyers Level 1	17,170	44,188	17,557	45,182	17,952	46,199	18,356	47,238	18,769	48,301	2.25%	11.25%	8,205	21,116	11,463	29,501	15,375	39,567
Data Entry Keyers Level 2	20,400	52,500	20,859	53,682	21,329	54,889	21,808	56,124	22,299	57,387	2.25%	11.25%	9,749	25,088	13,620	35,050	18,267	47,010
Word Processors & Typists Level 1	17,170	44,188	17,557	45,182	17,952	46,199	18,356	47,238	18,769	48,301	2.25%	11.25%	8,205	21,116	11,463	29,501	15,375	39,567
Word Processors & Typists Level 2	20,400	52,500	20,859	53,682	21,329	54,889	21,808	56,124	22,299	57,387	2.25%	11.25%	9,749	25,088	13,620	35,050	18,267	47,010

IL-Chicago	2008 (Min)	2008 (Max)	2009 (Min)	2009 (Max)	2010 (Min)	2010 (Max)	2011 (Min)	2011 (Max)	2012 (Min)	2012 (Max)	5-Year Average % Raise	5-Year Cumulative Raise Estimate**	20-Year Annual Pension Benefit Estimate (Min.)***	20-Year Annual Pension Benefit Estimate (Max.)	25-Year Annual Pension Benefit Estimate (Min.)	25-Year Annual Pension Benefit Estimate (Max.)	30-Year Annual Pension Benefit Estimate (Min.)	30-Year Annual Pension Benefit Estimate (Max.)
Principal Typist	60,730	83,008	62,097	84,875	63,494	86,785	64,922	88,738	66,383	90,734	2.25%	11.25%	30,962	42,319	43,257	59,124	58,016	79,298
Principal Systems Programmer	72,801	96,608	74,439	98,781	76,114	101,004	77,827	103,276	79,578	105,600	2.25%	11.25%	37,116	49,253	51,854	68,811	69,548	92,291
Senior Systems Programmer	60,730	83,008	62,097	84,875	63,494	86,785	64,922	88,738	66,383	90,734	2.25%	11.25%	30,962	42,319	43,257	59,124	58,016	79,298
Systems Programmer	49,853	69,676	50,975	71,244	52,122	72,847	53,294	74,486	54,493	76,162	2.25%	11.25%	25,416	35,523	35,509	49,629	47,625	66,562
Chief Systems Programmer	79,480	104,494	81,269	106,845	83,097	109,249	84,967	111,707	86,879	114,221	2.25%	11.25%	40,521	53,274	56,612	74,428	75,929	99,824
GIS Data Base Analyst	66,658	90,733	68,158	92,775	69,692	94,862	71,260	96,996	72,863	99,179	2.25%	11.25%	33,984	46,258	47,479	64,627	63,680	86,679
Chief Programmer/Analyst	79,480	104,494	81,269	106,845	83,097	109,249	84,967	111,707	86,879	114,221	2.25%	11.25%	40,521	53,274	56,612	74,428	75,929	99,824
Programmer/Analyst	49,853	69,676	50,975	71,244	52,122	72,847	53,294	74,486	54,493	76,162	2.25%	11.25%	25,416	35,523	35,509	49,629	47,625	66,562
Principal Programmer/Analyst	72,801	96,608	74,439	98,781	76,114	101,004	77,827	103,276	79,578	105,600	2.25%	11.25%	37,116	49,253	51,854	68,811	69,548	92,291
Senior Programmer/Analyst	60,730	83,008	62,097	84,875	63,494	86,785	64,922	88,738	66,383	90,734	2.25%	11.25%	30,962	42,319	43,257	59,124	58,016	79,298
Programmer/Analyst	49,853	69,676	50,975	71,244	52,122	72,847	53,294	74,486	54,493	76,162	2.25%	11.25%	25,416	35,523	35,509	49,629	47,625	66,562
Chief Data Base Analyst	79,480	104,494	81,269	106,845	83,097	109,249	84,967	111,707	86,879	114,221	2.25%	11.25%	40,521	53,274	56,612	74,428	75,929	99,824
Principal Data Base Analyst	72,801	96,608	74,439	98,781	76,114	101,004	77,827	103,276	79,578	105,600	2.25%	11.25%	37,116	49,253	51,854	68,811	69,548	92,291
Senior Data Base Analyst	60,730	83,008	62,097	84,875	63,494	86,785	64,922	88,738	66,383	90,734	2.25%	11.25%	30,962	42,319	43,257	59,124	58,016	79,298
Programmer	45,279	63,721	46,298	65,155	47,340	66,621	48,405	68,120	49,494	69,652	2.25%	11.25%	23,085	32,487	32,251	45,387	43,256	60,874
Data Base Analyst	49,853	69,676	50,975	71,244	52,122	72,847	53,294	74,486	54,493	76,162	2.25%	11.25%	25,416	35,523	35,509	49,629	47,625	66,562

State of Iowa	2008	2009	2010	2011	2012	5-Year Average % Raise	5-Year Cumulative Raise Estimate**	20-Year Annual Pension Benefit Estimate	25-Year Annual Pension Benefit Estimate	30-Year Annual Pension Benefit Estimate
Inform Technology Support Wkr 1	28,647	29,369	30,109	30,868	31,646	2.52%	12.60%	19,310	26,035	35,381
Inform Technology Support Wkr 2	34,451	35,319	36,209	37,121	38,057	2.52%	12.60%	23,222	31,309	42,549
Inform Technology Support Wkr 3	37,709	38,659	39,633	40,632	41,656	2.52%	12.60%	25,418	34,270	46,573
Inform Technology Support Wkr 4	40,682	41,707	42,758	43,835	44,940	2.52%	12.60%	27,422	36,971	50,245
Inform Technology Specialist 1	42,069	43,129	44,216	45,330	46,472	2.52%	12.60%	28,357	38,232	51,958
Inform Technology Specialist 2	50,838	52,120	53,433	54,780	56,160	2.52%	12.60%	34,268	46,202	62,789
Inform Technology Specialist 3	57,419	58,866	60,349	61,870	63,429	2.52%	12.60%	38,704	52,182	70,916
Inform Technology Specialist 4	68,581	70,309	72,081	73,897	75,759	2.52%	12.60%	46,228	62,326	84,702
Inform Technology Specialist 5	82,191	84,262	86,385	88,562	90,794	2.52%	12.60%	55,402	74,695	101,511
Inform Technology Supervisor 2	58,108	59,572	61,074	62,613	64,190	2.52%	12.60%	39,169	52,808	71,767
Inform Technology Enterprise Spec	110,952	113,748	116,614	119,553	122,566	2.52%	12.60%	74,789	100,832	137,033
Inform Technology Administrator 1	78,226	80,197	82,218	84,290	86,414	2.52%	12.60%	52,730	71,091	96,614
Inform Technology Administrator 2	90,387	92,665	95,000	97,394	99,848	2.52%	12.60%	60,927	82,143	111,634
Inform Technology Administrator 3	105,445	108,102	110,826	113,619	116,482	2.52%	12.60%	71,077	95,828	130,231
Inform Technology Administrator 4	111,844	114,662	117,552	120,514	123,551	2.52%	12.60%	75,390	101,643	138,134
Telecommunications Specilaist	53,303	54,646	56,023	57,435	58,882	2.52%	12.60%	35,930	48,441	65,833
Telecommunications Specilaist, Sr.	74,907	76,795	78,730	80,714	82,748	2.52%	12.60%	50,493	68,075	92,516
Telecommunications Engineer	54,733	56,112	57,526	58,976	60,462	2.52%	12.60%	36,893	49,741	67,598
Telecommunications Engineer, Sr.	72,802	74,636	76,517	78,445	80,422	2.52%	12.60%	49,073	66,162	89,915
Telecommunications Tech Enterprise Expert	88,619	90,853	93,142	95,489	97,896	2.52%	12.60%	59,735	80,537	109,451
Telecommunications Manager	73,127	74,970	76,859	78,796	80,781	2.52%	12.60%	49,292	66,457	90,317
Telecommunications Administrator	91,002	93,296	95,647	98,057	100,528	2.52%	12.60%	61,342	82,702	112,394

State of Maryland	2008 (Min)	2008 (Max)	2009 (Min)	2009 (Max)	2010 (Min)	2010 (Max)	2011 (Min)	2011 (Max)	2012 (Min)	2012 (Max)	5-Year Average % Raise	5-Year Cumulative Raise	20-Year Annual Pension Benefit Estimate (Min.)***	20-Year Annual Pension Benefit Estimate (Max.)	25-Year Annual Pension Benefit Estimate (Min.)	25-Year Annual Pension Benefit Estimate (Max.)	30-Year Annual Pension Benefit Estimate (Min.)	30-Year Annual Pension Benefit Estimate (Max.)
Computer Information Services Specialist Mgr	45,171	69,813	46,187	71,383	47,227	72,990	48,289	74,632	49,376	76,311	2.25%	11.25%	28,196	43,577	31,514	48,705	35,223	54,437
Computer Information Services Specialist Supv	42,362	65,392	43,315	66,864	44,290	68,368	45,286	69,906	46,305	71,479	2.25%	11.25%	26,442	40,818	29,554	45,621	33,032	50,990
Computer Information Services Specialist II	37,283	57,397	38,122	58,689	38,979	60,009	39,856	61,359	40,753	62,740	2.25%	11.25%	23,272	35,828	26,011	40,044	29,072	44,756
Computer Information Services Specialist I	32,846	50,414	33,585	51,549	34,340	52,709	35,113	53,894	35,903	55,107	2.25%	11.25%	20,502	31,469	22,915	35,172	25,612	39,311
Computer Network Specialist I	39,737	61,263	40,631	62,641	41,545	64,050	42,480	65,491	43,435	66,965	2.25%	11.25%	24,804	38,240	27,723	42,740	30,985	47,770
Computer Network Specialist II	42,362	65,392	43,315	66,864	44,290	68,368	45,286	69,906	46,305	71,479	2.25%	11.25%	26,442	40,818	29,554	45,621	33,032	50,990
Computer Network Specialist Trainee	37,283	57,397	38,122	58,689	38,979	60,009	39,856	61,359	40,753	62,740	2.25%	11.25%	23,272	35,828	26,011	40,044	29,072	44,756
Computer Network Specialist Supervisor	48,178	74,544	49,262	76,221	50,370	77,936	51,504	79,689	52,663	81,482	2.25%	11.25%	30,073	46,530	33,612	52,006	37,567	58,126
Computer Network Specialist Manager	51,394	79,606	52,550	81,397	53,733	83,229	54,942	85,101	56,178	87,016	2.25%	11.25%	32,080	49,690	35,855	55,538	40,075	62,073
Computer Network Specialist, Lead	45,171	69,813	46,187	71,383	47,227	72,990	48,289	74,632	49,376	76,311	2.25%	11.25%	28,196	43,577	31,514	48,705	35,223	54,437
Computer Operator Trainee	24,059	36,585	24,601	37,409	25,154	38,250	25,720	39,111	26,299	39,991	2.25%	11.25%	15,018	22,837	16,785	25,524	18,760	28,528
Computer Operator I	27,223	41,563	27,835	42,498	28,462	43,454	29,102	44,432	29,757	45,432	2.25%	11.25%	16,993	25,944	18,992	28,997	21,227	32,409
Computer Operator II	30,844	30,844	31,538	31,538	32,247	32,247	32,973	32,973	33,715	33,715	2.25%	11.25%	19,253	19,253	21,518	21,518	24,050	24,050
Computer Operator, Lead	32,846	50,414	33,585	51,549	34,340	52,709	35,113	53,894	35,903	55,107	2.25%	11.25%	20,502	31,469	22,915	35,172	25,612	39,311

State of Maryland	2008 (Min)	2008 (Max)	2009 (Min)	2009 (Max)	2010 (Min)	2010 (Max)	2011 (Min)	2011 (Max)	2012 (Min)	2012 (Max)	5-Year Average % Raise	5-Year Cumulative Raise	20-Year Annual Pension Benefit Estimate (Min.)***	20-Year Annual Pension Benefit Estimate (Max.)	25-Year Annual Pension Benefit Estimate (Min.)	25-Year Annual Pension Benefit Estimate (Max.)	30-Year Annual Pension Benefit Estimate (Min.)	30-Year Annual Pension Benefit Estimate (Max.)
Computer Operator Supervisor	34,990	53,793	35,777	55,004	36,582	56,241	37,405	57,507	38,247	58,801	2.25%	11.25%	21,841	33,578	24,411	37,529	27,284	41,946
Computer Operator Manager I	45,171	69,813	46,187	71,383	47,227	72,990	48,289	74,632	49,376	76,311	2.25%	11.25%	28,196	43,577	31,514	48,705	35,223	54,437
Computer Operator Manager II	51,394	79,606	52,550	81,397	53,733	83,229	54,942	85,101	56,178	87,016	2.25%	11.25%	32,080	49,690	35,855	55,538	40,075	62,073
Computer User Support Specialist I	27,223	41,563	27,835	42,498	28,462	43,454	29,102	44,432	29,757	45,432	2.25%	11.25%	16,993	25,944	18,992	28,997	21,227	32,409
Computer User Support Specialist II	30,844	47,262	31,538	48,326	32,247	49,413	32,973	50,525	33,715	51,661	2.25%	11.25%	19,253	29,501	21,518	32,973	24,050	36,853
Illustrator III	30,844	47,262	31,538	48,326	32,247	49,413	32,973	50,525	33,715	51,661	2.25%	11.25%	19,253	29,501	21,518	32,973	24,050	36,853
DP Technical Support Specialist Supervisor	48,178	74,544	49,262	76,221	50,370	77,936	51,504	79,689	52,663	81,482	2.25%	11.25%	30,073	46,530	33,612	52,006	37,567	58,126
Webmaster	39,737	61,263	40,631	62,641	41,545	64,050	42,480	65,491	43,435	66,965	2.25%	11.25%	24,804	38,240	27,723	42,740	30,985	47,770
Webmaster II	42,362	65,392	43,315	66,864	44,290	68,368	45,286	69,906	46,305	71,479	2.25%	11.25%	26,442	40,818	29,554	45,621	33,032	50,990
Webmaster Supervisor	48,178	74,544	49,262	76,221	50,370	77,936	51,504	79,689	52,663	81,482	2.25%	11.25%	30,073	46,530	33,612	52,006	37,567	58,126
Webmaster Trainee	37,283	57,397	38,122	58,689	38,979	60,009	39,856	61,359	40,753	62,740	2.25%	11.25%	23,272	35,828	26,011	40,044	29,072	44,756
DP Programmer Analyst Supervisor	48,178	74,544	49,262	76,221	50,370	77,936	51,504	79,689	52,663	81,482	2.25%	11.25%	30,073	46,530	33,612	52,006	37,567	58,126
DP Programmer Analyst, Lead/ Advanced	45,171	69,813	46,187	71,383	47,227	72,990	48,289	74,632	49,376	76,311	2.25%	11.25%	28,196	43,577	31,514	48,705	35,223	54,437

State of Nevada	2008 (Min)	2008 (Max)	2009 (Min)	2009 (Max)	2010 (Min)	2010 (Max)	2011 (Min)	2011 (Max)	2012 (Min)	2012 (Max)	5-Year Average % Raise	5-Year Cumulative Raise Estimate**	20-Year Annual Pension Benefit Estimate (Min.)***	20-Year Annual Pension Benefit Estimate (Max.)	25-Year Annual Pension Benefit Estimate (Min.)	25-Year Annual Pension Benefit Estimate (Max.)	30-Year Annual Pension Benefit Estimate (Min.)	30-Year Annual Pension Benefit Estimate (Max.)
Cartographic/ Graphics Tech 1	31,046	45,037	31,791	46,117	32,554	47,224	33,336	48,358	34,136	49,518	2.40%	12.00%	26,021	37,747	36,622	53,125	49,479	71,776
Cartographic/ Graphics Tech 2	33,652	49,109	34,459	50,288	35,286	51,494	36,133	52,730	37,000	53,996	2.40%	12.00%	28,205	41,161	39,695	57,928	53,631	78,266
Cartographic/ Graphics Tech 3	38,074	55,984	38,988	57,327	39,924	58,703	40,882	60,112	41,863	61,555	2.40%	12.00%	31,912	46,923	44,912	66,038	60,680	89,222
Cartographic/ Graphics Tech 4	43,154	63,975	44,189	65,510	45,250	67,083	46,336	68,693	47,448	70,341	2.40%	12.00%	36,169	53,621	50,904	75,464	68,775	101,959
Computer Info Systems Trainee	38,074	55,984	38,988	57,327	39,924	58,703	40,882	60,112	41,863	61,555	2.40%	12.00%	31,912	46,923	44,912	66,038	60,680	89,222
Computer Network Specialist 1	47,051	69,996	48,180	71,676	49,336	73,396	50,520	75,158	51,733	76,961	2.40%	12.00%	39,436	58,667	55,501	82,567	74,986	111,554
Computer Network Specialist 2	51,255	76,674	52,485	78,514	53,744	80,398	55,034	82,328	56,355	84,304	2.40%	12.00%	42,959	64,264	60,459	90,444	81,685	122,197
Computer Network Specialist 3	55,984	83,986	57,327	86,002	58,703	88,066	60,112	90,180	61,555	92,344	2.40%	12.00%	46,923	70,393	66,038	99,070	89,222	133,851
Computer Network Tech Trainee	38,074	55,984	38,988	57,327	39,924	58,703	40,882	60,112	41,863	61,555	2.40%	12.00%	31,912	46,923	44,912	66,038	60,680	89,222
Computer Network Technician 1	41,424	61,238	42,418	62,708	43,436	64,213	44,479	65,754	45,546	67,332	2.40%	12.00%	34,720	51,327	48,863	72,236	66,018	97,597
Computer Network Technician 2	45,037	66,909	46,117	68,515	47,224	70,159	48,358	71,843	49,518	73,567	2.40%	12.00%	37,747	56,080	53,125	78,925	71,776	106,634
Computer Network Technician 3	49,109	73,236	50,288	74,994	51,494	76,794	52,730	78,637	53,996	80,524	2.40%	12.00%	41,161	61,383	57,928	86,389	78,266	116,718
Computer Operations Spvr 1	43,154	63,975	44,189	65,510	45,250	67,083	46,336	68,693	47,448	70,341	2.40%	12.00%	36,169	53,621	50,904	75,464	68,775	101,959
Computer Operations Spvr 2	49,109	73,236	50,288	74,994	51,494	76,794	52,730	78,637	53,996	80,524	2.40%	12.00%	41,161	61,383	57,928	86,389	78,266	116,718
Computer Operations Spvr 3	53,575	80,221	54,861	82,146	56,178	84,117	57,526	86,136	58,907	88,204	2.40%	12.00%	44,904	67,237	63,197	94,628	85,384	127,849
Computer Operations Manager	58,523	87,927	59,928	90,038	61,366	92,199	62,839	94,411	64,347	96,677	2.40%	12.00%	49,051	73,696	69,034	103,718	93,270	140,132

State of Nevada	2008 (Min)	2008 (Max)	2009 (Min)	2009 (Max)	2010 (Min)	2010 (Max)	2011 (Min)	2011 (Max)	2012 (Min)	2012 (Max)	5-Year Average % Raise	5-Year Cumulative Raise Estimate**	20-Year Annual Pension Benefit Estimate (Min.)***	20-Year Annual Pension Benefit Estimate (Max.)	25-Year Annual Pension Benefit Estimate (Min.)	25-Year Annual Pension Benefit Estimate (Max.)	30-Year Annual Pension Benefit Estimate (Min.)	30-Year Annual Pension Benefit Estimate (Max.)
Computer Systems Programmer 1	43,154	63,975	44,189	65,510	45,250	67,083	46,336	68,693	47,448	70,341	2.40%	12.00%	36,169	53,621	50,904	75,464	68,775	101,959
Computer Systems Programmer 2	49,109	73,236	50,288	74,994	51,494	76,794	52,730	78,637	53,996	80,524	2.40%	12.00%	41,161	61,383	57,928	86,389	78,266	116,718
Computer Systems Programmer 3	53,575	80,221	54,861	82,146	56,178	84,117	57,526	86,136	58,907	88,204	2.40%	12.00%	44,904	67,237	63,197	94,628	85,384	127,849
Computer Systems Programmer 4	58,523	87,927	59,928	90,038	61,366	92,199	62,839	94,411	64,347	96,677	2.40%	12.00%	49,051	73,696	69,034	103,718	93,270	140,132
Computer Systems Tech Trainee	27,587	39,651	28,249	40,602	28,927	41,577	29,621	42,574	30,332	43,596	2.40%	12.00%	23,122	33,233	32,541	46,771	43,966	63,192
Computer Systems Technician 1	29,842	43,154	30,558	44,189	31,292	45,250	32,043	46,336	32,812	47,448	2.40%	12.00%	25,012	36,169	35,201	50,904	47,560	68,775
Computer Systems Technician 2	32,294	47,051	33,069	48,180	33,863	49,336	34,676	50,520	35,508	51,733	2.40%	12.00%	27,067	39,436	38,094	55,501	51,468	74,986
Computer Systems Technician 3	35,075	51,255	35,916	52,485	36,778	53,744	37,661	55,034	38,565	56,355	2.40%	12.00%	29,398	42,959	41,374	60,459	55,899	81,685
Computer Systems Technician 4	38,074	55,984	38,988	57,327	39,924	58,703	40,882	60,112	41,863	61,555	2.40%	12.00%	31,912	46,923	44,912	66,038	60,680	89,222
Database Admin. 1	43,154	63,975	44,189	65,510	45,250	67,083	46,336	68,693	47,448	70,341	2.40%	12.00%	36,169	53,621	50,904	75,464	68,775	101,959
Database Admin. 2	49,109	73,236	50,288	74,994	51,494	76,794	52,730	78,637	53,996	80,524	2.40%	12.00%	41,161	61,383	57,928	86,389	78,266	116,718
Database Admin. 3	53,575	80,221	54,861	82,146	56,178	84,117	57,526	86,136	58,907	88,204	2.40%	12.00%	44,904	67,237	63,197	94,628	85,384	127,849
Database Admin. 4	58,523	87,927	59,928	90,038	61,366	92,199	62,839	94,411	64,347	96,677	2.40%	12.00%	49,051	73,696	69,034	103,718	93,270	140,132
Data Processing Manager 1	61,238	92,109	62,708	94,320	64,213	96,584	65,754	98,902	67,332	101,275	2.40%	12.00%	51,327	77,201	72,236	108,651	97,597	146,797
Data Processing Manager 2	66,909	101,064	68,515	103,490	70,159	105,973	71,843	108,517	73,567	111,121	2.40%	12.00%	56,080	84,707	78,925	119,214	106,634	161,068
Digital Telecommunications Spc 1	41,424	61,238	42,418	62,708	43,436	64,213	44,479	65,754	45,546	67,332	2.40%	12.00%	34,720	51,327	48,863	72,236	66,018	97,597

State of Nevada	2008 (Min)	2008 (Max)	2009 (Min)	2009 (Max)	2010 (Min)	2010 (Max)	2011 (Min)	2011 (Max)	2012 (Min)	2012 (Max)	5-Year Average % Raise	5-Year Cumulative Raise Estimate**	20-Year Annual Pension Benefit Estimate (Min.)***	20-Year Annual Pension Benefit Estimate (Max.)	25-Year Annual Pension Benefit Estimate (Min.)	25-Year Annual Pension Benefit Estimate (Max.)	30-Year Annual Pension Benefit Estimate (Min.)	30-Year Annual Pension Benefit Estimate (Max.)
Digital Telecommunications Spc 2	45,037	66,909	46,117	68,515	47,224	70,159	48,358	71,843	49,518	73,567	2.40%	12.00%	37,747	56,080	53,125	78,925	71,776	106,634
Digital Telecommunications Spvr	49,109	73,236	50,288	74,994	51,494	76,794	52,730	78,637	53,996	80,524	2.40%	12.00%	41,161	61,383	57,928	86,389	78,266	116,718
Graphic Designer	35,075	51,255	35,916	52,485	36,778	53,744	37,661	55,034	38,565	56,355	2.40%	12.00%	29,398	42,959	41,374	60,459	55,899	81,685
Senior Graphic Designer	38,074	55,984	38,988	57,327	39,924	58,703	40,882	60,112	41,863	61,555	2.40%	12.00%	31,912	46,923	44,912	66,038	60,680	89,222
Information Systems Manager 1	58,523	87,927	59,928	90,038	61,366	92,199	62,839	94,411	64,347	96,677	2.40%	12.00%	49,051	73,696	69,034	103,718	93,270	140,132
Information Systems Manager 2	63,975	96,466	65,510	98,781	67,083	101,152	68,693	103,580	70,341	106,066	2.40%	12.00%	53,621	80,853	75,464	113,791	101,959	153,740
Information Systems Manager 3	66,909	101,064	68,515	103,490	70,159	105,973	71,843	108,517	73,567	111,121	2.40%	12.00%	56,080	84,707	78,925	119,214	106,634	161,068
Information Systems-Spec 1	43,154	63,975	44,189	65,510	45,250	67,083	46,336	68,693	47,448	70,341	2.40%	12.00%	36,169	53,621	50,904	75,464	68,775	101,959
Information Systems-Spec 2	49,109	73,236	50,288	74,994	51,494	76,794	52,730	78,637	53,996	80,524	2.40%	12.00%	41,161	61,383	57,928	86,389	78,266	116,718
Information Systems-Spec 3	53,575	80,221	54,861	82,146	56,178	84,117	57,526	86,136	58,907	88,204	2.40%	12.00%	44,904	67,237	63,197	94,628	85,384	127,849
Information Systems Spec 4	58,523	87,927	59,928	90,038	61,366	92,199	62,839	94,411	64,347	96,677	2.40%	12.00%	49,051	73,696	69,034	103,718	93,270	140,132
Master information Specialist 1	58,523	87,927	59,928	90,038	61,366	92,199	62,839	94,411	64,347	96,677	2.40%	12.00%	49,051	73,696	69,034	103,718	93,270	140,132
Master information Specialist 2	63,975	96,466	65,510	98,781	67,083	101,152	68,693	103,580	70,341	106,066	2.40%	12.00%	53,621	80,853	75,464	113,791	101,959	153,740
Telecommunications Coord 1	45,037	66,909	46,117	68,515	47,224	70,159	48,358	71,843	49,518	73,567	2.40%	12.00%	37,747	56,080	53,125	78,925	71,776	106,634
Telecommunications Coord 2	51,255	76,674	52,485	78,514	53,744	80,398	55,034	82,328	56,355	84,304	2.40%	12.00%	42,959	64,264	60,459	90,444	81,685	122,197

State of New Jersey	2008 (Min)	2008 (Max)	2009 (Min)	2009 (Max)	2010 (Min)	2010 (Max)	2011 (Min)	2011 (Max)	2012 (Min)	2012 (Max)	5-Year Average % Raise	5-Year Cumulative Raise Estimate**	20-Year Annual Pension Benefit Estimate (Min.)***	20-Year Annual Pension Benefit Estimate (Max.)	25-Year Annual Pension Benefit Estimate (Min.)	25-Year Annual Pension Benefit Estimate (Max.)	30-Year Annual Pension Benefit Estimate (Min.)	30-Year Annual Pension Benefit Estimate (Max.)
Com-munications Systems Technician	44,324	60,755	45,321	62,122	46,341	63,520	47,383	64,949	48,450	66,410	2.25%	11.25%	27,667	37,923	30,923	42,386	34,562	47,374
Computer Operator 1	38,678	52,840	39,548	54,029	40,438	55,245	41,348	56,488	42,278	57,759	2.25%	11.25%	24,143	32,983	26,984	36,865	30,159	41,203
Computer Operator 2	33,853	46,096	34,615	47,133	35,394	48,194	36,190	49,278	37,004	50,387	2.25%	11.25%	21,131	28,773	23,618	32,159	26,397	35,944
Computer Operator 3	31,011	42,106	31,708	43,054	32,422	44,022	33,151	45,013	33,897	46,026	2.25%	11.25%	19,357	26,283	21,635	29,376	24,181	32,833
Computer Operator Assistant	27,236	36,811	27,849	37,639	28,476	38,486	29,117	39,352	29,772	40,238	2.25%	11.25%	17,001	22,978	19,002	25,682	21,238	28,704
Data Base Analyst 1	61,048	84,171	62,422	86,065	63,826	88,001	65,262	89,981	66,731	92,006	2.25%	11.25%	38,106	52,540	42,591	58,723	47,603	65,633
Data Base Analyst 2	55,673	76,649	56,926	78,373	58,206	80,137	59,516	81,940	60,855	83,783	2.25%	11.25%	34,751	47,844	38,841	53,475	43,411	59,767
Data Entry Machine Operator	22,982	30,886	23,499	31,581	24,028	32,292	24,568	33,018	25,121	33,761	2.25%	11.25%	14,345	19,279	16,034	21,548	17,920	24,084
Data Processing Analyst 1	61,048	84,171	62,422	86,065	63,826	88,001	65,262	89,981	66,731	92,006	2.25%	11.25%	38,106	52,540	42,591	58,723	47,603	65,633
Data Processing Analyst 2	61,048	84,171	62,422	86,065	63,826	88,001	65,262	89,981	66,731	92,006	2.25%	11.25%	38,106	52,540	42,591	58,723	47,603	65,633
Data Processing Programmer 1	61,048	84,171	62,422	86,065	63,826	88,001	65,262	89,981	66,731	92,006	2.25%	11.25%	38,106	52,540	42,591	58,723	47,603	65,633
Data Processing Programmer 2	55,673	76,649	56,926	78,373	58,206	80,137	59,516	81,940	60,855	83,783	2.25%	11.25%	34,751	47,844	38,841	53,475	43,411	59,767
Data Processing Programmer 3	46,378	63,632	47,421	65,064	48,488	66,528	49,579	68,025	50,695	69,555	2.25%	11.25%	28,949	39,720	32,356	44,394	36,163	49,618
Data Processing Programmer Technician	29,689	40,261	30,357	41,167	31,040	42,094	31,739	43,041	32,453	44,009	2.25%	11.25%	18,532	25,131	20,713	28,089	23,150	31,394
Data Processing Systems Programmer 1	61,048	84,171	62,422	86,065	63,826	88,001	65,262	89,981	66,731	92,006	2.25%	11.25%	38,106	52,540	42,591	58,723	47,603	65,633

State of New Jersey	2008 (Min)	2008 (Max)	2009 (Min)	2009 (Max)	2010 (Min)	2010 (Max)	2011 (Min)	2011 (Max)	2012 (Min)	2012 (Max)	5-Year Average % Raise	5-Year Cumulative Raise Estimate**	20-Year Annual Pension Benefit Estimate (Min.)***	20-Year Annual Pension Benefit Estimate (Max.)	25-Year Annual Pension Benefit Estimate (Min.)	25-Year Annual Pension Benefit Estimate (Max.)	30-Year Annual Pension Benefit Estimate (Min.)	30-Year Annual Pension Benefit Estimate (Max.)
Data Processing Systems Programmer 2	53,176	73,153	54,372	74,799	55,596	76,482	56,847	78,202	58,126	79,962	2.25%	11.25%	33,193	45,662	37,099	51,036	41,464	57,041
Graphic Artist	35,384	48,250	36,180	49,335	36,994	50,445	37,826	51,580	38,677	52,741	2.25%	11.25%	22,087	30,118	24,686	33,662	27,591	37,623
Graphic Artist	36,992	50,481	37,824	51,617	38,675	52,778	39,545	53,966	40,435	55,180	2.25%	11.25%	23,090	31,510	25,808	35,218	28,845	39,363
Graphic Artist	40,448	55,334	41,358	56,579	42,289	57,852	43,240	59,154	44,213	60,485	2.25%	11.25%	25,248	34,540	28,219	38,604	31,540	43,147
Head Data Entry Machine Operator	37,042	50,551	37,875	51,688	38,727	52,851	39,599	54,040	40,490	55,256	2.25%	11.25%	23,122	31,554	25,842	35,267	28,884	39,417
Management Information Systems Coordinator	67,212	94,105	68,725	96,222	70,271	98,387	71,852	100,601	73,469	102,864	2.25%	11.25%	41,954	58,741	46,891	65,653	52,409	73,379
Management Information Systems Specialist 2	66,972	92,467	68,479	94,548	70,020	96,675	71,595	98,850	73,206	101,075	2.25%	11.25%	41,804	57,719	46,724	64,511	52,222	72,102
Management Information Systems Specialist 3	61,048	84,171	62,422	86,065	63,826	88,001	65,262	89,981	66,731	92,006	2.25%	11.25%	38,106	52,540	42,591	58,723	47,603	65,633
Network Admin. 1	61,048	84,171	62,422	86,065	63,826	88,001	65,262	89,981	66,731	92,006	2.25%	11.25%	38,106	52,540	42,591	58,723	47,603	65,633
Network Admin. 2	61,048	84,171	62,422	86,065	63,826	88,001	65,262	89,981	66,731	92,006	2.25%	11.25%	38,106	52,540	42,591	58,723	47,603	65,633
Principal Technician, Management Information Systems	44,324	60,755	45,321	62,122	46,341	63,520	47,383	64,949	48,450	66,410	2.25%	11.25%	27,667	37,923	30,923	42,386	34,562	47,374
Principal Data Entry Machine Operator	32,441	44,102	33,171	45,094	33,917	46,109	34,680	47,146	35,460	48,207	2.25%	11.25%	20,250	27,529	22,633	30,768	25,296	34,389
Principal Data Entry Machine Operator (Terminal)	32,441	44,102	33,171	45,094	33,917	46,109	34,680	47,146	35,460	48,207	2.25%	11.25%	20,250	27,529	22,633	30,768	25,296	34,389
Senior Data Entry Machine Operator	25,715	35,222	26,294	36,014	26,885	36,825	27,490	37,653	28,109	38,500	2.25%	11.25%	16,051	21,986	17,940	24,573	20,052	27,464
Senior Data Entry Machine Operator (Terminal)	26,096	35,222	26,683	36,014	27,283	36,825	27,897	37,653	28,525	38,500	2.25%	11.25%	16,289	21,986	18,206	24,573	20,348	27,464

State of New Jersey	2008 (Min)	2008 (Max)	2009 (Min)	2009 (Max)	2010 (Min)	2010 (Max)	2011 (Min)	2011 (Max)	2012 (Min)	2012 (Max)	5-Year Average % Raise	5-Year Cumulative Raise Estimate**	20-Year Annual Pension Benefit Estimate (Min.)***	20-Year Annual Pension Benefit Estimate (Max.)	25-Year Annual Pension Benefit Estimate (Min.)	25-Year Annual Pension Benefit Estimate (Max.)	30-Year Annual Pension Benefit Estimate (Min.)	30-Year Annual Pension Benefit Estimate (Max.)
Senior Technician, Management Information Systems	37,042	50,551	37,875	51,688	38,727	52,851	39,599	54,040	40,490	55,256	2.25%	11.25%	23,122	31,554	25,842	35,267	28,884	39,417
Software Development Specialist 1	42,367	58,023	43,320	59,329	44,295	60,664	45,291	62,029	46,310	63,424	2.25%	11.25%	26,445	36,218	29,557	40,481	33,036	45,244
Software Development Specialist 2	53,176	73,153	54,372	74,799	55,596	76,482	56,847	78,202	58,126	79,962	2.25%	11.25%	33,193	45,662	37,099	51,036	41,464	57,041
Software Development Specialist 3	61,048	84,171	62,422	86,065	63,826	88,001	65,262	89,981	66,731	92,006	2.25%	11.25%	38,106	52,540	42,591	58,723	47,603	65,633
Software Development Specialist 4	66,972	92,467	68,479	94,548	70,020	96,675	71,595	98,850	73,206	101,075	2.25%	11.25%	41,804	57,719	46,724	64,511	52,222	72,102
Software Development Specialist Assistant	35,384	48,250	36,180	49,335	36,994	50,445	37,826	51,580	38,677	52,741	2.25%	11.25%	22,087	30,118	24,686	33,662	27,591	37,623
Supervising Computer Operator	48,534	66,638	49,627	68,138	50,743	69,671	51,885	71,238	53,052	72,841	2.25%	11.25%	30,295	41,596	33,861	46,491	37,845	51,962
Supervisor, Data Processing Machine Operations 2	38,730	52,914	39,602	54,104	40,493	55,321	41,404	56,566	42,335	57,839	2.25%	11.25%	24,176	33,029	27,021	36,916	30,200	41,260
Supervisor, Data Processing Technical Support	61,048	84,171	62,422	86,065	63,826	88,001	65,262	89,981	66,731	92,006	2.25%	11.25%	38,106	52,540	42,591	58,723	47,603	65,633
Technical Support Specialist I	53,176	73,153	54,372	74,799	55,596	76,482	56,847	78,202	58,126	79,962	2.25%	11.25%	33,193	45,662	37,099	51,036	41,464	57,041
Technical Support Specialist 2	44,324	60,755	45,321	62,122	46,341	63,520	47,383	64,949	48,450	66,410	2.25%	11.25%	27,667	37,923	30,923	42,386	34,562	47,374
Telecommunications Systems Analyst 1	66,972	92,467	68,479	94,548	70,020	96,675	71,595	98,850	73,206	101,075	2.25%	11.25%	41,804	57,719	46,724	64,511	52,222	72,102
Telecommunications Systems Analyst 2	58,295	80,319	59,607	82,126	60,948	83,974	62,319	85,864	63,721	87,796	2.25%	11.25%	36,388	50,136	40,670	56,035	45,456	62,630

NY-NYC	2008 (Min)*	2008 (Max)	2009 (Min)	2009 (Max)	2010 (Min)	2010 (Max)	2011 (Min)	2011 (Max)	2012 (Min)	2012 (Max)	5-Year Average % Raise	5-Year	20-Year Annual Pension Benefit Estimate (Min.)***	20-Year Annual Pension Benefit Estimate (Max.)	25-Year Annual Pension Benefit Estimate (Min.)	25-Year Annual Pension Benefit Estimate (Max.)	30-Year Annual Pension Benefit Estimate (Min.)	30-Year Annual Pension Benefit Estimate (Max.)
Computer Aide Level I	35,215	39,637	36,061	40,589	36,926	41,563	37,812	42,560	38,720	43,582	2.40%	12.00%	18,351	20,655	25,826	29,069	34,893	39,275
Computer Aide Level II	38,146	49,220	39,062	50,401	39,999	51,611	40,959	52,850	41,942	54,118	2.40%	12.00%	19,878	25,649	27,976	36,097	37,797	48,770
Computer Associate Operations Level I	44,013	55,768	45,069	57,106	46,151	58,476	47,259	59,880	48,393	61,317	2.40%	12.00%	22,935	29,060	32,278	40,899	43,610	55,257
Computer Associate Operations Level II	52,809	68,421	54,077	70,063	55,375	71,744	56,704	73,466	58,065	75,229	2.40%	12.00%	27,519	35,654	38,729	50,178	52,326	67,795
Computer Associate Operations Level III	63,022	83,751	64,534	85,761	66,083	87,819	67,669	89,927	69,293	92,085	2.40%	12.00%	32,840	43,642	46,219	61,421	62,445	82,985
Computer Specialist Operations	65,829	89,351	67,408	91,496	69,026	93,692	70,683	95,940	72,379	98,243	2.40%	12.00%	34,303	46,561	48,277	65,528	65,227	88,534
Computer Programmer Analyst Trainee	35,242	35,242	36,087	36,087	36,954	36,954	37,840	37,840	38,749	38,749	2.40%	12.00%	18,364	18,364	25,845	25,845	34,919	34,919
Computer Programmer Analyst Level I	44,013	52,842	45,069	54,110	46,151	55,409	47,259	56,739	48,393	58,100	2.40%	12.00%	22,935	27,536	32,278	38,753	43,610	52,359
Computer Programmer Analyst Level II	51,346	62,557	52,578	64,058	53,840	65,596	55,132	67,170	56,455	68,782	2.40%	12.00%	26,756	32,598	37,656	45,878	50,876	61,985
Computer Associate Software Level I	57,211	68,969	58,584	70,624	59,991	72,319	61,430	74,055	62,905	75,832	2.40%	12.00%	29,813	35,940	41,958	50,580	56,688	68,338
Computer Associate Software Level II	61,603	74,557	63,081	76,346	64,595	78,179	66,146	80,055	67,733	81,976	2.40%	12.00%	32,101	38,851	45,178	54,679	61,039	73,875
Computer Associate Software Level III	65,792	83,751	67,371	85,761	68,988	87,819	70,644	89,927	72,339	92,085	2.40%	12.00%	34,284	43,642	48,250	61,421	65,190	82,985
Computer Specialist Software Level I	70,402	76,300	72,092	78,131	73,822	80,006	75,594	81,926	77,408	83,892	2.40%	12.00%	36,687	39,760	51,632	55,957	69,759	75,602
Computer Specialist Software Level II	73,394	82,164	75,156	84,136	76,959	86,156	78,806	88,223	80,698	90,341	2.40%	12.00%	38,245	42,816	53,826	60,258	72,723	81,413

NY-NYC	2008 (Min)*	2008 (Max)	2009 (Min)	2009 (Max)	2010 (Min)	2010 (Max)	2011 (Min)	2011 (Max)	2012 (Min)	2012 (Max)	5-Year Average % Raise	5-Year	20-Year Annual Pension Benefit Estimate (Min.)***	20-Year Annual Pension Benefit Estimate (Max.)	25-Year Annual Pension Benefit Estimate (Min.)	25-Year Annual Pension Benefit Estimate (Max.)	30-Year Annual Pension Benefit Estimate (Min.)	30-Year Annual Pension Benefit Estimate (Max.)
Computer Specialist Software Level III	79,223	89,351	81,124	91,496	83,071	93,692	85,065	95,940	87,107	98,243	2.40%	12.00%	41,283	46,561	58,101	65,528	78,499	88,534
Computer Specialist Software Level IV	84,964	102,306	87,003	104,762	89,091	107,276	91,229	109,851	93,419	112,487	2.40%	12.00%	44,275	53,312	62,311	75,029	84,187	101,371
	37,279	56,354	38,174	57,706	39,090	59,091	40,028	60,509	40,989	61,962	2.40%	12.00%	19,426	29,366	27,340	41,329	36,938	55,838
	52,018	61,992	53,266	63,480	54,545	65,003	55,854	66,563	57,194	68,161	2.40%	12.00%	27,106	32,304	38,149	45,464	51,542	61,425
	55,904	67,625	57,246	69,248	58,619	70,910	60,026	72,612	61,467	74,354	2.40%	12.00%	29,131	35,239	40,999	49,595	55,393	67,006
	62,424	84,727	63,922	86,761	65,456	88,843	67,027	90,975	68,636	93,158	2.40%	12.00%	32,529	44,151	45,780	62,137	61,853	83,952
Computer Service Technician Level I	35,215	39,637	36,061	40,589	36,926	41,563	37,812	42,560	38,720	43,582	2.40%	12.00%	18,351	20,655	25,826	29,069	34,893	39,275
Computer Service Technician Level II	38,146	49,220	39,062	50,401	39,999	51,611	40,959	52,850	41,942	54,118	2.40%	12.00%	19,878	25,649	27,976	36,097	37,797	48,770
Supvr. Computer Service Technician	52,809	68,421	54,077	70,063	55,375	71,744	56,704	73,466	58,065	75,229	2.40%	12.00%	27,519	35,654	38,729	50,178	52,326	67,795
Assistant Systems Analyst (EDP)	28,262	52,333	28,941	53,589	29,635	54,876	30,346	56,193	31,075	57,541	2.40%	12.00%	14,727	27,271	20,727	38,380	28,004	51,855
Systems Analyst (EDP)	30,584	56,168	31,318	57,516	32,070	58,896	32,839	60,310	33,627	61,757	2.40%	12.00%	15,937	29,269	22,430	41,192	30,304	55,654
Senior Systems Analyst (EDP)	33,829	63,189	34,641	64,706	35,472	66,259	36,324	67,849	37,196	69,477	2.40%	12.00%	17,628	32,928	24,810	46,342	33,520	62,611
Systems Administrator (CFB) Level 1	29,910	44,892	30,627	45,969	31,363	47,072	32,115	48,202	32,886	49,359	2.40%	12.00%	15,586	23,393	21,935	32,923	29,636	44,481
Systems Administrator (CFB) Level 2	38,696	64,480	39,624	66,028	40,575	67,612	41,549	69,235	42,546	70,897	2.40%	12.00%	20,164	33,600	28,379	47,288	38,342	63,890
Systems Administrator (CFB) Level 3	47,201	84,543	48,333	86,572	49,493	88,649	50,681	90,777	51,898	92,955	2.40%	12.00%	24,596	44,055	34,616	62,002	46,769	83,769
Certified Local Area Network Administrator Level 1	70,402	83,167	72,092	85,163	73,822	87,207	75,594	89,300	77,408	91,443	2.40%	12.00%	36,687	43,338	51,632	60,993	69,759	82,406
Certified Local Area Network Administrator Level 2	73,342	89,557	75,102	91,706	76,904	93,907	78,750	96,161	80,640	98,469	2.40%	12.00%	38,218	46,668	53,787	65,679	72,671	88,738

NY-NYC	2008 (Min)*	2008 (Max)	2009 (Min)	2009 (Max)	2010 (Min)	2010 (Max)	2011 (Min)	2011 (Max)	2012 (Min)	2012 (Max)	5-Year Average % Raise	5-Year	20-Year Annual Pension Benefit Estimate (Min.)***	20-Year Annual Pension Benefit Estimate (Max.)	25-Year Annual Pension Benefit Estimate (Min.)	25-Year Annual Pension Benefit Estimate (Max.)	30-Year Annual Pension Benefit Estimate (Min.)	30-Year Annual Pension Benefit Estimate (Max.)
Certified Local Area Network Administrator Level 3	79,202	97,393	81,103	99,730	83,049	102,124	85,043	104,575	87,084	107,085	2.40%	12.00%	41,272	50,751	58,085	71,426	78,478	96,502
Certified Local Area Network Administrator Level 4	84,964	111,514	87,003	114,190	89,091	116,931	91,229	119,737	93,419	122,611	2.40%	12.00%	44,275	58,110	62,311	81,782	84,187	110,494
Certified Wide Area Network Administrator Level 1	70,402	83,167	72,092	85,163	73,822	87,207	75,594	89,300	77,408	91,443	2.40%	12.00%	36,687	43,338	51,632	60,993	69,759	82,406
Certified Wide Area Network Administrator Level 2	73,342	89,557	75,102	91,706	76,904	93,907	78,750	96,161	80,640	98,469	2.40%	12.00%	38,218	46,668	53,787	65,679	72,671	88,738
Certified Wide Area Network Administrator Level 3	79,202	97,393	81,103	99,730	83,049	102,124	85,043	104,575	87,084	107,085	2.40%	12.00%	41,272	50,751	58,085	71,426	78,478	96,502
Certified Wide Area Network Administrator Level 4	84,964	111,514	87,003	114,190	89,091	116,931	91,229	119,737	93,419	122,611	2.40%	12.00%	44,275	58,110	62,311	81,782	84,187	110,494
Certified Applications Developer Level 1	70,402	83,167	72,092	85,163	73,822	87,207	75,594	89,300	77,408	91,443	2.40%	12.00%	36,687	43,338	51,632	60,993	69,759	82,406
Certified Applications Developer Level 2	73,342	89,557	75,102	91,706	76,904	93,907	78,750	96,161	80,640	98,469	2.40%	12.00%	38,218	46,668	53,787	65,679	72,671	88,738
Certified Applications Developer Level 3	79,202	97,393	81,103	99,730	83,049	102,124	85,043	104,575	87,084	107,085	2.40%	12.00%	41,272	50,751	58,085	71,426	78,478	96,502
Certified Applications Developer Level 4	84,964	111,514	87,003	114,190	89,091	116,931	91,229	119,737	93,419	122,611	2.40%	12.00%	44,275	58,110	62,311	81,782	84,187	110,494
Certified Database Administrator Level 1	70,402	83,167	72,092	85,163	73,822	87,207	75,594	89,300	77,408	91,443	2.40%	12.00%	36,687	43,338	51,632	60,993	69,759	82,406
Certified Database Administrator Level 2	73,342	89,557	75,102	91,706	76,904	93,907	78,750	96,161	80,640	98,469	2.40%	12.00%	38,218	46,668	53,787	65,679	72,671	88,738

State of New York	2007 (Min)*	2007 (Max)	2008 (Min)	2008 (Max)	2009 (Min)	2009 (Max)	2010 (Min)	2010 (Max)	2011 (Min)	2011 (Max)	5-Year Average % Raise	5-Year Cumulative Raise Estimate**	20-Year Annual Pension Benefit Estimate (Min.)***	20-Year Annual Pension Benefit Estimate (Max.)	25-Year Annual Pension Benefit Estimate (Min.)	25-Year Annual Pension Benefit Estimate (Max.)	30-Year Annual Pension Benefit Estimate (Min.)	30-Year Annual Pension Benefit Estimate (Max.)
Chief of Data Processing Services	76,142	96,429	77,977	98,753	79,856	101,133	81,780	103,570	83,751	106,066	2.41%	12.05%	36,568	46,311	51,490	65,209	69,600	88,145
Chief of Data Processing Technical Services	76,142	96,429	77,977	98,753	79,856	101,133	81,780	103,570	83,751	106,066	2.41%	12.05%	36,568	46,311	51,490	65,209	69,600	88,145
Computer Systems Programmer 1	57,087	70,292	58,463	71,987	59,872	73,721	61,315	75,498	62,793	77,318	2.41%	12.05%	27,417	33,759	38,604	47,534	52,183	64,254
Computer Systems Programmer 2	63,534	77,833	65,065	79,709	66,633	81,630	68,239	83,597	69,884	85,612	2.41%	12.05%	30,513	37,380	42,964	52,634	58,076	71,147
Data Base Programmer Analyst 1	57,087	70,292	58,463	71,987	59,872	73,721	61,315	75,498	62,793	77,318	2.41%	12.05%	27,417	33,759	38,604	47,534	52,183	64,254
Data Base Programmer Analyst 2	63,534	77,833	65,065	79,709	66,633	81,630	68,239	83,597	69,884	85,612	2.41%	12.05%	30,513	37,380	42,964	52,634	58,076	71,147
Data Communications Specialist 1	57,087	70,292	58,463	71,987	59,872	73,721	61,315	75,498	62,793	77,318	2.41%	12.05%	27,417	33,759	38,604	47,534	52,183	64,254
Data Communications Specialist 2	63,534	77,833	65,065	79,709	66,633	81,630	68,239	83,597	69,884	85,612	2.41%	12.05%	30,513	37,380	42,964	52,634	58,076	71,147
Data Machine Operator	23,400	30,707	23,964	31,447	24,542	32,205	25,133	32,981	25,739	33,776	2.41%	12.05%	11,238	14,747	15,824	20,765	21,390	28,069
Information Technology Specialist 1 (Programming)	35,108	44,833	35,954	45,914	36,821	47,020	37,708	48,154	38,617	49,314	2.41%	12.05%	16,861	21,532	23,741	30,318	32,092	40,982
Information Technology Specialist 2 (Programming)	43,914	54,656	44,972	55,973	46,056	57,322	47,166	58,704	48,302	60,119	2.41%	12.05%	21,090	26,249	29,696	36,960	40,141	49,961
Information Technology Specialist 1 (Database)	35,108	44,833	35,954	45,914	36,821	47,020	37,708	48,154	38,617	49,314	2.41%	12.05%	16,861	21,532	23,741	30,318	32,092	40,982
Information Technology Specialist 2 (Database)	43,914	54,656	44,972	55,973	46,056	57,322	47,166	58,704	48,302	60,119	2.41%	12.05%	21,090	26,249	29,696	36,960	40,141	49,961
Manager Data Processing Services	70,587	86,253	72,288	88,332	74,030	90,460	75,815	92,640	77,642	94,873	2.41%	12.05%	33,900	41,424	47,734	58,327	64,523	78,843

State of New York	2007 (Min)*	2007 (Max)	2008 (Min)	2008 (Max)	2009 (Min)	2009 (Max)	2010 (Min)	2010 (Max)	2011 (Min)	2011 (Max)	5-Year Average % Raise	5-Year Cumulative Raise Estimate**	20-Year Annual Pension Benefit Estimate (Min.)***	20-Year Annual Pension Benefit Estimate (Max.)	25-Year Annual Pension Benefit Estimate (Min.)	25-Year Annual Pension Benefit Estimate (Max.)	30-Year Annual Pension Benefit Estimate (Min.)	30-Year Annual Pension Benefit Estimate (Max.)
Manager Data Processing Technical Services	70,587	86,253	72,288	88,332	74,030	90,460	75,815	92,640	77,642	94,873	2.41%	12.05%	33,900	41,424	47,734	58,327	64,523	78,843
Manager Data Processing Technical Services (Database)	70,587	86,253	72,288	88,332	74,030	90,460	75,815	92,640	77,642	94,873	2.41%	12.05%	33,900	41,424	47,734	58,327	64,523	78,843
Manager Data Processing Technical Services (Data Comm)	70,587	86,253	72,288	88,332	74,030	90,460	75,815	92,640	77,642	94,873	2.41%	12.05%	33,900	41,424	47,734	58,327	64,523	78,843
Manager Data Processing	70,587	86,253	72,288	88,332	74,030	90,460	75,815	92,640	77,642	94,873	2.41%	12.05%	33,900	41,424	47,734	58,327	64,523	78,843
Senior Data Entry Machine Operator	27,681	34,214	28,348	35,039	29,031	35,883	29,730	36,748	30,447	37,634	2.41%	12.05%	13,294	16,432	18,719	23,137	25,303	31,275
Principal Data Entry Processing Operator	19,162	23,920	19,624	24,496	20,097	25,086	20,581	25,691	21,077	26,310	2.41%	12.05%	9,203	11,488	12,958	16,175	17,516	21,865
Head Data Entry Machine Operator	39,266	49,735	40,213	50,934	41,182	52,161	42,174	53,419	43,191	54,706	2.41%	12.05%	18,858	23,886	26,553	33,633	35,893	45,463
Supervisor, Data Processing	63,534	77,833	65,065	79,709	66,633	81,630	68,239	83,597	69,884	85,612	2.41%	12.05%	30,513	37,380	42,964	52,634	58,076	71,147
Telecommunications Analyst 1	35,108	44,833	35,954	45,914	36,821	47,020	37,708	48,154	38,617	49,314	2.41%	12.05%	16,861	21,532	23,741	30,318	32,092	40,982
Telecommunications Analyst 2	46,335	57,526	47,452	58,912	48,595	60,332	49,767	61,786	50,966	63,275	2.41%	12.05%	22,253	27,627	31,333	38,901	42,355	52,584
Associate Computer Programmer Analyst 1	57,087	70,292	58,463	71,987	59,872	73,721	61,315	75,498	62,793	77,318	2.41%	12.05%	27,417	33,759	38,604	47,534	52,183	64,254

State of Texas	2008 (Min)	2008 (Max)	2009 (Min)	2009 (Max)	2010 (Min)	2010 (Max)	2011 (Min)	2011 (Max)	2012 (Min)	2012 (Max)	5-Year Average % Raise	5-Year Cumulative Raise Estimate**	20-Year Annual Pension Benefit Estimate (Min.)***	20-Year Annual Pension Benefit Estimate (Max.)	25-Year Annual Pension Benefit Estimate (Min.)	25-Year Annual Pension Benefit Estimate (Max.)	30-Year Annual Pension Benefit Estimate (Min.)	30-Year Annual Pension Benefit Estimate (Max.)
Graphic Designer I	30,268	42,835	30,949	43,798	31,645	44,784	32,358	45,791	33,086	46,822	2.25%	11.25%	21,253	30,077	29,692	42,020	39,824	56,358
Graphic Designer II	34,029	48,316	34,794	49,403	35,577	50,515	36,378	51,652	37,196	52,814	2.25%	11.25%	23,894	33,925	33,382	47,397	44,772	63,570
Computer Operations Supervisor I	34,029	48,316	34,794	49,403	35,577	50,515	36,378	51,652	37,196	52,814	2.25%	11.25%	23,894	33,925	33,382	47,397	44,772	63,570
Computer Operations Supervisor II	38,445	58,450	39,310	59,765	40,195	61,110	41,099	62,485	42,024	63,891	2.25%	11.25%	26,994	41,041	37,714	57,338	50,582	76,903
Systems Support Specialist I	26,995	37,473	27,602	38,316	28,224	39,178	28,859	40,059	29,508	40,961	2.25%	11.25%	18,955	26,312	26,482	36,760	35,517	49,303
Systems Support Specialist II	30,268	42,230	30,949	43,181	31,645	44,152	32,358	45,145	33,086	46,161	2.25%	11.25%	21,253	29,652	29,692	41,427	39,824	55,562
Systems Support Specialist III	34,029	47,645	34,794	48,718	35,577	49,814	36,378	50,934	37,196	52,080	2.25%	11.25%	23,894	33,454	33,382	46,739	44,772	62,687
Programmer I	30,268	42,835	30,949	43,798	31,645	44,784	32,358	45,791	33,086	46,822	2.25%	11.25%	21,253	30,077	29,692	42,020	39,824	56,358
Programmer II	34,029	48,316	34,794	49,403	35,577	50,515	36,378	51,652	37,196	52,814	2.25%	11.25%	23,894	33,925	33,382	47,397	44,772	63,570
Programmer III	38,445	58,450	39,310	59,765	40,195	61,110	41,099	62,485	42,024	63,891	2.25%	11.25%	26,994	41,041	37,714	57,338	50,582	76,903
Programmer IV	43,492	66,113	44,471	67,600	45,471	69,121	46,494	70,677	47,540	72,267	2.25%	11.25%	30,538	46,421	42,665	64,855	57,223	86,985
Programmer V	49,210	74,813	50,317	76,497	51,449	78,218	52,607	79,978	53,791	81,777	2.25%	11.25%	34,553	52,530	48,274	73,390	64,745	98,432
Programmer VI	55,808	89,968	57,064	91,992	58,348	94,062	59,661	96,178	61,003	98,342	2.25%	11.25%	39,186	63,171	54,746	88,256	73,427	118,371
Programmer VII	63,326	102,086	64,750	104,383	66,207	106,732	67,697	109,133	69,220	111,589	2.25%	11.25%	44,464	71,680	62,121	100,145	83,317	134,315
Systems Analyst I	34,029	48,316	34,794	49,403	35,577	50,515	36,378	51,652	37,196	52,814	2.25%	11.25%	23,894	33,925	33,382	47,397	44,772	63,570
Systems Analyst II	38,445	58,450	39,310	59,765	40,195	61,110	41,099	62,485	42,024	63,891	2.25%	11.25%	26,994	41,041	37,714	57,338	50,582	76,903
Systems Analyst III	43,492	66,113	44,471	67,600	45,471	69,121	46,494	70,677	47,540	72,267	2.25%	11.25%	30,538	46,421	42,665	64,855	57,223	86,985
Systems Analyst IV	49,210	74,813	50,317	76,497	51,449	78,218	52,607	79,978	53,791	81,777	2.25%	11.25%	34,553	52,530	48,274	73,390	64,745	98,432
Systems Analyst V	55,808	89,968	57,064	91,992	58,348	94,062	59,661	96,178	61,003	98,342	2.25%	11.25%	39,186	63,171	54,746	88,256	73,427	118,371
Systems Analyst VI	63,326	102,086	64,750	104,383	66,207	106,732	67,697	109,133	69,220	111,589	2.25%	11.25%	44,464	71,680	62,121	100,145	83,317	134,315
Data Base Admin. I	34,029	48,316	34,794	49,403	35,577	50,515	36,378	51,652	37,196	52,814	2.25%	11.25%	23,894	33,925	33,382	47,397	44,772	63,570
Data Base Admin. II	38,445	58,450	39,310	59,765	40,195	61,110	41,099	62,485	42,024	63,891	2.25%	11.25%	26,994	41,041	37,714	57,338	50,582	76,903

State of Texas	2008 (Min)	2008 (Max)	2009 (Min)	2009 (Max)	2010 (Min)	2010 (Max)	2011 (Min)	2011 (Max)	2012 (Min)	2012 (Max)	5-Year Average % Raise	5-Year Cumulative Raise Estimate**	20-Year Annual Pension Benefit Estimate (Min.)***	20-Year Annual Pension Benefit Estimate (Max.)	25-Year Annual Pension Benefit Estimate (Min.)	25-Year Annual Pension Benefit Estimate (Max.)	30-Year Annual Pension Benefit Estimate (Min.)	30-Year Annual Pension Benefit Estimate (Max.)
Data Base Admin. III	43,492	66,113	44,471	67,600	45,471	69,121	46,494	70,677	47,540	72,267	2.25%	11.25%	30,538	46,421	42,665	64,855	57,223	86,985
Data Base Admin. IV	49,210	74,813	50,317	76,497	51,449	78,218	52,607	79,978	53,791	81,777	2.25%	11.25%	34,553	52,530	48,274	73,390	64,745	98,432
Data Base Admin. V	55,808	89,968	57,064	91,992	58,348	94,062	59,661	96,178	61,003	98,342	2.25%	11.25%	39,186	63,171	54,746	88,256	73,427	118,371
Data Base Admin. VI	63,326	102,086	64,750	104,383	66,207	106,732	67,697	109,133	69,220	111,589	2.25%	11.25%	44,464	71,680	62,121	100,145	83,317	134,315
Web Admin. I	38,445	58,450	39,310	59,765	40,195	61,110	41,099	62,485	42,024	63,891	2.25%	11.25%	26,994	41,041	37,714	57,338	50,582	76,903
Web Admin. II	43,492	66,113	44,471	67,600	45,471	69,121	46,494	70,677	47,540	72,267	2.25%	11.25%	30,538	46,421	42,665	64,855	57,223	86,985
Web Admin. III	49,210	74,813	50,317	76,497	51,449	78,218	52,607	79,978	53,791	81,777	2.25%	11.25%	34,553	52,530	48,274	73,390	64,745	98,432
Network Specialist I	34,029	48,316	34,794	49,403	35,577	50,515	36,378	51,652	37,196	52,814	2.25%	11.25%	23,894	33,925	33,382	47,397	44,772	63,570
Network Specialist II	38,445	58,450	39,310	59,765	40,195	61,110	41,099	62,485	42,024	63,891	2.25%	11.25%	26,994	41,041	37,714	57,338	50,582	76,903
Network Specialist III	43,492	66,113	44,471	67,600	45,471	69,121	46,494	70,677	47,540	72,267	2.25%	11.25%	30,538	46,421	42,665	64,855	57,223	86,985
Network Specialist IV	49,210	74,813	50,317	76,497	51,449	78,218	52,607	79,978	53,791	81,777	2.25%	11.25%	34,553	52,530	48,274	73,390	64,745	98,432
Network Specialist V	55,808	89,968	57,064	91,992	58,348	94,062	59,661	96,178	61,003	98,342	2.25%	11.25%	39,186	63,171	54,746	88,256	73,427	118,371
Telecommunications Specialist I	32,050	45,463	32,771	46,486	33,509	47,532	34,263	48,602	35,034	49,695	2.25%	11.25%	22,504	31,922	31,441	44,599	42,169	59,816
Telecommunications Specialist II	36,132	51,300	36,945	52,454	37,776	53,634	38,626	54,841	39,495	56,075	2.25%	11.25%	25,370	36,020	35,445	50,324	47,539	67,495
Telecommunications Specialist III	40,890	62,144	41,810	63,542	42,751	64,971	43,712	66,433	44,696	67,928	2.25%	11.25%	28,711	43,634	40,112	60,961	53,799	81,762
Telecommunications Specialist IV	46,240	70,292	47,280	71,873	48,344	73,491	49,431	75,144	50,544	76,835	2.25%	11.25%	32,467	49,356	45,360	68,955	60,837	92,483
Telecommunications Specialist V	52,378	84,448	53,556	86,348	54,761	88,291	55,993	90,278	57,253	92,309	2.25%	11.25%	36,777	59,296	51,381	82,842	68,913	111,109
Data Entry Operator I	19,767	25,630	20,212	26,207	20,667	26,796	21,132	27,399	21,607	28,016	2.25%	11.25%	13,880	17,996	19,391	25,142	26,007	33,721
Data Entry Operator II	21,751	28,309	22,240	28,946	22,740	29,597	23,252	30,263	23,775	30,944	2.25%	11.25%	15,272	19,877	21,337	27,770	28,617	37,246
Data Entry Operator III	24,164	33,346	24,707	34,096	25,263	34,863	25,832	35,648	26,413	36,450	2.25%	11.25%	16,967	23,414	23,704	32,712	31,792	43,873
Computer Operator I	22,951	29,889	23,467	30,561	23,996	31,249	24,535	31,952	25,087	32,671	2.25%	11.25%	16,115	20,987	22,515	29,320	30,197	39,325
Computer Operator II	25,542	35,356	26,117	36,152	26,704	36,965	27,305	37,797	27,920	38,647	2.25%	11.25%	17,935	24,825	25,056	34,684	33,606	46,518

Appendix A:
General Service Salary Schedule

SALARY TABLE 2006-GS
INCORPORATING THE 2.10% GENERAL SCHEDULE INCREASE

EFFECTIVE JANUARY 2006

Annual Rates by Grade and Step

Grade	Step 1	Step 2	Step 3	Step 4	Step 5	Step 6	Step 7	Step 8	Step 9	Step 10	WITHIN GRADE AMOUNTS
1	$ 16,352	$ 16,898	$ 17,442	$ 17,983	$ 18,527	$ 18,847	$ 19,383	$ 19,925	$ 19,947	$ 20,450	VARIES
2	18,385	18,822	19,431	19,947	20,169	20,762	21,355	21,948	22,541	23,134	VARIES
3	20,060	20,729	21,398	22,067	22,736	23,405	24,074	24,743	25,412	26,081	669
4	22,519	23,270	24,021	24,772	25,523	26,274	27,025	27,776	28,527	29,278	751
5	25,195	26,035	26,875	27,715	28,555	29,395	30,235	31,075	31,915	32,755	840
6	28,085	29,021	29,957	30,893	31,829	32,765	33,701	34,637	35,573	36,509	936
7	31,209	32,249	33,289	34,329	35,369	36,409	37,449	38,489	39,529	40,569	1040
8	34,563	35,715	36,867	38,019	39,171	40,323	41,475	42,627	43,779	44,931	1152
9	38,175	39,448	40,721	41,994	43,267	44,540	45,813	47,086	48,359	49,632	1273
10	42,040	43,441	44,842	46,243	47,644	49,045	50,446	51,847	53,248	54,649	1401
11	46,189	47,729	49,269	50,809	52,349	53,889	55,429	56,969	58,509	60,049	1540
12	55,360	57,205	59,050	60,895	62,740	64,585	66,430	68,275	70,120	71,965	1845
13	65,832	68,026	70,220	72,414	74,608	76,802	78,996	81,190	83,384	85,578	2194
14	77,793	80,386	82,979	85,572	88,165	90,758	93,351	95,944	98,537	101,130	2593
15	91,507	94,557	97,607	100,657	103,707	106,757	109,807	112,857	115,907	118,957	3050

Appendix B:
Competencies Required for
Federal IT Job Specialties

INFORMATION TECHNOLOGY MANAGEMENT, GS-2210
Specialty Competencies

Policy and Planning –
(PLCYPLN)
Work that involves a wide range of IT management activities that typically extend and apply to an entire organization or major components of an organization. This includes strategic planning, capital planning and investment control, workforce planning, policy and standards development, resource management, knowledge management, architecture and infrastructure planning and management, auditing, and information security management.
Functions commonly performed by employees in this specialty may include:
• developing and maintaining strategic plans;
• assessing policy needs and developing policies to govern IT activities;
• providing policy guidance to IT management, staff, and customers;
• defining current and future business environments;
• preparing IT budgets;
• managing IT investment portfolios;
• establishing metrics to measure and evaluate systems performance and total cost of ownership;
• identifying and addressing IT workforce planning and management issues, such as recruitment, retention, and training;
• conducting audits of IT programs and projects; and/or
• ensuring the rigorous application of information security/information assurance policies, principles, and practices in the delivery of planning and management services.
Common organizational or functional titles for positions in this specialty:
• enterprise resource planner
• IT policy and planning analyst
• IT program management specialist
• IT auditor

Security –
(INFOSEC)
Work that involves ensuring the confidentiality, integrity, and availability of systems, networks, and data through the planning, analysis, development, implementation, maintenance, and enhancement of information systems security programs, policies, procedures, and tools.
Functions commonly performed by employees in this specialty may include:
• developing policies and procedures to ensure information systems reliability and accessibility and to prevent and defend against unauthorized access to systems, networks, and data;
• conducting risk and vulnerability assessments of planned and installed information systems to identify vulnerabilities, risks, and protection needs;
• promoting awareness of security issues among management and ensuring sound security principles are reflected in organizations' visions and goals;
• conducting systems security evaluations, audits, and reviews;
• developing systems security contingency plans and disaster recovery procedures;
• developing and implementing programs to ensure that systems, network, and

177

data users are aware of, understand, and adhere to systems security policies and procedures;
• participating in network and systems design to ensure implementation of appropriate systems security policies;
• facilitating the gathering, analysis, and preservation of evidence used in the prosecution of computer crimes;
• assessing security events to determine impact and implementing corrective actions; and/or
• ensuring the rigorous application of information security/information assurance policies, principles, and practices in the delivery of all IT services.
Common organizational or functional titles for positions in this specialty:
• information systems security analyst/specialist
• information systems security officer
• network security officer
• information assurance analyst/specialist

Systems Analysis –
(SYSANALYSIS)
Work that involves applying analytical processes to the planning, design and implementation of new and improved information systems to meet the business requirements of customer organizations.
Functions commonly performed by employees in this specialty may include:
• performing needs analyses to define opportunities for new or improved business process solutions;
• consulting with customers to identify and specify requirements;
• developing overall functional and systems requirements and specifications;
• conducting business process reengineering;
• conducting feasibility studies and trade-off analyses;
• preparing business cases for the application of IT solutions;
• defining systems scope and objectives;
• developing cost estimates for new or modified systems;
• ensuring the integration of all systems components; e.g., procedures, databases, policies, software, and hardware;
• planning systems implementation; and/or
• ensuring the rigorous application of information security/information assurance policies, principles, and practices to the systems analysis process.
Common organizational or functional titles for positions in this specialty:
• systems analyst
• business analyst

Applications Software –
(APPSW)
Work that involves the design, documentation, development, modification, testing, installation, implementation, and support of new or existing applications software.
Functions commonly performed by employees assigned to this specialty may include:
• analyzing and refining systems requirements;
• translating systems requirements into applications prototypes;
• planning and designing systems architecture;
• writing, debugging, and maintaining code;
• determining and designing applications architecture;
• determining output media/formats;
• designing user interfaces;
• working with customers to test applications;
• assuring software and systems quality and functionality;
• integrating hardware and software components;
• writing and maintaining program documentation;
• evaluating new applications software technologies; and/or
• ensuring the rigorous application of information security/information assurance policies, principles, and practices to the delivery of application software services.
Common organizational or functional titles for positions in this specialty:
• programmer
• programmer analyst
• applications developer

• software engineer
• software developer
• software quality assurance specialist

Operating Systems –
(OS)
Work that involves the planning, installation, configuration, testing, implementation, and management of the systems environment in support of the organization's IT architecture and business needs.
Functions commonly performed by employees in this specialty may include:
• analyzing systems requirements in response to business requirements, risks, and costs;
• evaluating, selecting, verifying, and validating the systems software environment;
• evaluating, selecting, and installing compilers, assemblers, and utilities;
• integrating hardware and software components within the systems environment;
• monitoring and fine-tuning performance of the systems environment;
• evaluating new systems engineering technologies and their effect on the operating environment; and/or
• ensuring that information security/information assurance policies, principles, and practices are an integral element of the operating environment.
Common organizational or functional titles for positions in this specialty:
• systems programmer
• systems software programmer
• systems engineer
• systems software engineer

Network Services –
(NETWORK)
Work that involves the planning, analysis, design, development, testing, quality assurance, configuration, installation, implementation, integration, maintenance, and/or management of networked systems used for the transmission of information in voice, data, and/or video formats.
Functions commonly performed by employees in this specialty may include:
• analyzing and defining network requirements;
• defining and maintaining network architecture and infrastructure;
• configuring and optimizing network servers, hubs, routers, and switches;
• analyzing network workload;
• monitoring network capacity and performance;
• diagnosing and resolving network problems;
• developing network backup and recovery procedures;
• installing, testing, maintaining, and upgrading network operating systems software; and/or
• ensuring the rigorous application of information security/information assurance policies, principles, and practices in the delivery of network services.
Common organizational or functional titles for positions in this specialty:
• network administrator
• LAN/WAN administrator
• network analyst
• network designer
• network engineer

Data Management –
(DATAMGT)
Work that involves the planning, development, implementation, and administration of systems for the acquisition, storage, and retrieval of data.
Functions commonly performed by employees in this specialty may include:
• analyzing and defining data requirements and specifications;
• designing, normalizing, developing, installing, and implementing databases;
• maintaining, monitoring, performance tuning, backup, and recovery of databases;
• installing, configuring, and maintaining database management systems software;

• analyzing and planning for anticipated changes in data capacity requirements;
• developing and administering data standards, policies, and procedures;
• developing and implementing data mining and data warehousing programs;
• evaluating and providing recommendations on new database technologies and architectures; and/or
• ensuring the rigorous application of information security/information assurance policies, principles, and practices in the delivery of data management services.

Common organizational or functional titles for positions in this specialty:
• database developer
• database administrator
• data analyst
• data administrator
• data architect
• data storage specialist
• data warehouse specialist

Internet –
(INET)
Work that involves the technical planning, design, development, testing, implementation, and management of Internet, intranet, and extranet activities, including systems/applications development and technical management of Web sites. This specialty only includes positions that require the application of technical knowledge of Internet systems, services, and technologies.
In most cases, the term Internet is used in this standard to refer generically to Internet, intranet, and extranet systems and services.
Functions commonly performed by employees in this specialty may include:
• determining overall technical design and structure of Internet services;
• monitoring functionality, security, and integrity of Internet services;
• troubleshooting and resolving technical problems with the design and delivery of Internet services;
• collecting and analyzing Internet services usage and performance statistics;
• evaluating new Internet services and technologies;
• providing technical advice to Internet content providers; and/or
• ensuring the rigorous application of information security/information assurance policies, principles, and practices in the delivery of Internet services.

Common organizational or functional titles for positions in this specialty:
• Web developer
• Webmaster
• Web manager
• Web site administrator
• Web operations specialist
• Internet specialist
• Internet developer
• Internet architect
NOTE: This specialty does not include positions referred to as Webmaster, Web manager, and Web page manager that do not require a paramount knowledge of IT principles, concepts, and methods. Classify such positions in other occupational series requiring paramount knowledge of the subject matter involved.

Systems Administration –
(SYSADMIN)
Work that involves planning and coordinating the installation, testing, operation, troubleshooting, and maintenance of hardware and software systems.
Functions commonly performed by employees in this specialty may include:
• planning and scheduling the installation of new or modified hardware and operating systems and applications software;
• managing accounts, network rights, and access to systems and equipment;
• managing systems resources including performance, capacity, availability, serviceability, and recoverability;
• implementing security procedures and tools;
• developing and documenting systems administration standard operating procedures;
• resolving hardware/software interface and interoperability problems;

• ensuring systems availability, functionality, integrity, and efficiency;
• maintaining systems configuration;
• managing the installation and integration of systems fixes, updates, and
enhancements; and/or
• ensuring the rigorous application of information security/information
assurance policies, principles, and practices in the delivery of systems
administration services.
Common organizational or functional titles for positions in this specialty:
• systems administrator
• site administrator
• UNIX/Windows systems administrator

Customer Support –
(CUSTSPT)
Work that involves the planning and delivery of customer support services,
including installation, configuration, troubleshooting, customer assistance, and/or
training, in response to customer requirements.
Functions commonly performed by employees in this specialty may include:
• diagnosing and resolving problems in response to customer reported incidents;
• researching, evaluating, and providing feedback on problematic trends and
patterns in customer support requirements;
• developing and maintaining problem tracking and resolution databases;
• installing, configuring, troubleshooting, and maintaining customer hardware
and software;
• developing and managing customer service performance requirements;
• developing customer support policies, procedures, and standards;
• providing customer training; and/or
• ensuring the rigorous application of information security/information assurance

Appendix C:
U.S. Federal Government
Definitions of Pay Grade Factors
Determining Job Title Classification
& Pay Grade

Knowledge Required by the Position:
This factor covers **the nature and extent of the work;** the nature and extent of **information or facts** that an employee must understand to do acceptable work **(e.g., steps, procedures, practices, rules, policies, theories, principles, and concepts)** and the nature and extent of the skills necessary to apply that knowledge.

The Role of Competencies:
"Information technology as a field of work is finely attuned to the competencies it requires. By competency, it means an observable, measurable pattern of skills, knowledge, abilities, behaviors, and other characteristics that an individual needs to perform work roles or occupational functions successfully. The rapid pace of change in information technology results in constantly evolving competencies. This is true both in terms of the specific knowledge and skills that are changing and in terms of the way technological advances change the pattern of abilities and behaviors, as well as work and work roles," (USOPM, 2001, 2003). **(See Appendix B: Competencies Required for Federal IT Job Specialties).**

Supervisory Factors
This factor covers nature and extent of direct or indirect controls exercised by the supervisor or another individual over the work performed, the employee's responsibility, and the review of completed work will be considered. The supervisor determines how much information the employee needs to perform the assignments; e.g., instructions, priorities, deadlines, objectives, and boundaries. The employee's responsibility depends on the extent to which the supervisor expects the employee to develop the sequence and timing of the various aspects of the work, to modify or recommend modification of instructions, and to participate in establishing priorities and defining objectives. The degree of review of completed work depends upon the nature and extent of the review; e.g., close and detailed review of each phase of the assignment; detailed review of the completed assignment; spot check of finished work for accuracy; or review only for adherence to policy. The primary components of this factor are: How Work Is Assigned, Employee Responsibility, and How Work Is Reviewed.

Judgment Factors
This factor covers the nature of guidelines and the judgment employees need to apply them. Individual assignments may vary in the specificity, applicability, and availability of guidelines; thus, the judgment that employees use similarly varies. The existence of detailed plans and other instructions may make innovation in planning and conducting work unnecessary or undesirable. However, in the absence of guidance provided by prior agency experience with the task at hand or when objectives are broadly stated, the employee may use considerable judgment in developing an approach or planning the work. Here are examples of guidelines used in administrative work in the Information Technology Group:

Policies and Guidance – Several policy and guidance statements influence and direct how the Government manages its information resources. The primary components of this factor are: **Guidelines Used** and **Judgment Needed**.

Nature of Assignment Factors
This factor covers the nature, number, variety, and intricacy of tasks, steps, processes, or methods in the work performed; the difficulty in identifying what needs to be done; and the difficulty and originality involved in performing the work. The primary components of this factor are: Nature of Assignment, What Needs To Be Done, and Difficulty and Originality Involved.

Scope of the Work
Effect of the Work Relationship between Nature of Work and Output

This factor covers the relationships between the nature of work, i.e., the purpose, breadth and depth of the assignment, and the effect of work products or services both within and outside the organization. Effect measures such things as whether the work output facilitates the work of others, provides timely services of a personal nature, or impacts on the adequacy of research conclusions. The primary components of this factor are: **Scope of the Work** and **Effect of the Work**.

Scope of Contacts – Purpose of Contacts

These factors include face-to-face and remote dialogue – e.g., telephone, email, and video conferences – with persons not in the supervisory chain. The levels of these factors consider and take into account what is necessary to make the initial contact, the difficulty of communicating with those contacted, the setting in which the contact takes place, and the nature of the discourse. The setting describes how well the employee and those contacted recognize their relative roles and authorities. The nature of the discourse defines the reason for the communication and the context or environment in which the communication takes place. For example, the reason for a communication may be to exchange factual information or to negotiate. The communication may take place in an environment of significant controversy and/or with people of differing viewpoints, goals, and objectives (U.S. Federal Government, Office of Personnel Management, "Job Family Position Classification Standard for Administrative Work in the Information Technology Group GS-2200", GS-2200, 2001, 2003; http://www.opm.gov/FEDCLASS/gs2200a.pdf).

REFERENCES

U.S. Federal Government, Office of Personnel Management, "Job Family Position Classification Standard for Administrative Work in the Information Technology Group GS-2200", GS-2200, 2001, 2003; http://www.opm.gov/FEDCLASS/gs2200a.pdf .

Appendix D:
Sample Federal Job Announcements

Deputy Assistant Secretary for Information & Technology
Department: **Department Of Veterans Affairs**
Agency: **Deputy Assistant Secretary for Information & Technology**
Job Announcement Number:
DS117475-BM

INFORMATION TECHNOLOGY SPECIALIST (APPLICATION SOFTWARE)
Salary Range: 74,074.00 - 96,292.00 USD per year Open Period: (Sample only)
Series & Grade: GS-2210-13 Position Information: Full Time Career/Career Conditional
Promotion Potential: 13 Duty Locations: 1 vacancy - Austin, TX
Who May Be Considered: U.S. Citizens

Job Summary: The mission of the Department of Veterans Affairs, Austin Automation Center is to provide One-VA world-class service to veterans and their families by delivering results-oriented, secure, highly available, and cost effective IT services. *This position is located at the VA Austin Automation Center (AAC) Enterprise Systems Division, located in Austin, Texas. The division develops and maintain a application software to automate franchise fund business functions. The division serves internal customers and other federal agencies by analyzing customer's requests for information and implementing methods for customers to have easy access to the information they need.*

Full Performance Level: 13
Key Requirements: U.S. Citizenship

Major Duties: Individuals within the Application Developer job family are responsible for the design, development, testing, documentation, maintenance, and integration of application software. Incumbents within the Application Developer job family obtain and refine business requirements through interaction with the Requirements Analysts and the customer. Application developer personnel are also required to provide Tier II and Tier III support for the Help Desk. In addition, the incumbents work as individual contributors, team members or serve as project task managers.

Qualifications: Applicants must have one or more years of specialized experience as Information Technology Specialist (Application Software), completing computer project assignments that involve design, development, testing, documentation, maintenance and integration of application software; participation in technology planning, product evaluation and report development; and serving as a project manager. This experience must be equivalent to the GS-12 level in the Federal service, but could have been gained in the public or private sectors. *In addition, the following skills and experience is required:* 1) Skill in administering a clustered BEA WebLogic Server environment in a RedHat Linux environment *and* 2) Skill in installing, configuring, tuning, troubleshooting, clustering, and deploying applications to WebLogic Server.

Veterans Health Administration
Department: Department Of Veterans Affairs
Agency: Veterans Health Administration
Job Announcement Number:
VZ119102TLC

INFORMATION TECHNOLOGY SPECIALIST (NETWORK)
Salary Range: 74,074.00 - 100,554.00 USD per year Open Period: (Sample only)
Series & Grade: GS-2210-13 Position Information: Full Time Term NTE 2 years
Promotion Potential: 13 Duty Locations: 1 vacancy - St. Louis Metro area, MO 1 vacancy - Washington, DC
Who May Be Considered: U.S. Citizens

Job Summary: Be a member of a team providing compassionate healthcare to veterans.

SALARY RANGES:

St. Louis, MO: $74,074 - $96,292 annually

Washington, DC: $77,353 - $100,554 annually

THE FOLLOWING DOCUMENTS ARE REQUIRED TO APPLY FOR THIS POSITION:

1. OF 306 – DECLARATION OF FEDERAL EMPLOYMENT (January 2001 or later version

required)

2. OF 612 – Optional Application for Federal Employment OR Resume

3. OPM 1203 FX – Occupational Questionnaire

4. Veterans Preference:

a. CPS, CP (10PT) – required documents: SF 15, DD214 – Member 4 copy which reflects CHARACTER OF

SERVICE (i.e. Honorable), VA disability letter dated 1991 or later

b. TP (5PT) – required documents: DD214 - Member 4 copy which reflects CHARACTER OF SERVICE

(i.e. Honorable)

c. XP OR XPP (10PT) – refer to SF 15 for required documents

5. College Transcripts (*see Qualifications/Evaluations section*)

Major Duties: The VA Learning University (VALU) is a Department-wide, comprehensive, virtual, education-focused staff supporting VA continuing learning objectives through all-employee training, education, performance support, development and consultation. The incumbent will serve as the Senior Network Administrator responsible for technical support of live satellite-based Internet Protocol (IP) video to the desktop and Content Distribution Network (CDN) video on-demand across the entire Veterans Health Administration (VHA) healthcare system and other Department of Veterans Affairs offices as required. This support will frequently entail troubleshooting and direct customer support to assist CDN clients with all aspects of CDN video to the desktop including Content Library administration. In collaboration with the Employee Education System (EES) CDN Project Manager and the EES Media and Learning Technology Coordinator, plans, designs, and installs telecommunications hardware/software related to the design and implementation of IP desktop video and CDN within the VHA. This entails the selection, implementation and administration of telecommunications equipment inclusive of routers, hubs, switches, video interface units, video gateways, and specialized CDN equipment such as Cisco Content Engines. Incumbent serves as liaison to the Veterans Integrated Service Network (VISN) Chief Information Office (CIO) technical staff with regard to installation and the support of VALU IP video as well as other education support initiatives. Some examples include Internet Protocol Television, Content Distribution, Satellite uplink/downlink systems, Internet Protocol Multicast, and networking devices (LAN, WAN, and MAN). Supports and maintains telecommunications (WAN, LAN, MAN) operating systems, database management systems, programming languages, application software systems, programming utilities systems programming support, video communications software and associated integrated subsystems associated with VAKN satellite video downlinks/uplinks and the delivery of Internet Protocol television and distribution of on-demand content. Tests and administers video telecommunications systems used for implementation of IP desktop video and CDN within the VHA. Specialized technical skills in the area of H.320 communications and IP based H.323 will be required. The incumbent must be familiar with WAN network transport protocols and equipment that may be used for support of video communications, i.e. ATM switch equipment utilizing Synchronous Optical Network (SONET) transport, Protocol Independent Multicasting (PIM), and IP precedence tagging for the provision Class of Service (COS) WAN transport. Creates written materials to assist users and support staff in hardware, software, and network operation activities where required. Incumbent assists in the creation and implementation of the network support and maintenance plan, and must maintain accurate documentation of demographic information for the express purpose of supporting the Content Distribution and Internet Protocol Television network. Incumbent trains VAKN operations staff and end users in CDN network administration duties as required to manage network activity in individual services/applications and in telecommunications hardware technology. Incumbent must be capable of providing end user training in networking hardware and multiple software applications as relevant to the support of VHA broadcast initiatives. Incumbent acts as a contingent support person for local duty station LAN and WAN network engineers. This may entail operating systems support (Microsoft NT Workstation/Server, Exchange Server, SMS Server, etc.), software applications support (Microsoft BackOffice Suite, etc.), and network troubleshooting such as providing assistance in troubleshooting TCP/IP protocol routing problems in WAN environment.

Delivers technical presentations related to the VAKN CDN as requested. These may be in a formal classroom/conference setting. They may also be to Veterans Affairs Central Office (VACO) program offices and national VA committees and organizations such as the VA Learning University (VALU), a VISN, facility level stakeholders and customers, or internal EES leadership and committees.

Qualifications: GS-13 SPECIALIZED EXPERIENCE: One (1) year of specialized experience that equipped you with the knowledge, skills and ability to successfully perform, and that are related to the duties of this position. Specialized experience includes: Demonstrated accomplishment of computer project assignments that required a wide range of knowledge of computer requirements and techniques pertinent to this position. This knowledge is generally demonstrated by assignments where you analyzed a number of alternative approaches in the process of advising management concerning major aspects of ADP system design, such as what system interrelationships must be considered, or what operating mode, system software, and/or equipment configuration is most

Appendix E:
U.S. States & Major Cities
Sample IT Job Descriptions & Qualifications

STATE OF CALIFORNIA
Personnel website:
http://www.governmentguide.com/govsite.adp?bread=*Main*&url=http:
//www.my.ca.   gov/
Job Application Website:
http://www.governmentguide.com/govsite.adp?bread=*Main*&url=http:
//www.my.ca.gov/
*See Charts for Salary & Pension Information

ASSOCIATE PROGRAMMER ANALYST (SPECIALIST)
Job Description & Qualifications: Under general supervision, independently performs programming and analysis work and or acts as leader of a team of programmers and/or participates with other programmer analysists on projects of a very complex nature of unusually broad scope. One year of experience in the California state service performing duties comparable to a Programmer II. Or eighteen months of progressively responsible experience in information technology systems study, design, and programming, which shall have included responsibility on an information technology system project for analyzing operational methods and developing computer programs to meet desired results. One year of experience in this pattern must include responsibilities under general supervision to plan and develop programs to be processed on information technology systems equipment, perform systems analysis, or systems programming work. Or equivalent to graduation from a recognized college or university with a minimum of 24 semester or 36 quarter units in information technology-related coursework.

ASSOCIATE PROGRAMMER ANALYST (SUPERVISOR)
Under general supervision, acts as a supervisor of a team of programmers.One year of experience in the California state service performing duties comparable to a Programmer II. Or eighteen months of progressively responsible experience in information technology systems study, design, and programming, which shall have included responsibility on an information technology system project for analyzing operational methods and developing computer programs to meet desired results. One year of experience in this pattern must include responsibilities under general supervision to plan and develop programs to be processed on information technology systems equipment, perform systems analysis, or systems programming work. Or equivalent to graduation from a recognized college or university with a minimum of 24 semester or 36 quarter units in information technology-related coursework. (Registration as a senior in a recognized institution will admit applicants to the examination, but they must produce evidence of graduation or its equivalent before they can be considered eligible for appointment.)

STAFF PROGRAMMER ANALYST (SPECIALIST)
Under general supervision, acts as a project leader on complex applications and/or on complex information technology system problems and works independently as a technical specialist. One year of experience in the California state service performing duties comparable to an Associate Programmer Analyst (Specialist) or Associate Programmer Analyst (Supervisor). Or Two years of progressively responsible experience in information technology systems study, design, and programming, which shall have included responsibility on a project for analyzing operational methods and developing computer programs to meet desired results. One year of experience in this pattern must include independent performance of programming and analysis work, lead of a programming team, or participation as a team member on projects of a very complex nature or broad scope. Or Thirty semester units or 45 quarter units of graduate work in information technology-related coursework from a recognized college or university.

STAFF PROGRAMMER ANALYST (SUPERVISOR)
Under general supervision, acts as a supervisor on complex applications. One year of experience in the California state service performing duties comparable to an Associate Programmer Analyst (Specialist) or Associate Programmer Analyst (Supervisor). Or two years of progressively responsible experience in information technology systems study, design, and programming, which shall have included responsibility on a project for analyzing operational methods and developing computer programs to meet desired results. One year of experience in this pattern must include

187

independent performance of programming and analysis work, lead of a programming team, or participation as a team member on projects of a very complex nature or broad scope. Or thirty semester units or 45 quarter units of graduate work in information technology-related coursework from a recognized college or university.

SENIOR PROGRAMMER ANALYST (SPECIALIST)

Under general direction, acts as a project leader on the most complex applications and/or on the most complex information technology system problems; and works independently as a high level technical specialist. One year of experience in the California state service performing duties comparable to a Staff Programmer Analyst (Specialist) or Staff Programmer Analyst (Supervisor). Or Two years of experience in the California state service performing duties comparable to an Associate Programmer Analyst (Specialist) or Associate Programmer Analyst (Supervisor). Or Thirty months of progressively responsible experience in information technology systems study, design, and programming, which shall have included responsibility on a project for analyzing operational methods and developing computer programs to meet desired results. One year of experience in this pattern must include responsibility as a project leader on complex applications, or resolution of complex information technology systems problems, and working independently as a technical specialist.

SENIOR PROGRAMMER ANALYST (SUPERVISOR)

Under general direction, acts as a supervisor on the most complex applications. One year of experience in the California state service performing duties comparable to a Staff Programmer Analyst (Specialist) or Staff Programmer Analyst (Supervisor). Or two years of experience in the California state service performing duties comparable to an Associate Programmer Analyst (Specialist) or Associate Programmer Analyst (Supervisor). Or thirty months of progressively responsible experience in information technology systems study, design, and programming, which shall have included responsibility on a project for analyzing operational methods and developing computer programs to meet desired results. One year of experience in this pattern must include responsibility as a project leader on complex applications, or resolution of complex information technology systems problems, and working independently as a technical specialist.

TELECOMMUNICATIONS SYSTEMS ANALYST I

Education: The following education is required when non-State experience is used to qualify at any level: Equivalent to graduation from college, prefereably with major specialization in electronics or related technical subject area. (Additional qualifying experience may be substituted for education on a year for year basis. Experience: One year of experience performing telecommunications systems work which shall have included analyzing and making written reports or recommendations on radio/microwave and/or wire service staffing or systems; or Four years' experience in the California state service coordinating, operating, and/or maintaining telecommunications systems, such as performed by incumbents in the classes of Supervising Telephone Operator, Radio Dispatch Supervisor, or Communications Supervisor, California Highway Patrol; or Six months of experience performing the duties of a Management Services Technician, Range B, in a State service telecommunications operation; or Two years' experience in the California state service in a formal telecommunications training and development assignment to a class equivalent to Management Services Technician.

TELECOMMUNICATIONS SYSTEMS ANALYST II

Education: The following education is required when non-State experience is used to qualify at any level: Equavalent to graduation from college, prefereably with major specialization in electronics or related technical subject area. (Additional qualifying experience may be subtituted for education on a yar for year basis. Experience: One year of experience in the California state service performing the duties of a Telecommunications Systems Analyst I, Range C; or Three years of analytical experience in planning, organizing and coordinating maintenance and upgrade activities for telecommunications systems such as radio/microwave and/or wire service systems. (Experience in California state service applied toward this requirement must include at least one year performing the duties of a class at a level of responsibility not less than that of Telecommunications Systems Analyst I, Range C.)

TELECOMMUNICATIONS SYSTEMS MANAGER I (SPECIALIST)

Education: The following education is required when non-State experience is used to qualify at any level: Equavalent to graduation from college, prefereably with major specialization in electronics or related technical subject area. (Additional qualifying experience may be subtituted for education on a year for year basis. Experience: Either One year of experience in the California state service performing the duties of a Telecommunications Systems Analyst I or Five years of analytical experience in planning, organizing and coordinating maintenance and upgrade activities for telecommunications equipment such as dio/microwave and/or wire service systems. (Experience in California state service applied toward this requirement must include one year performing the duties of a class with a level of responsibility not less than that of Telecommunications Systems Analyst II.)

TELECOMMUNICATIONS SYSTEMS MANAGER I (SUPERVISOR)

Education: The following education is required when non-State experience is used to qualify at any level: Equavalent to graduation from college, prefereably with major specialization in electronics or related technical subject area. (Additional qualifying experience may be subtituted for education on a year for year basis. Experience: Either One year of experience in the California state service performing the duties of a Telecommunications Systems Analyst I or Five years of analytical experience in planning, organizing and coordinating maintenance and upgrade activities for telecommunications equipment such as dio/microwave and/or wire service systems. (Experience in California state service applied toward this requirement must include one year performing the duties of a class with a level of responsibility not less than that of Telecommunications Systems Analyst II.)

New York - New York City
Personnel website: http://www.nyc.gov
Job Application Website: http://www.nyc.gov/html/recruit/home.html
*See Chart s Salary & Pension Information for Complete List of IT Job Titles
Residency: City residency is not required for this position.
English Requirement: Candidates must be able to understand and be understood in English.
Sample Job Descriptions. Not intended to list all Job Descriptions.

COMPUTER AIDE (LEVELS I-III)
Job Description: Responsibilities will include: provide desktop support and software programming to all agency locations including the 311 Call Center, NYC.gov and NYC-TV; handling desktop PC support for the Agency; troubleshooting and resolving user problems, hardware deployment, software installation and programming, asset inventory and management, and ensuring that all agency desktops are set up within required specifications and agency standards.
Preferred Skills: Candidate should have knowledge in troubleshooting and PC problems and providing technical desktop support; Experience in windows 2003/XP environments a plus.
CIVIL SERVICE QUALIFICATION REQUIREMENTS
1. An Associates Degree from an accredited college (60 credits) including or supplemented by 12 credits in computer operations. -OR-
2. A four year high school diploma or its equivalent, plus (A) six months of full-time computer operations experience acquired in the past year or (B) graduation from an approved technical school (approximately 675 hours) with specialization in computer operations. -OR-
3. Education and/or experience equivalent. However, all candidates must have a four year high school diploma or its equivalent.

COMPUTER ASSOCIATE OPERATIONS (LEVELS I-III)
WHAT THE JOB INVOLVES: Computer Associates (Operations) under general supervision, with very considerable latitude for independent initiative and judgment, supervise the activities of subordinates in one or more computer operating units of considerable size; serve as technical resource persons in the monitoring, troubleshooting, diagnosis, and problem resolution of mainframe computer operations. Computer Associates (Operations) may be required to work shifts, including nights, Saturdays, Sundays, and holidays.
Education and Experience Requirements:
(1) A certificate from an accredited technical school (approximately 675 hours) with a specialization in computer operations, and two years of satisfactory, full-time large-scale mainframe computer operations or mainframe data communication network experience in a mainframe environment gained since February, 1996; or
(2) A baccalaureate degree from an accredited college and three years of satisfactory, full-time experience as described in "1" above; or
(3) A four year high school diploma or its educational equivalent and four years of satisfactory, fulltime experience as described in "1" above; or
(4) A satisfactory combination of education and/or experience which is equivalent to "1", "2", or "3" above. However, all candidates must have at least two years of full-time large scale mainframe computer operations or mainframe data communication network experience in a mainframe environment gained since February, 1996.

COMPUTER SPECIALIST (OPERATIONS)
WHAT THE JOB INVOLVES: Computer Specialists (Operations), under supervision, with considerable latitude for independent action or the exercise of independent judgment, are responsible for providing management with state-of-the-art technical assistance in all aspects of data processing operations; provide supervision or senior staff support of computer operations in a large-scale, multi-programmed mainframe computer environment, or the conduct of similar duties within a large network of distributed minicomputer and microcomputer systems. All personnel perform related work. Computer Specialists (Operations) may be required to work shifts, including nights, Saturdays, Sundays, and holidays.
Education and Experience Requirements:
(1) A four-year high school diploma or its educational equivalent plus a certificate from an accredited technical school (approximately 675 hours) with a specialization in computer operations, and three years of satisfactory, full-time large-scale mainframe computer operations or three years of satisfactory data communication network experience in a

mainframe environment, gained since June, 1996, one year of which must have been in a project leader capacity or as a major contributor on a complex project; or

(Note: If you have a certificate from an accredited technical school (approximately 675 hours)with a specialization in computer operations, indicate the Name of the School, Number of Hours Completed, and the Date of Graduation in Section A.4 [Courses] on page 2 of the Education and Experience Test Paper).

(2) A baccalaureate degree from an accredited college and four years of satisfactory, full-time experience as described in "1" above, including one year of which must have been in a project leader capacity or as a major contributor on a complex project; or

(3) A four-year high school diploma or its educational equivalent and five years of satisfactory, fulltime experience as described in "1" above, including one year of which must have been in a project leader capacity or as a major contributor on a complex project; or

(4) A satisfactory combination of education and/or experience which is equivalent to "1," "2," or "3" above. However, all candidates must have at least a four-year high school diploma or its educational equivalent and three years of satisfactory, full-time large-scale mainframe computer operations or three years of satisfactory data communication network experience in a mainframe environment, gained since June, 1996, one year of which must have been in a project leader capacity or as a major contributor on a complex project. NOTE: In order to have your experience accepted as Project Leader or Major Contributor experience, you must explain in detail how your experience qualifies you as a project leader or as a major contributor. Experience in computer software development and maintenance, technical support, quality assurance (QA), hardware installation, or as an end user will not be accepted for meeting the minimum qualification requirements.

COMPUTER PROGRAMMER ANALYST (LEVELS I-III)

WHAT THE JOB INVOLVES: Computer Programmer Analysts, under general supervision, with some latitude for independent or unreviewed action or decision, perform work in the design, development, implementation, maintenance, and enhancement of database management systems, operating systems, data communication systems, and/or computer applications; may supervise work in the development of computer programs; and perform related work.

Education and Experience Requirements:

(1) A baccalaureate degree from an accredited college, including or supplemented by twenty-four (24) semester credits in computer science or a related computer field; or

(2) A four year high school diploma or its educational equivalent plus (3) years of satisfactory fulltime computer programming experience; or

(3) A satisfactory combination of education and experience that is equivalent to (1) or (2) above. College education may be substituted for up to one year of the experience required in (2) above on the basis that sixty (60) semester credits from an accredited college is equated to one year of experience. In addition, twenty-four (24) credits from an accredited college or graduate school in computer science or a related computer field, or a certificate of at least 625 hours in computer programming from an accredited technical school (post high school) may be substituted for one year of experience. However, all candidates who attempt to qualify under option (3) must have at least a four year high school diploma or its educational equivalent and at least (1) year of satisfactory full-time computer programming experience. To receive credit, all college credits in computer science or a related computer field and/or the certificate in computer programming must be listed in Section A.2 on page 2 of the Education and Experience Test Paper.

COMPUTER ASSOCIATE (SOFTWARE LEVELS I-III)

WHAT THE JOB INVOLVES: Computer Associates(Software)under direct supervision, with moderate latitude for independent initiative and judgment, are responsible for the design, development, testing, implementation, maintenance, and enhancement of database management systems, operating systems, data communications and/or computer applications through product lifecycle. May supervise work in the development of computer programs. All Computer Associates (Software) perform related work..

Education and Experience Requirements:

(1) A baccalaureate degree from an accredited college, including or supplemented by twenty-four (24) semester credits in computer science or a related computer field and one (1) year of satisfactory fulltime computer software experience in computer systems development and analysis, applications programming, database administration, systems programming or data communications; or

(2) A four year high school diploma or its educational equivalent and five (5) years of full-time satisfactory computer software experience as described in "1" above; or

(3) A satisfactory combination of education and experience that is equivalent to "1" or "2" above. College education may be substituted for up to two years of the required experience in "2" above on the basis that sixty(60) semester credits from an accredited college is equated to one year of experience. In addition, twenty-four (24) semester credits from an accredited college or graduate school in computer science or a related field, or a certificate of at least 625 hours in computer programming from an accredited technical school (post high school), may be substituted for one year of experience. However, all candidates who attempt to qualify under option "3" must have at least a four year high school diploma or its educational equivalent .

COMPUTER SPECIALIST (SOFTWARE LEVELS I-IV)

WHAT THE JOB INVOLVES: Computer Specialists (Software), under varying degrees of supervision or direction, with varying degrees of latitude for independent initiative and judgment perform software functions of a highly complex, technical nature in the maintenance, design, implementation and enhancement of database management systems, operating systems, data communication systems, and/or computer applications; may supervise a unit engaged in work related to these areas; and perform related work.

Experience & Education Requirements:

(1) A baccalaureate degree from an accredited college, including or supplemented by twenty-four (24) semester credits in computer science or a related computer field and two (2) years of satisfactory full-time software experience in designing, programming, debugging, maintaining, implementing, and enhancing computer software applications, systems programming, systems analysis and design, data communication software, or database design and programming, including one year in a project leader capacity or as a major contributor on a complex project; or

(2) A four-year high school diploma or its educational equivalent and six   (6) years of full-time satisfactory software experience as described in "1" above, including one year in a project leader capacity or as a major contributor on a complex project; or

(3) A satisfactory combination of education and experience that is equivalent to (1) or (2) above. College education may be substituted for up to two years of the required experience in (2) above on the basis that sixty (60) semester credits from an accredited college is equated to one year of experience. A masters degree in computer science or a related computer field may be substituted for one year of the required experience in (1) or (2) above. However, all candidates must have a four year high school diploma or its educational equivalent, plus at least one (1) year of satisfactory full-time software experience in a project leader apacity or as a major contributor on a complex project.

TELECOMMUNICATIONS ASSOCIATE (LEVELS I-III)

WHAT THE JOB INVOLVES: At Assignment Level I: Telecommunications Associates under supervision , with some latitude for the exercise of independent judgement and initiative, perform other than engineering functions for delivery of voice (telephone) and/or data telecommunications service. They perform assignments of moderate difficulty in the procurement, set-up, operation, and/or maintenance of voice and/or data telecommunications systems or serve as a voice and /or data telecommunications analyst, member of a project team, or project manager for voice and/or data telecommunications projects of moderate scope; and perform related work. Some of the physical activities performed by Telecommunications Associates and environmental conditions experienced are: Walking to and from sites; climbing and descending from ladders or stairs; standing for an extended period of time; bending and stooping during surveys; working in confined areas; distinguishing colors; communicating orally; carrying clipboard, equipment and tools weighing up top 50 pounds; climbing around and over various objects; walking in areas that may be damp, dark, smoky or acrid; working outdoors in all kinds of weather; may drive a motor vehicle to and from sites; work nights and weekends.

Education and Experience Requirements:

Voice Telecommunications

1. A baccalaureate degree from an accredited college including or supplemented by 24 semester credits in voice telecommunications (telephone, radio, microwave, fiber optic and cell service), telecommunications technology, electronics, physics, and/or planning and analysis of electronic systems, and one year of satisfactory full-time experience in the performance of analytical, planning, operational, technical, and/or administrative duties in a voice telecommunications or closely-related electronics planning, electronics management, and/or electronics service environment; or

2. An associate degree from an accredited college including or supplemented by 12 semester credits in voice telecommunications (telephone, radio, microwave, fiber optic and cell service), telecommunications technology, electronics, physics, and/or planning and analysis of electronic systems, and two years of experience as described in "1" above; or

3. A four-year high school diploma or its educational equivalent and three years of experience as described in "1" above; or

4. A satisfactory combination of education and/or experience which is equivalent to "1", "2" or "3" above. College education may be substituted for experience on the basis of six months of experience as described in "1" above for each 30 semester credits of undergraduate college education including or supplemented by 6 semester credits in voice telecommunications (telephone, radio, microwave, fiber optic and cell service), telecommunications technology, electronics, physics, and/or planning and analysis of electronic systems. However, all candidates must have at least one year of the experience as described in "1" above.   Examples of acceptable experience in voice telecommunications are as follows: installing and servicing voice telecommunications systems; planning and analyzing of voice communications systems; and preparing proposals for voice telecommunications systems.

Data Communications

1. A baccalaureate degree from an accredited college including or supplemented by 24 semester credits in data telecommunications/networking or in a pertinent scientific, technical, electronic or related area and one year of satisfactory full-time experience in the performance of analytical, planning, operational, technical, and/or administrative duties in a data telecommunications or closely-related electronics planning, electronics management, and/or electronics service environment; or

2. An associate degree from an accredited college including or supplemented by 12 semester credits in data telecommunications/networking or in a pertinent scientific, technical, electronic or related area and two years of experience as described in "1" above; or

3. A four-year high school diploma or its educational equivalent and three years of experience as described in "1" above; or

4. Education and/or experience equivalent to "1", "2" or "3" above. College education may be substituted for experience on the basis of six months of experience as described in "1" above for each 30 semester credits of undergraduate college education including or supplemented by 6 semester credits in data telecommunications/networking or in a pertinent scientific, technical, electronic or related area. However all candidates must have at least one year of the experience as described in "1" above.

Examples of acceptable course work are: data telecommunications, computer science, electronics, and electrical engineering.

Examples of acceptable experience in data telecommunications are as follows: operating data telecommunications computer consoles and peripheral devices; computer equipment planning; automation planning; computer programming; and computer system installation and service.

TELECOMMUNICATIONS SPECIALIST (LEVELS I-III)

Rresponsible non-engineering work as specialists in voice (telephone) and/or data communications. Education & Experience Qualifications: similar to those or Telecommunications Analyst, requiring more years experience. See New York City website for specifics.

COMPUTER SERVICE TECHNICIAL (LEVELS I-III)

WHAT THE JOB INVOLVES: At Assignment Level I: Computer Service Technicians, under supervision, with some latitude for independent initiative and judgement, perform routine service functions in maintaining, troubleshooting and repairing computers, computer peripheral equipment and/or networking technology equipment; may be required to drive a motor vehicle in the performance of these functions in field locations; and perform related work.

Education and Experience Requirements:

1. A four-year high school diploma or its educational equivalent and one year of satisfactory, full-time experience in computer maintenance and repair; or

2. A four-year high school diploma or its educational equivalent and graduation from a certified technical training program in computer maintenance and repair; or

3. A satisfactory combination of education, training and/or experience equivalent to "1" or "2" above. Experience of the type described in "1" above may be substituted for high school on the basis of one year of experience for each year of high school. However, all candidates must have either one year of the type of experience described in "1" above, or graduation from a certified technical training program as described in "2" above.

LOCAL AREA NETWORK ADMINISTRATOR (LEVELS I-IV)

Job Description: Provide second-level workstation problem identification, diagnosis and resolution. Perform analysis concerning the agency's MIS operations; analyze, support and administer existing Windows based systems and provide troubleshooting strategies; supervise staff and assist in the ongoing deployment of the desktop PC hardware and software; provide technical support and maintenance for common business related technologies; document and maintain a complete inventory of Agency hardware and software assets.

REQUIRED VENDOR CERTIFICATION: Microsoft Certified Desktop Support Technician (MCDST), Plus 1. A baccalaureate degree from an accredited college, and two years of satisfactory, full-time (not classroom-based) experience in local area network planning, design, configuration, installation, troubleshooting, integration, performance monitoring, maintenance, enhancement, and security management; or

2. A four year high school diploma or its educational equivalent and six years of satisfactory, full-time (not classroombased) information technology experience of which at least 2 years must have been as described in "1" above; or

3. A master's degree in computer science or a related field from an accredited college may substitute for one year of experience. However, all candidates must have at least one year of satisfactory (not classroom-based) full-time information technology experience as described in "1" above.

WIDE AREA NETWORK ADMINISTRATOR (LEVELS I-IV)

Job Description: Under supervision, with latitude for the exercise of independent judgment and initiative. Responsible for planning, designing, configuring, installing, troubleshooting, testing, integrating, performance monitoring, maintaining, enhancing, security management, and support of ALL aspects of the Department's Wide Area Network. Develop and implement advanced network management programs and services in support of the Department of Finance's (DOF) Wide Area Network; Review and evaluate current and future network management platforms and configurations and provide rapid and effective troubleshooting capability for operators and network engineers for the Intranet / Internet Infrastructure; Interface with other groups both inside and outside of DOF in order to meet network management requirements of the DOF network; Design and configure network management platforms in order to meet the requirements of the DOF network, including but not limited to: CiscoWorks 2000, configure network devices for SNMP traps and conditions as required; responsible for troubleshooting the Agency's Internet / intranet based routers; responsible for insuring the Agency's VPN (Virtual Private Network) is active at all times; produce network device performance/utilization reports at the direction of the Manager of Network Management; provide advanced-level technical support for problems on all DOFowned network management platforms.

REQUIRED VENDOR CERTIFICATION: Cisco Certified Network Professional (CCNP)

1. A baccalaureate degree from an accredited college, and two years of satisfactory, full-time (not classroom-based) experience in wide area network planning, design, configuration, installation, troubleshooting, integration, performance monitoring, maintenance, enhancement, and security management; or

2. A four year high school diploma or its educational equivalent and six years of satisfactory, full-time (not classroom-based) information technology experience of which at least 2 years must have been as described in "1" above; or

3. A master's degree in computer science or a related field from an accredited college may substitute for one year of experience. However, all candidates must have at least one years of satisfactory (not classroom-based) full-time information technology experience as described in "1" above.

APPLICATIONS DEVELOPER (LEVELS I-IV)

Job Description: Under general supervision, performs a full range of computer systems functions including: manage programmers and systems analysts, work with the business community to ensure that programming specifications meet their requirements, provide technical leadership in supporting on-line CICS transactions and a nightly batch billing process to meet the mainframe application programming needs of the bureau's client community, the Water Board and the City's oversight agencies, assist in the implementation of changes to the bureau's interactive voice response system (IVR) which provides billing payment meter reading information to our customers and allows customers to enter meter readings; assist in the development and implementation of an agency intranet and in developing browser applications.

Experience & Education Requirements:

(1) Professional/vendor certifications in computer applications programming that s required for the position to be filled.

Required Vendor Certification: Microsoft Certified Applications Developer for. Net (MCAD); Microsoft Certified Solutions Developer for .Net (MCSD); Microsoft Certified Solutions Developer for Visual Studio 6.0 (MCSD). In addition, all candidates must have the following:

A baccalaureate degree from an accredited college, and two years of satisfactory full-time (not classroom-based) experience in computer applications development planning, design, configuration, installation, troubleshooting, integration, performance monitoring, maintenance, enhancement, and security management; or

(2) A four-year high school diploma or its educational equivalent and six years of satisfactory full-time (not classroom based) information technology experience of which at least 2 years must have been as described in "1" above; or

(3) A master's degree in computer science or a related field from an accredited college may substitute for one year of experience. However, all candidates must have at least one year of satisfactory full-time information technology experience as described in "1" above.

DATABASE ADMINISTRATOR (LEVELS I-IV)

Job Description: Under general supervision, with wide latitude for the exercise of independent initiative and judgment, supervises a unit engaged in planning, designing, configuring, installing, testing, troubleshooting, integrating, performance monitoring, maintaining, enhancing, security management, and support of database systems and performs related functions. Responsible for installation, configuration, customization, upgrades of AIX/AIX5L operating systems associated server based products. Perform analysis, ongoing monitoring of equipment for availability and proper operation concerning the agency's MIS operations; analyze, support and administer existing AIX/AIX5L based systems and provide troubleshooting strategies; assist in the ongoing deployment of server and desktop hardware and software; provide technical support and maintenance for common business related technologies; document and maintain a complete inventory of associated agency hardware and software assets. Perform AIX/UNIX commands, Tivoli Netview, Tivoli Enterprise Console (TEC2), Tivoli Frameworks, including application and systems software; install and configure base operating systems for product agents for RS6000/AIX, Windows 2000/3, Linux, and other operating systems. Develop and maintain databases to store and manage spatial and non-spatial data for various Departmental initiatives. Work closely with end-users, project managers, and other technical staff to design and build both new databases and enhancements to existing databases.

REQUIRED VENDOR CERTIFICATION: Microsoft Certified Database
Administrator (MCDBA)

1. A baccalaureate degree from an accredited college, and two years of satisfactory full-time (not classroom based) experience in database administration planning, design, configuration, installation, troubleshooting, integration, performance monitoring, /maintenance, enhancement, and security management; or

2. A four-year high school diploma or its educational equivalent and six years of satisfactory full-time (not classroom based) information technology experience of which at least 2 years must have been as described in "1" above; or

3. A master's degree in computer science or a related field from an accredited college may substitute one year of experience. However, all candidates must have at least one year of satisfactory (not classroom based) full-time information technology experience as described in "1" above.

ADMINISTRATIVE GRAPHIC ARTIST (LEVEL M-I)

Job Description: Directs graphic art staff and is responsible for the timely completion of all graphic related projects, including printed material and web development. Examples of printed material include: flyers, manuals, brochures, posters, banners, exhibitions, signs, directories, maps, charts, presentations, invitations, programs, business cards, logos, permits, schedules, forms, newsletters, advertisements, and more. Directs artwork performed under contract and manages the execution of contractual work to assure conformance to specifications and highest standards of quality.

Qualification Requirements:

1.High school graduation or equivalent and two years of training in an approved technical school in oils, water colors, painting, design, black and white, layout and other art media and seven years full-time paid experience as a commercial artist, four years of which must have been in supervision and planning of art work done by a staff; or

2 .Education and/or experience which is equivalent to "1". However, all candidates must have the four years of supervisory experience as described above.

PROCUREMENT ANALYST I-IV

WHAT THE JOB INVOLVES: At Assignment Level I: Procurement Analysts, under supervision, with some latitude for independent initiative and decision making, assist procurement personnel in purchasing goods, services, construction and/or construction-related services, and/or in processing procurement documents and contracts; confer with, advise and assist operational, technical and professional staff in the procurement process, and manage contracts for services as assigned; and perform related work.

Education and Experience Requirements:

1. A baccalaureate degree from an accredited college and six months of satisfactory full-time professional experience in procurement of goods, services, construction or construction-related services, or professional, technical or administrative experience in contract negotiation/management; or

2. An associate degree or completion of 60 semester credits from an accredited college, and 18 months of satisfactory, full-time professional experience as described in "1" above; or

3. A four-year high school diploma or its educational equivalent and two and one-half years of satisfactory full-time professional experience as described in "1" above; or

4. A combination of education and/or experience equivalent to "1", "2" or "3" above. College education may be substituted for professional experience under "2" or "3" above at the rate of 30 semester credits from an accredited college for 6 months of experience. However, all candidates must have at least a four-year high school diploma or its educational equivalent and 6 months of experience as described in "1" above.

ASSOCIATE STAFF ANALYST & STAFF ANALYST

WHAT THE JOB INVOLVES: Staff Analysts perform professional and supervisory work of varying degrees of difficulty and responsibility in the preparation and administration of agency budgets and the conduct of economic research and studies; in the preparation and conduct of administrative, procedural and operational studies and analyses concerning the agency organization and operations; and in personnel administration. Staff Analysts utilize computers in the performance of these duties. All personnel perform related work.

Education and Experience Requirements: Education Requirements must be met by June 30, 2004. Experience Requirements must be met by the last day of the Application Period.

1. A master's degree from an accredited college in economics, finance, accounting, business or public administration, human resources management, management science, operations research, organizational behavior, industrial psychology, statistics, personnel administration, labor relations, psychology, sociology, human resources development, political science, or closely related field; or

2. A baccalaureate degree from an accredited college and two years of satisfactory full-time professional experience working with the budget of a large public or private concern in budget administration, accounting, economic or financial administration, or fiscal or economic research; or in management or methods analysis, operations research, organizational research or program evaluation; or in personnel or public administration, recruitment, position classification, personnel relations, labor relations, employee benefits, staff development, employment program planning/administration, labor market research, economic planning, fiscal management, or in a related area; or

3. A four-year high school diploma or its educational equivalent and six years of satisfactory full-time professional experience working for the City of New York in the areas described in "2" above; or

4. A combination of education and/or experience equivalent to "1", "2", or "3" above. All candidates who qualify under "1" or "2" above must possess a baccalaureate degree from an accredited college, and all candidates who qualify under "3"above must possess a four-year high school diploma or its educational equivalent. To be credited under "3" above, experience must have been with the City of New York. Education above the high school level may be substituted for City experience under "3" above at the rate of 30 semester credits from an accredited college for one year of experience. Graduate education may be substituted for experience beyond the baccalaureate degree on the basis of 24 graduate credits for one year of experience. You may be given the test before we check your qualifications.

Appendix F:
Locating Federal Jobs at Direct Hire Authority and Excepted Service Agencies

EXCEPTED SERVICE AGENCIES

Most Federal Government civilian positions are part of the competitive civil service. To obtain a Federal job, you must compete with other applicants in open competition.

Some agencies are excluded from the competitive civil service procedures. This means that these agencies have their own hiring system which establishes the evaluation criteria they use in filling their internal vacancies. These agencies are called *excepted service agencies*.

If you are interested in employment with an *excepted service agency*, you should contact that agency directly. The U.S. Office of Personnel Management does not provide application forms or information on jobs in excepted service agencies or organizations. Below is a list of excepted service agencies, departments and public international organizations. This list is not all-inclusive and is subject to change.

MAJOR EXCEPTED SERVICE DEPARTMENTS AND AGENCIES

Federal Reserve System, Board of Governors
20th & C Street, NW.
Washington, DC 20551
www.federalreserve.gov
(202) 452-3038

Central Intelligence Agency
Office of Public Affairs
Washington, D.C. 20505
www.cia.gov
703-82-0623

Defense Intelligence Agency
Civilian Personnel Office DAH-2
100 MacDill Blvd
Washington, DC 20340-5100
www.dia.mil
202-231-8228

U.S. Department of State
2201 C Street NW
Washington, DC 20520
www.state.gov
202-647-4000

MAJOR EXCEPTED SERVICE DEPARTMENTS AND AGENCIES

Federal Bureau of Investigation
J. Edgar Hoover Building
935 Pennsylvania Avenue, NW
Washington, D.C. 20535-0001
www.fbi.gov
202-324-3000

Government Accountability Office
441 G Street, NW., Room 1157
Washington, DC 20548

www.gao.gov
202-512-6092

Agency for International Development
2401 E Street, NW., Room 1127
Washington, DC 20523
www.usaid.gov
202-712-4810

National Security Agency
College Relations Branch
Fort Meade, MD 20750
www.nsa.gov
1-866-672-4473
U.S. Nuclear Regulatory Commission
Division of Organization of Personnel
Resources and Employment Program
Washington, DC 20555
www.nrc.gov
301-415-1534

Post Rate Commission
Administrative Office, Suite 300
Washington, DC 20268-0001
www.prc.gov
(202) 789-6800

Postal Service
(Contact your local Postmaster) www.usps.gov

Tennessee Valley Authority
Knoxville Office Complex
400 West Summit Hill Drive

Knoxville, TN 37902
www.tva.gov
865-632-2101

United States Mission to the United Nations
140 East 45th Street
New York, N.Y. 10017
www.un.int/usa
212-415-4050

U.S. Department of Veterans Affairs
810 Vermont Avenue, NW.
Washington, DC 20420
www.va.gov

JUDICIAL BRANCH

The Judicial Branch of the Federal
Government
includes all legal entities except the
U.S. Claims Court. For Judicial Branch
employment information contact:

United States Supreme Court Building
Personnel Office
1 First Street, NE.
Washington, DC 20543
202-479-3211

Office of Public Affairs
Administrative Office of the U.S. Courts
Washington, D.C. 20544
www.uscourts.gov
202-502-2600

United States Court of Federal Claims
717 Madison Place, NW.
Washington, DC 20005
www.uscfc.uscourts.gov
202-357-6400

LEGISLATIVE BRANCH

The Legislative Branch of the Federal
Government
includes Senators' and
Representatives' offices,
the Library of Congress and the U.S.
Capitol. For employment
information contact:

U.S. Senate
Senate Placement Office
Senate Hart Building, Room 142B
Washington, DC 20510
www.senate.gov
(202) 224-3121

U.S. House of Representatives
House Placement Office
House Office Building, Annex 2, Room 219
Third & D Street, SW.
Washington, DC 20515-6609
www.house.gov

202-224-3121

Library of Congress
Employment Office
Room 107, Madison Building
Washington, DC 20540
www.loc.gov
202-707-5627

PUBLIC INTERNATIONAL ORGANIZATIONS

The United States holds membership in numerous
international organizations which are not part of the Federal
Government. For employment information and application
procedures contact:

International Monetary Fund
Recruiting and Training Division
700 19th Street, NW.
Washington, DC 20431
www.imf.org
202-623-7000

Pan American Health Organization
Pan American Sanitary Bureau
Regional Office of the
World Health Organizations
525 23rd Street, NW.
Washington, DC 20037
www.paho.org
202- 974-3000

United Nations Children's Fund
333 East 38th Street
(Mail Code: GC-6)
New York, New York 10016
www.unicef.org
212-686-5522

United Nations Development Program
One United Nations Plaza
New York, NY 10017
www.undp.org
212-906-5000

United Nations Institute for Training and
Research
One United Nations Plaza
Room DC1-603,
New York, NY, 10017-3515
www.unitar.org
212-963-9196

United Nations Population Fund
220 East 42nd Street
New York, NY 10017
www.unfpa.org
212-297-5000

United Nations Secretariat
Office of Personnel Services
Recruitment Programs Section
New York, NY 10017
www.un.org/documents/st.htm

World Bank, IFC and MIGA*
Recruitment Division
International Recruitment
1818 H Street, NW.
Washington, DC 20433
www.worldbank.org
(202) 473-1000

* IFC-International Finance Corporation
MIGA-Multilateral Investment Guarantee
Agency

Form Approved
OMB No. 3206-0219

OPTIONAL APPLICATION FOR FEDERAL EMPLOYMENT - OF 612

You may apply for most jobs with a resume, this form, or other written format. If your resume or application does not provide all the information requested on this form and in the job vacancy announcement, you may lose consideration for a job.

1 Job title in announcement	2 Grade(s) applying for	3 Announcement number

4 Last name	First and middle names	5 Social Security Number - -

6 Mailing address	7 Phone numbers (include area code) Daytime ( )
City	State	ZIP Code -	Evening ( )

WORK EXPERIENCE

8 Describe your paid and nonpaid work experience related to the job for which you are applying. Do **not** attach job descriptions.

1) Job title (if Federal, include series and grade)

From (MM/YY)	To (MM/YY)	Salary $	per	Hours per week
Employer's name and address				Supervisor's name and phone number ( )

Describe your duties and accomplishments

2) Job title (if Federal, include series and grade)

From (MM/YY)	To (MM/YY)	Salary $	per	Hours per week
Employer's name and address				Supervisor's name and phone number ( )

Describe your duties and accomplishments

9 May we contact your current supervisor?

YES ☐   NO ☐ è   If we need to contact your current supervisor before making an offer, we will contact you first.

EDUCATION

10 Mark highest level completed.   **Some HS** ☐   **HS/GED** ☐   **Associate** ☐   **Bachelor** ☐   **Master** ☐   **Doctoral** ☐

11 Last high school (HS) or GED school. Give the school's name, city, State, ZIP Code (if known), and year diploma or GED received.

12 Colleges and universities attended. Do **not** attach a copy of your transcript unless requested.

	Name			Total Credits Earned		Major(s)	Degree - Year
1)				Semester	Quarter		(if any) Received
	City	State	ZIP Code				
			-				
2)							
			-				
3)							
			-				

OTHER QUALIFICATIONS

13 **Job-related** training courses (give title and year). **Job-related** skills (other languages, computer software/hardware, tools, machinery, typing speed, etc. **Job-related** certificates and licenses (current only). **Job-related** honors, awards, and special accomplishments(publications, memberships in professional/honor societies, leadership activities, public speaking, and performance awards.) Give dates, but do **not** send documents unless requested.

GENERAL

14 Are you a U.S. citizen?   **YES** ☐   **NO** ☐ è   Give the country of your citizenship.

15 Do you claim veterans' preference?   **NO** ☐   **YES** ☐ è   Mark your claim of 5 or 10 points below.

   5 points ☐ è   Attach your DD 214 or other proof.   **10 points** ☐ è   Attach an *Application for 10-Point Veterans' Preference* (SF 15) and proof required.

16 Were you ever a Federal civilian employee?

			Series	Grade	From (MM/YY)	To (MM/YY)

NO ☐   **YES** ☐ è   For highest civilian grade give:

17 Are you eligible for reinstatement based on career or career-conditional Federal status?

NO ☐   **YES** ☐ è   If requested, attach SF 50 proof.

APPLICANT CERTIFICATION

18 **I certify** that, to the best of my knowledge and belief, all of the information on and attached to this application is true, correct, complete and made in good faith. **I understand** that false or fraudulent information on or attached to this application may be grounds for not hiring me or firing me after I begin work, and may be punishable by fine or imprisonment. **I understand** that any information I give may be investigated.

SIGNATURE   **DATE SIGNED**

Appendix H:
Sample Knowledge, Skills Abilities Statement

Knowledge, Skills, Abilities Statement
(Sample KSA Statement for Job Announcement
#DS117475-BM
See Job Description in Appendix D: Sample Federal Jobs

Information Technology Specialist (Application Software)
Job Announcement #DS117475-BM
Duties:
Individuals within the Application Developer job family are :
1. -Responsible for the design, development, testing, documentation, maintenance,
and integration of application software

I have worked for 6 years, from 2001-2006, in Applications Development. In my position as Application Development Manager for Quad States Developers, from 2003-2006, I worked for 3 years in customized IT/IS applications development. As Applications Development Manager, I supervised a team of 3 application developers in the design of an application for a large Utility company. Strengths include programming knowledge, database knowledge, and experience with open architectures for application usage and growth.

I have been responsible for the design, development, testing, documentation, maintenance, and integration of application software for multiple clients with a variety of software tools. From 2001-2003, in my position as Application Developer with Quad States Developers, I worked as Project Leader of Application Development Team for Large Utility Company and managed 3 developers. I have worked as Individual Contributor and Team Member on Application Development projects for U.S. mid-sized companies, using Oracle, Java in J2EE server environments, and with Linux and Windows. Part of a 6-member team from Quad States that enhanced and retooled financial applications for a Life Insurance company, a Bond Company, and an IT manufacturer, using Java.

Knowledge/Education:
Operating Systems: UNIX (AIX, HP-UX, Sun Solaris, RedHat Linux, BEA WebLogic); WINDOWS 2000 to Current; WINDOWS NT
DBMS: Oracle 7/8/8i, , Java, Java Beans (Developer, Designer, DBA); MS SQL Server; MS Access; O2 (Object DBMS), J3EE, BEA WebLogic, Linux, Windows Operating System Training
Languages/Tools: SQL, PL/SQL, SQL Server, ASP, Active X, VB Script, Jscript, HTML, XML
Specialty: Specialize in developing custom software applications to combine accounting, finance, and logistics, to process information on customer usage of product and services. Developed a reputation of making clients happy by completing projects easily, facilitating retrieval of information, and reducing costs.
Supervisory Controls & Leadership: I have worked for 6 years in Applications Development. In my position as Application Development Manager for Quad States Developers, from 2003-2006, I worked for 3 years in customized IT/IS applications development. As Applications Development Manager from 2003-2006, I supervised a team of 3 application developers in the design of an application for a large Utility company. Strengths include programming knowledge, database knowledge, and experience with open architectures for application usage and growth. I have been responsible for the design, development, testing, documentation, maintenance, and integration of application software for multiple clients with a variety of software tools. From 2001-2003, in my position as Application Developer with Quad States Developers, I worked as Project Leader of Application Development Team for Large Utility Company and managed 3 developers. I have worked as Individual Contributor and Team Member on Application Development projects for U.S. mid-sized companies, using Oracle, Java in J2EE server environments, and with Linux and Windows. Part of a 6-member team from Quad States that enhanced and retooled financial applications for a Life Insurance company, a Bond Company, and an IT manufacturer, using Java.

Nature of Work & Scope of Difficulty: Responsible for analysis, design, and implementation of customized Application Software for Utility Company, Mid-Sized U.S. Manufacturer, and Bond Rating Company. References available on request.

2. -Obtain and refine business requirements through interaction with the
Requirements Analysts and the customer

I have worked for 6 years, from 2001-2006, in Applications Development. In my position as Application Development Manager for Quad States Developers, from 2003-2006, I worked for 3 years in customized IT/IS applications development. As Applications Development Manager, I supervised a team of 3 application developers in the design of an application for a large Utility company. Strengths include programming knowledge, database knowledge, and experience with open architectures for application usage and growth.

I have been responsible for the design, development, testing, documentation, maintenance, and integration of application software for multiple clients with a variety of software tools. From 2001-2003, in my position as Application Developer with Quad States Developers, I worked as Project Leader of Application Development Team for Large Utility Company and managed 3 developers. I have worked as Individual Contributor and Team Member on Application Development projects for U.S. mid-sized companies, using Oracle, Java in J2EE server environments, and with Linux and Windows. Part of a 6-member team from Quad States that enhanced and retooled financial applications for a Life Insurance company, a Bond Company, and an IT manufacturer, using Java.

Business requirements drove the design, development, testing, documentation, maintenance, and integration of application software with Oracle, Java Beans, MS Access, SQL Server and other software tools for business applications.
Knowledge/Education:
Supervisory Controls & Leadership: Part of a 3-member team from Quad States that enhanced and retooled financial applications for a Life Insurance company, a Bond Company, and an IT manufacturer, using Java.
Nature of Work & Scope of Difficulty: Analyzed existing systems, performance shortfalls, new module creation and migrations. Increased usability of existing database information.

3. Provide Tier II and Tier III support for the Help Desk.

In my position as Application Developer with Quad States Developers for multiple clients, from 2001-2002, I was responsible for the design, development, testing, documentation, maintenance, and integration of Help Desk software, including the installation of Network Solutions Support Magic and Peregrine Service Center. Installed and configured software on local machines. Supported desktop environment distributed in different buildings.
Knowledge/Education: Network Solutions Support Magic and Peregrine Service Center Training.
Specialty: 2+ Years experience in Help Desk application development and support. Management experience as Lead for the Help Desk team in initial phases, conducting training and support, productivity analysis, and performance assessments.
Supervisory Controls & Leadership: Managed and trained Help Desk supervisor in installation and use of Network Solutions Support Magic. Managed and trained
a team of helpdesk analysts to provide first and second-level support to more than 350 end-users, explaining software components and escalation techniques.
Nature of Work & Scope of Difficulty: Implemented Help Desk application through system life-cycle, including Feasibility, System Design, Software Purchase and Customization, Installation and Use.

4. -Work as individual contributors, team members or serve as project task
managers.

I have worked for 6 years, from 2001-2006, in Applications Development. In my position as Application Development Manager for Quad States Developers, from 2003-2006, I worked for 3 years in customized IT/IS applications development. As Applications Development Manager, I supervised a team of 3 application developers in the design of an application for a large Utility company. Strengths include programming knowledge, database knowledge, and experience with open architectures for application usage and growth.
I have been responsible for the design, development, testing, documentation, maintenance, and integration of application software for multiple clients with a variety of software tools. From 2001-2003, in my position as Application Developer with Quad States Developers, I worked as Project Leader of Application Development Team for Large Utility Company and managed 3 developers. I have worked as Individual Contributor and Team Member on Application Development projects for U.S. mid-sized companies, using Oracle, Java in J2EE server environments, and with Linux and Windows. Part of a 6-member team from Quad States that enhanced and

retooled financial applications for a Life Insurance company, a Bond Company, and an IT manufacturer, using Java.

Knowledge/Education:

Supervisory Controls & Leadership: Worked as Project Leader of Application Development Team for Large Utility Company. Worked as Individual Contributor and Team Member on Application Development projects for U.S. Mid-sized companies, using Oracle, Java in J2EE server environments, and with Linux and Windows operating systems.

Nature of Work & Scope of Difficulty: Application Development for Large Utility company, finance system; Mid-sized Manufacturing DBMS systems.

5. -Have a solid understanding of software, data structure, data management, and/or database design principles, system development life cycle, and prototyping methodology and techniques

-Managed a team of 3 developers
-Managed the server team
-Installed and upgraded Oracle servers on several UNIX systems
-Created, configured, backed up, and tuned database instances
-Defined a common logical architecture for Oracle database and developed PL/SQL interfaces.
-Performed logical and physical data modeling
-Project Leader with overall responsibility for defining business requirements (interviews and meetings with end-users), design, development and selection of software tools. Brought application to fruition in system life cycle from client-customer need, through design, development of database, population of database, migration of database, interfaces and end-user implementation

Knowledge/Education:

Specialty: Mid-sized Manufacturing DBMS systems

Supervisory Controls & Leadership:

-Project Leader with overall responsibility for defining business requirements (interviews and meetings with end-users), design, development and selection of software tools. Brought application to fruition in system life cycle from client-customer need, through design, development of database, population of database, migration of database, interfaces and end-user implementation

Nature of Work & Scope of Difficulty:

-Project Leader with overall responsibility for defining business requirements (interviews and meetings with end-users), design, development and selection of software tools. Brought application to fruition in system life cycle from client-customer need, through design, development of database, population of database, migration of database, interfaces and end-user implementation

6. -Responsible for applying project management principles to their individual project work

-Demonstrated leadership and project management skills as Project Leader for design, development of database, population of database, migration of database, interfaces and end-user implementation
-Improved overall application performance on several applications, reducing the memory footprint over original specifications by applying object-oriented methodologies
-Utilized object-oriented design principles in ASPs, to create higher performance, improvements in speed, and easier code maintenance.
-Prepared and utilized Microsoft Project Management Timelines with Client-Customers for resource management and to estimate and carry out proper project management of development work

Knowledge/Education:

Supervisory Controls & Leadership:

-Project Leader with overall responsibility for defining business requirements (interviews and meetings with end-users), design, development and selection of software tools. Brought application to fruition in system life cycle from client-customer need, through design, development of database, population of database, migration of database, interfaces and end-user implementation

Nature of Work & Scope of Difficulty:

-Project Leader with overall responsibility for defining business requirements (interviews and meetings with end-users), design, development and selection of software tools. Brought application to fruition in system life cycle from client-customer need, through design, development of database, population of database, migration of database, interfaces and end-user implementation

7. -Provide client support, consultation, and subject mater expertise for application development, maintenance and administration

I have worked for 6 years, from 2001-2006, in Applications Development. In my position as Application Development Manager for Quad States Developers, from 2003-2006, I worked for 3 years in customized IT/IS applications development. As Applications Development Manager, I supervised a team of 3 application developers in the design of an application for a large Utility company. Strengths include programming knowledge, database knowledge, and experience with open architectures for application usage and growth.

I have been responsible for the design, development, testing, documentation, maintenance, and integration of application software for multiple clients with a variety of software tools. From 2001-2003, in my position as Application Developer with Quad States Developers, I worked as Project Leader of Application Development Team for Large Utility Company and managed 3 developers. I have worked as Individual Contributor and Team Member on Application Development projects for U.S. mid-sized companies, using Oracle, Java in J2EE server environments, and with Linux and Windows. Part of a 6-member team from Quad States that enhanced and retooled financial applications for a Life Insurance company, a Bond Company, and an IT manufacturer, using Java.

Knowledge/Education:

Supervisory Controls & Leadership:

-Project Leader with overall responsibility for defining business requirements (interviews and meetings with end-users), design, development and selection of software tools. Brought application to fruition in system life cycle from client-customer need, through design, development of database, population of database, migration of database, interfaces and end-user implementation

Nature of Work & Scope of Difficulty:

-Project Leader with overall responsibility for defining business requirements (interviews and meetings with end-users), design, development and selection of software tools. Brought application to fruition in system life cycle from client-customer need, through design, development of database, population of database, migration of database, interfaces and end-user implementation

8. -Demonstrate autonomous work environment flexiblity in work assignments, and exhibit customer orientation skills.

Demonstrated autonomous work environment flexibility in work assignments with many clients, by making and meeting appointments at client-customer schedule, working with client support and technical teams on various schedules, adjusting work and work loads to accommodate timetables for required work.

Managed applications development team-member assignments to accommodate and account for required flexibility in work assignments, schedules, timetables for required work.

Knowledge/Education:

Supervisory Controls & Leadership:

-Project Leader with overall responsibility for defining business requirements (interviews and meetings with end-users), design, development and selection of software tools. Brought application to fruition in system life cycle from client-customer need, through design, development of database, population of database, migration of database, interfaces and end-user implementation

Nature of Work & Scope of Difficulty:

Demonstrated autonomous work environment flexibility in work assignments with many clients, by making and meeting appointments at client-customer schedule, working with client support and technical teams on various schedules; adjusting work and work loads to accommodate timetables for required work.

Managed applications development team-member assignments to accommodate and account for required flexibility in work assignments, schedules, timetables for required work.

<u>Qualifications for GS-13:</u>

1. -Applicants must have one or more years of specialized experience as Information Technology Specialist (Application Software), completing computer project assignments that involve design, development, testing, documentation, maintenance and integration of application software; participation in technology planning, product evaluation and report development; and serving as a project manager. This experience must be equivalent to the GS-12 level in the Federal service, but could have been gained in the public or private sectors.

I have worked for 6 years, from 2001-2006, in Applications Development. In my position as Application Development Manager for Quad States Developers, from 2003-2006, I worked for 3 years in customized IT/IS applications development. As Applications Development Manager, I supervised a team of 3 application developers in the design of an application for a large Utility company. Strengths include programming knowledge, database knowledge, and experience with open architectures for application usage and growth.

I have been responsible for the design, development, testing, documentation, maintenance, and integration of application software for multiple clients with a variety of software tools. From 2001-2003, in my position as Application Developer with Quad States Developers, I worked as Project Leader of Application Development Team for Large Utility Company and managed 3 developers. I have worked as Individual Contributor and Team Member on Application Development projects for U.S. mid-sized companies, using Oracle, Java in J2EE server environments, and with Linux and Windows. Part of a 6-member team from Quad States that enhanced and retooled financial applications for a Life Insurance company, a Bond Company, and an IT manufacturer, using Java.

Knowledge/Education:

Operating Systems: UNIX (AIX, HP-UX, Sun Solaris, RedHat Linux, BEA WebLogic); WINDOWS 2000 to Current; WINDOWS NT

DBMS: Oracle 7/8/8i , Java, Java Beans (Developer, Designer, DBA); MS SQL Server; MS Access; O2 (Object DBMS), J3EE, BEA WebLogic, Linux, Windows Operating System Training

Languages/Tools: SQL, PL/SQL, SQL Server, ASP, Active X, VB Script, Jscript, HTML, XML

Specialty: Specialize in developing custom software applications to combine accounting, finance, and logistics, to process information on customer usage of product and services. Developed a reputation of making clients happy by completing projects easily, facilitating retrieval of information, and reducing costs.

Supervisory Controls & Leadership: I have worked for 6 years in Applications Development. In my position as Application Development Manager for Quad States Developers, from 2003-2006, I worked for 3 years in customized IT/IS applications development. As Applications Development Manager from 2003-2006, I supervised a team of 3 application developers in the design of an application for a large Utility company. Strengths include programming knowledge, database knowledge, and experience with open architectures for application usage and growth. I have been responsible for the design, development, testing, documentation, maintenance, and integration of application software for multiple clients with a variety of software tools. From 2001-2003, in my position as Application Developer with Quad States Developers, I worked as Project Leader of Application Development Team for Large Utility Company and managed 3 developers. I have worked as Individual Contributor and Team Member on Application Development projects for U.S. mid-sized companies, using Oracle, Java in J2EE server environments, and with Linux and Windows. Part of a 6-member team from Quad States that enhanced and retooled financial applications for a Life Insurance company, a Bond Company, and an IT manufacturer, using Java.

Nature of Work & Scope of Difficulty: Responsible for analysis, design, and implementation of customized Application Software for Utility Company, Mid-Sized U.S. Manufacturer, and Bond Rating Company. References available on request.

As Applications Development Manager from 2003-2006, I supervised a team of 3 application developers in the design of an application for a large Utility company. Strengths include programming knowledge, database knowledge, and experience with open architectures for application usage and growth.

2. -In addition, the following skills and experience is required: 1) Skill in administering a clustered BEA WebLogic Server environment in a RedHat Linux environment and 2) Skill in installing, configuring, tuning, troubleshooting, clustering, and deploying applications to WebLogic Server.

In my position as Application Developer, with Quad-State Developers for multiple clients, I worked from 2003-2006 in Linux environments and with BEA WebLogic Servers, and was responsible for the design, development, testing, documentation, maintenance, and integration of application software with BEA WebLogic software tools.

Knowledge: Knowledge of the fundamentals of distributed development using Enterprise JavaBeans 2.0. Knowledge of EJB deployment, and the general use of Java Message Service (JMS) and how to write messaging clients. In addition, knowledge of BEA WebLogic Administration Console.

Education: BEA WebLogic Server Training

Specialty: Utilized BEA WebLogic Server 9.1 new BEA Smart Update tool to download, apply and manage maintenance updates, including patches, to the BEA WebLogic Servers. Utilized other new updates in the areas of security (SAML), diagnostics, messaging, web services and other.

Nature of Work & Scope of Difficulty: Enabled enterprise to achieve faster time-to-value for critical business applications using open standards, web services and a Service-Oriented Architecture (SOA) of BEA WebLogic Server.

BIBLIOGRAPHY

AFSCME, CWA Local 1180, 2006, http://www.cwa1180.org/civil/civil.shtml

Americas Job Bank, http://www.ajb.org

Anderson Ross A., Security Engineering: A Guide to Building Dependable Distributed Systems, 2005.

Anderson, Ronald E., Ethics in Digital Government, in Digital Government, Principles and Best Practices, ed. Pavlichev, Alexei, and Garson, David, A., Idea Group Inc., 2004, 218-235
Association for Computing Machinery (ACM), http://www.acm.org/globalizationreport

Career One Stop Centers, http://www.careeronestop.org
Chabrow, Eric, Information Technology Hiring Hits an All-time High, Infromation Week, July 17, 2006

Chabrow, Eric, More U.S. Workers Have IT Jobs Than Ever Before, Information Week, Apr 24, 2006, August 8, 2006.

Chang, K.S., Introduction to Geographic Information System, McGraw Hill, 3rd edition, 2005.

Corbett, Christopher, The Future of Digital Government, in Digital Government, Principles and Best Practices, ed. Pavlichev, Alexei, and Garson, David, A., Idea Group Inc., 2004, 344-367.

Crain's Business New York, Number of Vacant Computer Jobs Rises: Survey, Amanda Fung, March 29, 2006.

Fletcher, Patricia Diamond, Portals and policy: Implications of Electronic Access to U.S. Federal Government Information and Services, in Digital Government, Principles and Best Practices, ed. Pavlichev, Alexei, and Garson, David, A., Idea Group Inc., 2004, 52-62.

Franzel, Joshua M. and Coursey, David H., Government Web Portals: Management Issues and the Approaches of Five States, in Digital Government, Principles and Best Practices, ed. Pavlichev, Alexei, and Garson, David, A., Idea Group Inc., 2004, 63-77.

Friedman, Thomas, The World Is Flat, Farrar, Strauss and Giroux, 2006.

Gant, Jon and Ijams, Donald S., Digital Government and Geographic Information Systems, in Digital Government, Principles and Best Practices, ed. Pavlichev, Alexei, and Garson, David, A., Idea Group Inc., 2004, 248-262.

Garson, David A., The Promise of Digital Government, in Digital Government, Principles and Best Practices, ed. Pavlichev, Alexei, and Garson, David, A., Idea Group Inc., 2004, 2-15.

Gore, Al, quoted in Fletcher, Patricia Diamond, Portals and policy: Implications of Electronic Access to U.S. Federal Government Information and Services, in Digital Government, Principles and Best Practices, ed. Pavlichev, Alexei, and Garson, David, A., Idea Group Inc., 2004, 52-62.

Gross, Daniel, "Why 'Outsourcing' May Lost Its Power as a Scare Word," The New York Times, August 13, 2006.
Harper, Franklin Maxwell, Data Warehousing and the Organization of Governmental Databases, in Digital Government, Principles and Best Practices, ed. Pavlichev, Alexei, and Garson, David, A., Idea Group Inc., 2004, 236-247.

Hood, C., The Tools of Government, London, MacMillan, 1983.

Info Tech Employment, "Employment Survey," 2007, http://www.infotechemployment.com.

Info Tech Employment, "IT Federal Jobs Survey," 2007, http://www.infotechemployment.com.

Info Tech Employment, "Survey of IT Job Titles in U.S. States & Major U.S. Cities," 2007, http://www.infotechemployment.com.

Info Tech Employment, Editors, Computer Jobs with the Growing Information Technology Professional Services Sector, William Briggs Publishing, 2007, http://www.infotechemployment.com .

Info Tech Employment, Editors, IT Jobs-IT Prospects- Companies-Contacts-Links: Get Hired by Companies Winning New Business and Requiring New Staff (2007), William Briggs Publishing, 2006, http://www.infotechemployment.com .

InformationWeek, More U.S. Workers Have IT Jobs Than Ever Before, Eric Chabrow, April 24, 2006

Krysiak, Mark E.; Tucker, Carla; Spitzer, David; and Holland, Kevin, E-Procurement: State Government Learns from the Private Sector, in Digital Government, Principles and Best Practices, ed. Pavlichev, Alexei, and Garson, David, A., Idea Group Inc., 2004, 149-168.

Latchford, Michael, Lowry, Alexander, Roberts, Ian, PA Consulting Group, "Successful Program Management in a Complex Outsourcing Environment," quoted in CMP Global Services, July 24, 2006, http://www.globalservicesmedia.com/sections/sm/showArticle.jhtml?articleID=190500432

Lawson, Roy, InformationWeek, 2006, More U.S. Workers Have IT Jobs Than Ever Before, Eric Chabrow, InformationWeek, Apr 24, 2006

Levy, Frank and Murnane, Richard, The New Division of Labor: How Computers are Creating the Next Job Market, Princeton University Press, 2004.

Liston, Robert A., Your Career in Civil Service, Messner Publishers, 1967.

Margetts, Helen, Information Technology in Government: Britain and America, Routledge Press, 1999.

Marlin, John Tepper, City Economist, 2006, http://www.cityeconomist.com/pdf/CityEconomist06-04-01.pdf quoted in Crain's Business New York, February 2006, Number of Vacant Computer Jobs Rises: Survey, Amanda Fung, March 29, 2006.

McClure, C.R., Sprehe, T. and Eschenfelder, K. Performance Measures for Federal Agencies: Final Report. Retrieved December 13, 2001 from http://www.access.gpo.gov/su_docs/index.html

McDougall, Paul, U.S. Tech Workers In Hot Demand Despite More Outsourcing

Mullen, Patrick R., Digital Government and Individual Privacy, in Digital Government, Principles and Best Practices, ed. Pavlichev, Alexei, and Garson, David, A., Idea Group Inc., 2004, 134-148.

National Research Council (NRC), Funding a Revolution: Government Support for Computing Research, National Academy Press, 1999.

O'Looney, J.A., Wiring Governments, Challenges and Possibilities for Public Managers, Quorum Books, 2002.

Patterson, David A., Association for Computing Machinery, 2006, http://www.acm.org/globalizationreport; http://www.acm.org/pubs/cacm/

Registered Contract between 23 Companies and Client Company, 2006 from one Large U.S. Municipality, Published as Registered Contract in Municipal Government Public Records.

Relyea, Harold C. and Hogue, Henry B., A Brief History of the Emergence of Digital Government in the United States, in Digital Government, Principles and Best Practices, ed. Pavlichev, Alexei, and Garson, David, A., Idea Group Inc., 2004, 16-33.

Richardson, Ronald E., Digital Government: Balancing Risk and Reward through Public/Private Partnerships, in Digital Government, Principles and Best Practices, ed. Pavlichev, Alexei, and Garson, David, A., Idea Group Inc., 2004, 200-217.

Rose, Barbara, Tech Workers Plugging Back in to a Changed Job Marke, Chicago Tribune, July 2006

Society for Information Management, 2006, http://www.simnet.org

Stowers, Genie, Issues in E-Commerce and E-Government Service Delivery, in Digital Government, Principles and Best Practices, ed. Pavlichev, Alexei, and Garson, David, A., Idea Group Inc., 2004, 169-185.

Sun Microsystems, http://www.sunmicrosystems.com

U.S. Bureau of Labor Statistics, U.S. Government, 2006, 2007; http://www.bls.gov

U.S. Federal Government, Office of Personnel Management, 15 Executive Agencies & 101 Other Federal Agencies, 2006, http://www.loc.gov/rr/news/fedgov.html.

U.S. Federal Government, Office of Personnel Management, Administrative Careers with America -ACWA), http://www.opm.gov/qualifications/SEC-V/sec-v.asp

U.S. Federal Government, Office of Personnel Management, Career Transition Resources, 2006, http://www.careeronestop.org.

U.S. Federal Government, Office of Personnel Management, Detail and Transfer of Federal Employees to International Organizations, 2006, http://www.opm.gov/employ/internat/.

U.S. Federal Government, Office of Personnel Management, Direct Hiring Authority and by Excepted Agencies, http://www.apps.opm.gov

U.S. Federal Government, Office of Personnel Management, Federal Executive Boards, http://www.opm.gov

U.S. Federal Government, Office of Personnel Management, Form C Section C. Form C, it may be downloaded from http://www.opm.gov/forms/pdf_fill/OPM1203fx.pdf.

U.S. Federal Government, Office of Personnel Management, Form OF-612 may be downloaded and printed from http://www.opm.gov/forms/pdf_fill/of612.pdf.

U.S. Federal Government, Office of Personnel Management, General Services Salary Schedule, 2006, http://www.opm.gov.

U.S. Federal Government, Office of Personnel Management, Individual Development Plans (IDP), 2006, http://www.opm.gov/hcaaf_resource_center/assets/Lead_tool3.pdf.;

U.S. Federal Government, Office of Personnel Management, Intergovernmental Personnel Act Mobility Program, 2006, http://www.opm.gov/programs/ipa/.

U.S. Federal Government, Office of Personnel Management, Introduction to the Position Classifications Standard,1995, http://www.opm.gov/fedclass/gsintro.pdf.

U.S. Federal Government, Office of Personnel Management, Job Family Position Classification Standard for Administrative Work in the Information Technology Group GS-2200, GS-2200, 2001, 2003; http://www.opm.gov/FEDCLASS/gs2200a.pdf.

U.S. Federal Government, Office of Personnel Management, Leadership & Knowledge Management Programs, 2006, http://apps.opm.gov/HumanCapital/standards/lkmq5b.html

U.S. Federal Government, Office of Personnel Management, Student Employment; http://www.studentjobs.gov

U.S. Federal Government, Office of Personnel Management, The Classifier's Handbook, 1991, http://www.opm.gov/fedclass/clashnbk.pdf

U.S. Federal Government, Office of Personnel Management, The Executives in Residence Program, 2006, http://www.leadership.opm.gov/content.cfm?CAT=EIRP.

U.S. Federal Government, USAJOBS.gov, Official Jobs Web Portal, http://www.USAjobs.gov

U.S. Government, Department of Justice, U.S. Freedom of Information Act, 2006.

VARBusiness, March 2006.

Zieger, Robert H., American Workers, American Unions, Second Edition, Johns Hopkins University Press, 1994.

Index

CPSIA information can be obtained at www.ICGtesting.com
Printed in the USA
LVOW09s0231261114

415722LV00001B/3/P